Reading Evangelicals

How Christian Fiction Shaped a Culture and a Faith

Daniel Silliman

WILLIAM B. EERDMANS PUBLISHING COMPANY

GRAND RAPIDS, MICHIGAN

Wm. B. Eerdmans Publishing Co.
4035 Park East Court SE, Grand Rapids, Michigan 49546
www.eerdmans.com

27 26 25 24 23 22 21   1 2 3 4 5 6 7

ISBN 978-0-8028-7935-6

Library of Congress Cataloging-in-Publication Data

Names: Silliman, Daniel, 1982– author.
Title: Reading evangelicals : how Christian fiction shaped a culture
    and a faith / Daniel Silliman.
Description: Grand Rapids, Michigan : Wm. B. Eerdmans Publish-
    ing Co., [2021] | Includes bibliographical references and index.
    | Summary: "A historical examination of evangelical identity
    through a close look at five best-selling evangelical novels and
    the Christian publishing and bookselling industry they helped
    build"—Provided by publisher.
Identifiers: LCCN 2021012168 | ISBN 9780802879356
Subjects: LCSH: Evangelicalism—United States—History. | Chris-
    tian fiction, American—History and criticism. | Publishers and
    publishing—United States.
Classification: LCC BR1642.U5 S459 2021 | DDC 277.3/082—dc23
LC record available at https://lccn.loc.gov/2021012168

Contents

Acknowledgments

I feel a little like I've gotten away with something here. Any book is a feat. A good book is even harder, and depends on a staggering amount of generosity, good will, creativity, and collaboration. I tried to write a good book and also a strange one. It's a history of novels. It's an American studies project undertaken by an American in Germany at a German university, and it is deeply interdisciplinary, at a time when academia has decided it cannot afford thinking that happens in multiple categories at once. This book attempts to show the complexity of the architecture of American evangelicalism, insisting that the weird side doors, the stairway that doesn't seem to go anywhere, and the rooms that appear not to connect are not incidental to the structure but important to understanding what it is. There are good reasons to think that kind of book shouldn't work. I was told a bunch of times over the years why it wouldn't, and that it didn't fit, and also that there wasn't a place for me. That seems eminently reasonable when I think about it. But it also makes me incredibly grateful for the many, many people—really it is astonishing how many—who saw the weird thing I was trying to do and responded with enthusiasm, encouragement, and joy. Again and again, without a thought of how or whether they'd be acknowledged, much less rewarded, people gave their time, talent, and skill to make this book better and make it real. Now that I'm done, the finished product feels like nothing so much as a magic trick that I don't know how I did, which is just a way of saying it was accomplished through a million acts of generosity and even more of grace. Thank you.

Thank you, Jan Stievermann, my doctoral supervisor, who started this project with a simple question about why *Left Behind* was fiction and what readers were doing when they read a novel about the apocalypse instead of a political or theological tract about the apocalypse. Your integrity, rigor, and intellectual honesty are unmatched, and I'm proud to call you my *Doktorvater* and my friend.

Thanks to the Stievermanners, who were in it with me in Heidelberg, especially Jennifer Adams-Massmann, Heike Jablonski, Ryan Hoselton, and Johanna Müller.

Thanks to the scholars who supported me even when it didn't seem that there would be anything in it for them. Academia is bad for the soul, but you valued higher things. I want to especially name Timothy E. W. Gloege, Matthew Avery Sutton, Darren Dochuk, Heath Carter, Mark Noll, Kathryn Lofton, Kate Bowler, and Kristin Kobes Du Mez.

Thanks to my conversation partners in the University of Notre Dame's Colloquium on Religious and History: Jonathan Riddle, Phillip Byers, Suzanna Krivulskaya, and Benjamin Wetzel, as well as Peter Cajka and Philipp Gollner. That was a terrible year for me, redeemed a little by your kindnesses and collaborative spirit.

Thank you to the people who made the Lilly Postdoctoral Fellows Program possible, especially Joe Creech, Mark Schwehn, Dorothy Bass, and Joe Goss. And a huge thanks to my fellow Lillies: Chelsea Wagenaar, Elizabeth Fredericks, Pat Gardner, Ashleigh Elser, Christine Hedlin, Jason Gehrke, and Jillian Snyder. You can't know how much it meant to me and I miss you every Monday at 4.

Acknowledgments

I also want to thank the friends who made sure I knew I was worth more than what I wrote in a day. You made my life so much better: Shawn Huelle, Johanna Roering, Tyler and Shalynn Crawford, Pam and Nathan Heald, Chris Godwin, Emily and Max Bartenbach, Erin Mehaffey Harper, Julia Kopp, Tony Cole, and especially my sister Valerie.

Thanks to my editor David Bratt, marketing director Laura Bardolph Hubers, and the folks at Eerdmans, who bought into this project with such enthusiasm.

And thank you, most of all, to my wife Beth. Your belief in this work from beginning to end has astounded me. Your love means everything. And remember when you got me the best cat? That was a good day and there have been so many good days.

From the bottom of my heart, thank you all.

Introduction

Defining Evangelicals in a Christian Bookstore

The sign says, "Closing. Everything 10-40% Off!"
The parking lot is slushy with yesterday's snow, and inside,
people drip. They open their coats, put gloves in pockets, and smile
at the clerk who greets them.

The store is more crowded than it has been in a long time. It
has the happy hum of Christmas shopping, even though it's March
2017. The store's sound system plays a bouncy, upbeat song:

> I got an old church choir singing in my soul
> I got a sweet salvation and it's beautiful
> I got a heart overflowing 'cause I been restored
> There ain't nothing gonna steal my joy.[1]

Despite the cheer, the regular ring of the register signals the
end of the Mishawaka, Indiana, bookstore. This is one of 240
Family Christian Bookstore outlets across the country. And the
chain—"the world's largest retailer of Christian-themed merchandise"—is going out of business.

Evangelical bookstores like Family Christian have been a
curious feature of the American cultural landscape since the
1970s, when the number of these little stores doubled and then

tripled across suburbia and annual sales swelled to an estimated $770 million per year.[2] By the early 1990s, evangelical retail was a $3 billion business.[3] Now, across the country, this industry is collapsing, and all these stores are closing. Family Christian is covered in signs that say, "SALE! SALE! SALE!"

I'm here to browse, people-watch, and think about a question I've been working over for a number of years: What is an evangelical?

The question emerges at particular moments in the public conversation that is always rolling and roiling in America. More often than not, it's because of politics. When Jerry Falwell Sr., a Baptist minister from Virginia, launched a series of "I Love America" rallies in 1976 and started talking about how he used to believe Christians shouldn't be involved in politics but now thought they should be because they needed to defend traditional family values, people asked, "What is an evangelical?" Journalists asked, and scholars, and regular people, some of whom were evangelical and had strong feelings about how the question was answered and some of whom weren't, but they also had opinions about the right answer and felt, with some urgency, that it was important to have the right answer.

The question reemerged in 2000, when presidential candidate George W. Bush said he was an evangelical and his favorite philosopher was Christ. Then Bush went on to win the White House, and there was a sense that you had to be able to define "evangelical" in order to understand what was going on in the world.

People asked again in 2016, with the election of Donald Trump. It was widely reported that a lot of evangelicals voted for Trump, which raised the question of what an evangelical was. Trump himself didn't seem to know. A few days before his inauguration, he asked two ministers from a liberal Presbyterian church near his offices in Manhattan if they were evangelicals, and when they said no, he seemed confused. Other people seemed confused too, none more than the many people who thought they were evangelical but didn't vote for Trump or support Trump, and actually found him pretty repulsive and couldn't understand how other evangelicals could support him with such fervor.

It made them wonder if they knew what they thought they did, so they asked again: What is an evangelical?

Of course, it was never only big public conversations where this would come up, and never only conversations about politics. A lot of young people have asked what an evangelical is as they try to figure out what they are, comparing the particularities of their childhoods with other people's childhoods and trying to articulate for themselves their views, value commitments, and ways of being in the world. And adults also have experiences— sometimes as mundane as moving to a new town, sometimes as profound as a new relationship with God—and those experiences raise the question.

Historians have been fighting over the definition of the "evangelical" pretty much since the emergence of a distinct field of history that focused on evangelicals. Some of them got interested in the question as young people who moved out into the world, went to college and then grad school, and decided to try to use the things they were learning to understand their own past and the place they came from. Others saw evangelicals from a distance and got intrigued and thought, "I can explain this. I *need* to explain this."

I feel that kind of urgency now. I've always been invested in American politics and feel the need to understand this bloc to understand what is going on. And I'm someone who grew up in a particular, peculiar church but found my own Christian faith as an adult. I'm also a historian who specializes in twentieth-century American evangelicals, yet I was surprised Trump won and surprised so many evangelicals liked him so much. The problem of this persistent question feels very real to me. And I think the answer may be in the bookstore.

The upbeat song about the church choir in your soul is for sale at a discount on a rack of CDs. Right now, it's the number four hit on *Billboard*'s chart of "Hot Christian Songs."[4] A young woman in a loosened scarf stands at the rack, flipping the cases with her index finger. In her other hand is a copy of one of Christian hip-hop's recent big successes, Lecrae's seventh studio album, *Anomaly*. It's sold half a million copies, garnered two Grammy nominations, and earned the Christian rapper an appearance on *The Late Night Show with Jimmy Fallon*.[5]

Asked the message of his hip-hop, Lecrae says, "No matter how bad you mess up, God loves you and there's nothing you can do about it."[6]

Behind the teen, a whole shelf is dedicated to C. S. Lewis books. There are several different editions of his beloved fantasy series The Chronicles of Narnia. The seven novels are sold separately, or in a single volume with an introduction by Lewis's stepson, or in two different box sets, one with still photos from the third Narnia movie, *The Voyage of the Dawn Treader*. The film made $105 million in the United States, which wasn't enough, since it cost $155 million to make.[7]

Another of Lewis's novels has also been repackaged. *The Great Divorce* has a new cover with a red bus on a blue field. The novel starts at a bus stop in hell, on a rainy street where damnation's time seems suspended in "that dismal moment when only a few shops have lit up and it is not yet dark enough for their windows to look cheering."[8] Next to that is Lewis's most famous work of nonfiction, *Mere Christianity*. Across the country, *Mere Christianity* will sell about eight thousand copies this month.[9]

On the back wall are Bibles. The whole wall. A man and woman are looking at the *ESV Large Print Value Thinline Bible*. The English Standard Version, first published in 2001, is a translation that aims to be "essentially literal" and "transparent to the original."[10] There are more than two hundred versions of the ESV, and a dozen or so are stocked in this store alongside many other translations, including the King James Version, New International Version, New Living Translation, New American Standard Bible, New Revised Standard Version, New King James Version, and The Message. The woman says she thinks she wants Jesus's words printed in red. The large-print "thinline" feels nice, and it's easy to read, but Jesus's words aren't in red. The man says, "Is there one like that?" and bends down to look on a lower shelf.

A nearby section of the store sells church supplies: little plastic communion cups and offering plates and pew cards with a box to check if you're new to the church and another if you want a visit from a pastor. Another section sells home decor, like a wooden sign that has Joshua 24:15 in a cursive script. "As for me and my house," it says, "we will serve the Lord." The sign is, according to the tag, Bible Love Rustic Decor Farmhouse Style.

Does any of that help me answer the question, What is an evangelical? Maybe. This isn't the approach most people have taken. But then, I'm not happy with their definitions. They feel insufficient to me. Most answers can be sorted into two groups. Some people define evangelicals by their political beliefs, others by their theological beliefs.

Historian Frances FitzGerald, for example, wrote a 712-page history of evangelicals that critics called magisterial and epic.[11] For her, evangelicals are essentially political actors—the people rallied by Jerry Falwell, the people who voted for Bush and Trump. Evangelicals are those, she says, who "have reintroduced religion into public discourse, polarized the nation, and profoundly changed American politics."[12]

Historian Thomas Kidd, on the other hand, argues that evangelicalism has nothing to do with voting and everything to do with ideas about the proper human relationship to God. In his recent, well-reviewed book *What Is an Evangelical?*, he defines evangelicals as people who believe in conversion, the primacy of the Bible, and a personal relationship with Jesus Christ and the Holy Spirit.[13]

I'm in the minority among evangelical historians in that I don't think these kinds of belief-based definitions work. For one thing, they don't help you identify who is and who is not an evangelical, unless you already kind of know.

The political definitions never grapple with the evangelicals who are politically progressive, for example. Or the many who don't vote. Or the fact that politics actually doesn't take up all the space in the lives and the homes and the conversations of regular evangelicals. A recent study of fifty thousand sermons preached over three months found that about 20 percent of evangelical congregations heard a preacher mention abortion. That's a lot, but that means four out of five evangelical churches didn't hear a sermon that mentioned abortion, which is a lot more.[14] Making politics the focus seems to require us to ignore the majority of what evangelicals care about.

The theological definitions, on the other hand, tend to lump a bunch of things together that are actually pretty different while also excluding things that, on the face of it, are pretty similar. The "primacy of the Bible," for example, can mean everything from an emphasis on the importance of daily devotional reading to an insistence on the historic fact that the earth was created in six days, six thousand years ago. It can mean that a church should not have bishops. Or that a church should have bishops. At the same time, Christians who reject the doctrine of the Trinity because it's not explicitly mentioned in the Bible are generally *not* considered evangelical. The same is true of Christians who believe they should worship on Saturday, such as the Seventh-day Adventists and the Seventh Day Baptists, and Christians who don't believe in hell, such as the Primitive Baptist Universalists, commonly known as the "No-Hellers." The "primacy of the Bible" isn't as useful as it needs to be, as an identifying mark.

There are a couple of bigger problems too. Belief-based definitions don't identify the mechanism that forms evangelicals as a group. How do evangelicals become evangelicals? How does evangelicalism exist? Catholics have an institutional apparatus, as do Southern Baptists, Republicans, Rotarians, Mary Kay consultants, Walmart employees, and Amazon Prime members. Belonging is structured, for each of these, by some mechanism that forms the group as a group. A definition should help us understand that structuring as it happens in the world, and understand the practices of participation and belonging. You don't have that with "evangelical."

Belief-based definitions also don't account for change over time. For historians, it's not enough to state facts that are true. It's necessary to explain contingencies (how things happened to happen) and narrate change (how they happened to happen differently). A good historical definition should help people understand evangelicals even as particular beliefs fade in importance and others emerge with new urgency. Today evangelicals care about abortion, but one hundred years ago it was prohibition. Premillennialism used to be a dividing line, and now it almost never comes up. A good definition should even help people understand why a particular belief can seem essential sometimes and inessential other times, directing attention to the internal dynamic responding to external pressures in particular—and maybe even predictable—ways.

It's a mistake to confuse the content of a conversation with the conversation itself. My wife and I, for example, have been talking a lot about our garden. Two years ago, though, we didn't have a garden. Two years from now, we also might not. Defining our family as people who care a lot about their gardens, then, would be right in a sense but not particularly helpful as we change over time. Rather than focusing on what we talk about, it would be better to pay attention to why we keep talking, and how the conversation shifts and flows.

The German philosopher Jürgen Habermas has an idea about "discourse communities," an academic term that just means a group involved in a conversation. Habermas says a discourse community is formed by the practices that make the discussion possible. How do people communicate? Where? What do they have to do to keep participating in the conversation? The reality of access and the limits of accessibility also shape the group's imagination, according to Habermas: how it conceives of itself, the unspoken rules of the discussion, and the recurring questions that orient it as it moves forward.

You can see that happening at an evangelical bookstore. It's visible: the formation and ongoing evolution of a discourse community. Here is a mechanism that forms a group as a group, bringing people into a conversation. That conversation is both open and limited, which gives rise to the internal dynamics that govern responses to change. Imagination happens in a bookstore. It is a place to remember your questions and reframe them slightly as you engage others involved in the same process, changing over time even as the community identity grows stronger in the cascade of contingency.

There are of course other hubs of evangelical conversation. Magazines organize discourse into community. So do conferences. Camps. Seminaries and Bible colleges. Celebrities do this in a way. Anyone on a "circuit." A bookstore—and the broader book market—isn't singularly powerful, sustaining and shaping discussion. It's one institution that does it. The record of this hub of discussion, however, is in books that aren't hard to find, and you can reconstruct the conversation and communal imagination pretty well.

In a bookstore, it turns out, browsing the shelves, people watching, and asking the question "What is an evangelical?" can all be the same thing. One definition of evangelical is people who shop at Christian bookstores. Or maybe better: evangelicals are people who are a part of the ongoing conversation that is represented by Christian bookstores.

As I look around the store, I'm drawn to the fiction section, possibly because I'm particularly interested in the imagination. Fiction, more than the theology books or the home decor or the Christian music, starts with an invitation to suspend disbelief and think about how the world might be, *if.* There's a lot of fiction, and it sells really well. It's the largest category of sales in the Christian bookstore, after Bibles. Some of these books have been read by millions, and that makes me think they're important for this "discourse community."

I move to the fiction and find a freckled boy sitting cross-legged in the aisle. He has a novel by Ted Dekker open in his lap. Dekker is more known for his horror fiction, but this is a fantasy titled *Black.* It has been rated more than twenty-five thousand times on the social-cataloguing website GoodReads. Nearly half the readers give the book five stars. Another 30 percent give it four stars. The boy, for his part, seems engrossed. He flips a page.

This section of the store is crowded. One aisle over, a woman in boots and red plaid looks at Tosca Lee's *The Legend of Sheba: The Rise of a Queen*, while her friend holds a Lynette Eason novel about a woman hunting a serial killer. Next to them, a man in khakis opens Joel Rosenberg's latest political thriller, *Without Warning*, which has been blurbed by a famous pastor and a famous right-wing talk-show host. Across from him, a woman has a small stack of books held to her chest and tells a teen with Debbie Viguie's vampire novel *Kiss of Night* that it "might be too scary." Another woman holds two different novels set in the American Civil War like she's weighing them with her hands.

It's pretty easy to see how a reader and an author are in conversation. But there's also a wider conversation going on. Authors are, first of all, readers. Their books are responding to other books, which are, in turn, in dialogue with other books.[15]

And no author produces a volume singlehandedly. This is the cliché of the acknowledgments page, but often not acknowledged by historians and cultural critics who imagine books springing fully formed from the mind of a writer-genius. Give authors their due, but publishers also exist. Then, between the author and the publisher sometimes stands an agent, who has a role managing that relationship, and deciding how people communicate and what they have to do to keep participating in that conversation. The publisher is also typically in a publishing house, which includes various editors, a board that makes decisions about acquisitions, and a marketing team that decides how a book will be sold.

Even all these people together don't produce a book by themselves, of course. There have to be a printer, a paper producer, an ink manufacturer, and those who contribute the material and labor to produce the object itself. Then the object has to be distributed, and this process, historically, has set the limits of discourse communities as much or more than any other activity. Then the book gets to the bookseller. And the relationship between the bookseller and the book buyer also shapes the conversation, starting with who is served and not served by the store.

It's worth noting as well that even when a reader reads a book, she is not alone. The individual reader is in a conversation with the author, of course—a relationship intermediated by all the others involved in that process of production and distribution—but the reader is also in conversation with other readers. Often this is literal: people read books together, discuss what they're reading with friends and family, and often pass books and recommendations about books back and forth. It is not uncommon for a book to come with some familial obligation, a debt of friendship, or a commitment to conversation upon completion.

There's also an imaginative communal aspect of reading. Built into the experience of engaging with a text is the experience of thinking about other readers. As an individual reads, he positions himself in relationship to other possible responses to the text, the differences allowing an assertion of identity in terms of taste, preference, and even values. As much as reading allows you to imagine what it would be like to be someone else, it also allows you to imagine what it is like to be yourself, though distinguished from others, who are also imagined.

Some crude cultural analysis will treat an audience as a singular, homogeneous mass. Critics will interpret a text, cite the number of readers, and then imply with a wave of the hand that all those readers agree with what they read and with what the critic said the text said. A lot of what passes for cultural studies—in academia and journals of thought and in popular analysis—consists of this one move. It's not really plausible, though, if you've ever read a book and not liked it. Or read a book and had a different opinion than someone else. These critics would seem to think that it's normal for everyone everywhere to respond to a text in the one way, when in fact that would be astounding if that happened.

The best and most careful studies of readers show, in fact, that they can be quite creative in interpreting a text, and there is always a lot of variety in how people respond to what they're reading.[16] Further, readers are almost always aware of other possible readings, and so readers, and that imagined community, are part of the normal interpretive process as people read.

I want to tell the story of American evangelicalism that captures this: the freedom of the individual readers, their imagination, and how they're also part of this larger community, which is real and imagined, and how that ongoing conversation is shaped and given structure by institutions and networks, which limit the discussion but also make it possible. I want to tell the story of how all that works together to produce this religious identity, evangelical.

In the store, I pick out five novels published over four decades. *Love Comes Softly* came out in 1979; *This Present Darkness*, 1986; *Left Behind*, 1995, and *The Shunning*, 1998; and *The Shack*, 2008.

Each of these has sold more than a million copies. Each has marked a change in the history of publishing and bookselling, and each invites the reader into a conversation and a community. If I tell the story of these books—how they were written, how they were published, how they were sold, and how they were read—I think I can tell the story of evangelicalism at the end of the twentieth century and the beginning of the twenty-first.

The register keeps ringing, as the going-out-of-business sale keeps going. I hear an older woman in line ask the Family Christian clerk, "Did I hear Beth Moore has a novel now? Do you have that?"

Moore has written more than a dozen popular Bible studies and speaks about Scripture to sold-out convention centers around the country. *The Undoing of Saint Silvanus* is her first novel. Asked about the message of her novel, Moore says, "We just accept things how they are and don't realize how dramatically God can change us."[17]

The clerk looks up the book, but it wouldn't be out until September. By then, this Family Christian will be a Halloween City. For now, though, the store hums with the life of a conversation being formed, sustained, and changing.

The Romance of Abundant Life

Janette Oke's *Love Comes Softly*

The station wagon sped across the Canadian prairie in the summer of 1977. Inside was a full and happy family of six headed for vacation at a nearby lake. Four teenage children were in the back. Edward Oke, the president of Mountain View Bible College in Didsbury, Alberta, was driving. And in the front passenger seat, Janette Oke, forty-two, with a pad of paper on her knees, was writing. This was her novel. Her dream novel. She was writing a romance, set on a prairie like the one rolling by, where a woman found love through hardship—human love but also divine. It was a simple story but filled with Oke's faith that God wanted people to flourish in their everyday lives and that they could live their best lives if they would submit and accept God's love. She didn't know it, but this novel would shape the evangelical imagination. It would sell more than one million coupes, inspire countless new authors, and launch an industry of religious fiction that would serve as the site for an ongoing discussion about what it means to believe in Jesus and live out the reality of that relationship in modern-day life. But at the moment, Oke was just trying to get her plot on paper.[1]

Oke (pronounced "oak," like the tree) was not a professional writer. She worked at a newspaper once while her husband was in seminary in Indiana, but she was in the accounting department. She had written stories as a child. She had written some poetry over the years too. She was so busy, though, with her children and church work and accounting jobs, that she couldn't really write seriously. She once looked at a mail-order writing course offered by the Christian Writers Institute, in Wheaton, Illinois. She scored well on the aptitude test but decided the course was too expensive.

But she had an idea for a novel—"I don't know if a writer can tell you how he or she gets ideas," Oke would later say. "Ideas come"[2]—and she felt like she had to write it. She didn't know whether one could write a romance novel that had this theme—a religious romance, where the narrative of falling in love is intertwined with a story about finding faith. She read a lot of romances, usually more than one hundred per year.[3] She got them at shopping centers in Calgary, the only place near her home where you could buy books at that time. None of them were Christian. The authors didn't seem to see or know how human love could be an analogy for one's relationship to God. In fact, few of the characters in the novels ever prayed or went to church or read the Bible, though the books were often set in very religious periods of time.

They didn't have religion in those books. What they did have was sex.

There had been a notable shift in the popular romances of the time. The first really successful commercial paperbacks had been gothic romances, starting with Phyllis Whitney's *Thunder Heights* and Victoria Holt's *Mistress of Mellyn*, both published in 1960. They were novels about mansions and isolated women falling in love with wealthy, mysterious men. The market was soon flooded with similar stories. Between 1969 and 1972, about four hundred new gothic romances were published every year. They were primarily sold in department stores and grocery stores—sometimes even packaged in deals with laundry soap. Women could buy them even on the prairie in Alberta, where there were no regular booksellers. The romances did good business, but a slump in sales in the early

1970s prompted publishers to look for something new. Soon, the book racks in Calgary were stocked with alternatives, which industry experts called "sweet savage" or "erotic historical" romances. They were also called, more popularly, "bodice rippers." The first one, Kathleen E. Woodiwiss's novel *The Flame and the Flower*, starts with a rape. The heroine's clothes—notably the bodice of her dress—are ripped off in one early scene by the man she will, by the novel's happy resolution, love and live with ever after.[4]

Oke didn't like these books. She didn't like the sexual violence, but it wasn't just that. She understood that life was a struggle and bad things happen. She understood sorrow. She liked stories about women faced with real challenges. But in her own life she overcame through faith, and that never happened in the romance novels. For her love was also about belief, and how you lived out your belief in practice, in your "Christian walk," and she wanted a novel with a story like that.

So she wrote one. Then she sent it to one of the publishers that published the paperbacks stocked in the Calgary stores, and got a rejection note. She put the manuscript in a drawer. "I'll give it to you," she told God, "so you'll be free to bless it, Lord."[5]

Six months later her husband brought home a book about how to get published and a list of evangelical publishing houses. Would they print it? Did they publish romance novels? She didn't know, but the answer was no. At the time, there were no Christian publishers regularly publishing any fiction, let alone popular romance novels. But that was about to change. Oke sent off six query letters and waited.

The History of Evangelical Publishing

The time was right for an evangelical romance novel. Evangelical publishing was coming into its own, emerging out of the history of American publishing as a solution to a particular market problem.

At the end of the nineteenth century, general trade publishing was booming, and the number of new titles printed in America every year tripled between 1880 and 1900. Population growth and rising literacy rates meant an increasing number of readers. Advances in printing technology meant that mass publishing was cheaper, improving profit margins. At the same time, family-owned publishers such as Lippincott, Harper, Scribner, and Houghton Mifflin reorganized as corporations. They professionalized, capitalized, and made bookselling a big business.

But the burgeoning book industry was constrained by problems of distribution. "Book distribution," writes historian Michael Winship, "has often posed a more difficult problem for publishers than book production. This is especially true in a country like the United States in which production facilities, largely concentrated in eastern urban publishing centers, had to reach a diverse population spread over an extensive area."[6] Winship counts only 3,500 bookstores in America in 1914.[7] These were mostly in urban centers, inaccessible to a lot of people. There were other ways to sell books, however. Publishers used traveling salesmen to peddle subscriptions across the country. This worked well for certain titles—Ulysses S. Grant's memoirs, for example—but not for the thousands of new books published every year.

The problem of distribution was felt, especially, with religious titles. It wasn't profitable to produce a book that would, by its very nature, exclude potential readers. If you could sell a title at only a few places across the country, you didn't want one that would only interest Methodists. So there wasn't a lot of religious publishing, even if people were pretty religious overall. In 1900, American publishers released 6,356 new titles. About 7 percent of these were categorized as religious. Religious books sold a little better than poetry and drama, though not nearly as well as fiction.[8]

Where religious publishing thrived was with denominational publishers. This is because a denomination could double as a distribution network. Clergy across the country were linked through their institutions, and they were interested in buying books. Thus, at the start of the twentieth century, religious books were mostly produced by denominational presses. In 1915, the *Federal Council Year Book* identified 389 Protestant presses—but not for Protestants generally, or even for broad groups of Protestants. The publishers were divided by denomination. The prolific Methodists printed sixty-nine newspapers and had several book publishers. The smallest Protestant group on the list, the six-hundred-member Church of God, Adventist, had two papers.[9] "Denominations were," writes historian William Vance Trollinger Jr., "the organizational structure for American Protestantism between 1880 and 1940, and they were the critical locus of identity."[10]

Whatever theological similarities a Methodist might have had with a Mennonite, Methodists and Mennonites were distinct textual communities. These religious groups can both be called "evangelical," and will be by historians who use an ahistorical theological definition of the term. In their historical, day-to-day reality, however, Methodists and Mennonites were separated. Methodists, according to Trollinger, put out "a cascade of hymnals, Sunday School and Vacation Bible School materials, evangelical tracts and a variety of other religious books and booklets."[11] They were by and for Methodists. The publishers might occasionally turn an eye to non-Methodist book buyers, but they couldn't really reach them. Just getting books to non-Methodists would be an immense practical problem, requiring new, non-Methodist channels of distribution. To appeal to a non-Methodist book buyer, further, they would presumably need to produce books that were less distinctively Methodist. If they did that, they ran the risk of alienating their core clientele.[12]

The same was true for Mennonites. The Mennonite Publishing House put out 262 books and pamphlets between 1908 and 1945.[13] It was a small business, but it was successful because it served a niche market. These were Mennonite publications, produced, distributed, and consumed by Mennonites. They were not readily available to "evangelicals" generally, and it wouldn't have worked, financially, to try to sell Mennonite books as evangelical books and to stop serving their distinctive niche.

Some religious print material crossed denominational lines, of course. A number of ambitious publishing projects at the start of the century brought together various Protestant groups into cooperative enterprises. Significant examples include the American Bible Society, the American Tract Society, and the Bible Institute Colportage Association,[14] all of which used colporteurs—book peddlers—to distribute books. Dwight L. Moody's Bible Institute Colportage Association, for instance, had about one hundred of these booksellers in 1906. Funding came from multiple denominations and from Christians across the denominational spectrum. According to historian Candy Gunther Brown, however, these cooperative Protestant publishing ventures "at no point supplanted denominational identity."[15] Joint publishing endeavors worked only if the books were sold very cheaply, and if the stream of texts didn't create a print culture that challenged the denominations subsidizing the cost of the books. This was sometimes stated explicitly. Moody's group, for example, made it clear that the goal was to "carry the Gospel, by means of the printed page, where church privileges are wanting or not embraced."[16] The books were not meant to be read by Mennonites or Methodists, or even by Christians who might identify with Moody. They were tools for evangelism, meant for people who had no religious identity at all.

A new, transdenominational print culture emerged with the fundamentalist-modernist controversies. As Protestant denominations divided in theological disputes, the fighting factions sometimes discovered they had allies in other denominations. They sometimes identified more with these allies than with people in their own religious groups. New textual communities encouraged these people to talk to each other and to establish new conversations across denominational lines, establishing new religious identities.

Fundamentalists, for example, could subscribe to the series of books from which they took their name, *The Fundamentals*. Historian Timothy E. W. Gloege writes that the editors of *The Fundamentals* sought to "create a generic, nonsectarian, 'conservative' Protestantism free from denominational controls."[17] The editors developed a mailing list of 175,000 religious leaders who belonged to very different religious groups and who disagreed with each other—sometimes fiercely—about theological issues that they considered to be of the utmost importance. *The Fundamentals* told them that what they had in common was more important than what they disagreed about. Some concurred, identifying with this new religious brand. They subscribed to *The Fundamentals* and, in doing so, identified themselves with this new conversation. After the first volume of *The Fundamentals* was published, the editors reportedly receiving three hundred or more grateful letters per day. Pastors from around the country said they didn't feel alone anymore. The publication, Gloege writes, "created an imagined community of Protestants united in their opposition to theological modernism."[18] Periodicals such as *Moody Monthly*, the *Pilot*, the *King's Business*, and the *Sunday School Times* served the same function.[19]

Some denominational booksellers also joined this new, transdenominational Protestant identity. Notable here are the Dutch Reformed publishers in Grand Rapids, Michigan. At first a company like Eerdmans was strictly denominational. William B. Eerdmans Sr. himself was affiliated with the Christian Reformed Church, and so was the company to which he gave his name. The company served the Dutch Reformed immigrants of western Michigan, selling theology books to students at Calvin College and Seminary and then later publishing the school's professors.[20] As

Eerdmans expanded, the company relied on the immigrant church as a distribution network. Calvin graduates became pastors around the Midwest, and they and their congregations bought Eerdmans books. As Dutch Reformed immigrants transitioned into English and found their place in America's religious landscape, Eerdmans helped them maintain their distinct identity.[21] The publisher acted as gatekeeper. In this role, however, it also started selling non–Dutch Reformed books to Dutch Reformed readers. The Eerdmans brand guaranteed the orthodoxy of American authors who might have otherwise been suspect to devout members of the Christian Reformed Church. In the 1930s, Eerdmans sold the works of fundamentalist Presbyterians such as A. A. Hodge and B. B. Warfield, and people associated with Moody, such as Harry Ironside, a Plymouth Brethren preacher.[22]

Zondervan, another Grand Rapids publisher, followed this model. The bookseller was founded when two brothers, Pat and Bernie Zondervan, left the company of their uncle William Eerdmans Sr. and started their own in 1931. The first book they sold was *The Virgin Birth of Christ* by J. Gresham Machen, a fundamentalist champion in the Presbyterian church.[23] *Virgin Birth* had been published by Harper & Brothers the year before, to disappointing sales. It was supposed to be a great salvo in the fundamentalist-modernist controversies, but the New York publisher hadn't marketed the book successfully. Harper & Brothers thought only academics would really be interested in questions of the historicity of Jesus's birth and the problem of the relationship between what German theologians termed *Historie* and *Geschichte*. The publisher priced *Virgin Birth* at $5 at the height of the Great Depression and sent it out for review to the *Times Literary Supplement*, *Christian Century*, the *Anglican Theological Review*, and *Deutsche Literaturezeitung*.[24] It was also advertised to ministers with a notice in the *Religious Book Club Bulletin*, a journal associated with the Federal Council of Churches, an institutional enemy of the fundamentalists.[25] The publisher was apparently unaware that across Depression-ridden America, there were religious farmers, shopkeepers, and housewives, not to mention Calvinist clergy, who were very interested in these questions and might be interested in this book. The Zondervan brothers knew Dutch immigrants in Michigan would be interested. They saw an opportunity. They bought the remaindered stock for $1 per book and resold the books through Dutch Reformed distribution networks for $1.95.[26] The nascent company turned enough profit to prove that their business model, catering to this religious readership, was potentially successful.

The model had its limitations, though. Zondervan could typically sell only about a thousand books to the names taken from denominational yearbooks and business contacts developed from the brothers' time at Eerdmans.[27] Zondervan also had to compete with the more established and more trusted Eerdmans, and sell books to a niche of book buyers who were already pretty well served. Zondervan needed new markets, so the company tapped into new fundamentalist distribution channels. Zondervan started advertising books through the *Sunday School Times*, the popular fundamentalist periodical. Then the company bought its own fundamentalist periodical, the *Christian Digest*, a monthly magazine with thousands of subscribers. The publisher started selling books to and through the Gideons, traveling Christian businessmen known for putting Bibles in hotel rooms. Zondervan opened a bookstore at the Winona Lake Bible Conference, a Christian retreat center in Indiana affiliated with Moody and popularized by the tent revivalist Billy Sunday, and it established a publishing relationship with Sunday, winning the rights to publish one of his books in a prayer competition.[28]

With these new distribution channels opened, Zondervan started selling an unprecedented number of books. Zondervan had its first big hit with *John and Betty Stam: Martyrs*. The Stams were missionaries to China, with the China Inland Mission, who were killed by Communists in 1934. A Christian Reformed Church missionary wrote up the story of the Stams' death. He sent the manuscript to Zondervan because he knew the Zondervan brothers personally. The publisher got the president of Moody Bible Institute to write an introduction and printed an unprecedented five thousand copies. *John and Betty Stam: Martyrs* sold out within a year.[29]

The books sold to fundamentalists. There were men and women across the country who now thought of themselves as part of this transdenominational Protestant movement, thanks to a transdenominational print culture. The religious identity was also a growing book-market category. Zondervan published a second run of *John and Betty Stam* in 1936, and a third run in 1937. By the end of the decade, the publisher had sold about twenty thousand copies, more than twenty times the number Zondervan could typically sell to Dutch Reformed readers. The publisher all but shed its denominational identity and became a major supporter of fundamentalism and, later, evangelicalism. The company expressed this in a credo in 1941: "We have pledged ourselves to publish only the soundest of fundamental, evangelical literature."[30]

With these new distribution channels opened, publishers' market incentives changed. A book that appealed specifically to Methodists or Mennonites or the Dutch Reformed was not going to sell as well as a book that appealed to a broad transdenominational audience. Subjects that divided denominations also divided markets. Books on ecclesiology or the sacraments would have a more limited appeal. Personal testimonies and books on practical issues like marriage and children and how to live day-to-day would have a broader appeal and a larger potential market.

Not everyone involved in evangelical publishing was happy about this—complaints about the dumbing down of religious publishing were perennial. But the market was the market. The changing dynamics of the market organized an evangelical identity and shaped a specifically evangelical imagination, which cared especially about spiritual fulfillment in the mundanity of day-to-day living. Attention to immanent things was encouraged and rewarded.

Eerdmans followed Zondervan, mostly shedding its denominational identity. Baker, another Dutch Reformed publisher from Grand Rapids, started putting out evangelical books in 1939. The Bible Institute Colportage Association rebranded itself Moody Press and began selling "Christian Classics" to this network of book buyers in 1941. With the boom of the postwar economy and a new generation of fundamentalists trying out the term "evangelical," more publishers entered the market. By 1950, there were about fifty evangelical publishers.[31]

Over the next twenty years, growth was steady. Royal Publishers—which later acquired Thomas Nelson and took its name—started in 1961. Tyndale House started in 1962. Gospel Light, a Sunday school curriculum publisher, began a line of evangelical books under the name Regal Books in 1965. Word Books, spun off from a music publisher, started the same year. Bethany House—the publishing arm of a Minnesota church-turned-commune, where families lived cheaply to pool their resources to support foreign missionaries—was founded in 1966. Multnomah Press started in 1969. Whitaker House began in 1970, and Harvest House in 1974. Good News, a tract publishing company, started a book division called Crossway at the end of the 1970s.

This growth was supported by a rapid increase in the number of evangelical bookstores in America. When evangelical booksellers first organized with the Christian Booksellers Association in 1950, there were 279 stores.[32] The number grew to 725 by the mid-1960s and reached 1,850 by the mid-1970s.[33] By the end of the 1970s, there were about 3,000 evangelical bookstores in the United States.[34]

Not all these bookstores were successful. Many were run by people with little to no business experience who were more interested in ministry than money. One Bible wholesaler recalled that some bookstore owners refused to fill out the credit applications necessary to stock Bibles in their stores. They would just write "the Lord will provide" on the top of the form.[35] These mom-and-pop operations frequently found themselves in financial trouble. And even well-financed operations could flounder. The evangelical publisher Tyndale House, for example, started a doomed bookstore chain with three stores in suburban Chicago malls. The stores attracted new customers for evangelical books, but not enough of them to pay the shopping centers' high rents. The stores operated at a loss until the threat of bankruptcy forced Tyndale House to divest.[36]

As a whole, though, the religious retailing industry boomed in the 1970s. Perhaps the most successful chain, Family Christian Bookstores, doubled its number of retail outlets between 1969 and 1973, and again from 1973 to 1978. By 1980, the corporation had fifty-seven outlets across America and brought in annual revenues of $18 million.[37] That was the trend. The number of evangelical bookstores increased, and the amount each store was selling increased too.[38] Religious book sales increased 112 percent between 1972 and 1977.[39] At the end of the decade, religious bookstores brought in an estimated $770 million.[40]

The market expansion was notable—and noted. The *New York Times* reported that religious books were the "fastest growing segment of U.S. publishing," reflecting the "spirit of the 70's." In fact, the paper reported, "firms that emphasize the evangelical and inspirational aspects of religion have been growing by leaps and bounds." There were one hundred publishing houses turning out religious books, and only two of them were big, general trade publishers from New York. There were 607 new religious titles released in the fall of 1976, but, the *New York Times* observed, "you'll find few of them in bookstores on New York's Fifth Avenue."[41] They were, instead, sold in little evangelical bookstores in the suburbs of America, where evangelical books were established as a distinct and independent book market.

The new religious titles were different from the ones that came before. Increasingly, these weren't books for seminarians or ministers. The bookstores catered to laypeople, and particularly middle-class white women in the suburbs. This wasn't an accident. The stores were almost all in the suburbs, where credit was freely available for commercial development. The suburbs were mostly white, as the result of white flight and the government policies, notably redlining, that made white flight possible.[42] The suburbs fueled the growth of the middle class and encouraged upward mobility. And in the single-family homes that ringed every city in America, most people embraced the ideal of the nuclear family with distinct social roles for men and women, with the men responsible for earning money and the women responsible for managing household consumption. Most shopping was done by women.[43] The new and expanding religious retail industry was born in this context and catered to people living in this world.

A survey of the best-selling books in these bookstores shows a distinct evangelical sensibility emerging in this specific market. There were a lot of evangelical books about sex and marriage, for example. *The Marriage Affair*, by J. Allan Petersen, was published in 1971, followed by *God, Sex, and You*, by M. O. Vincent, in 1972. The most successful sex-and-marriage manual was Marabel Morgan's *The Total Woman*, published in 1973 and a best seller by 1974. Morgan told women that the secret to a "superlative" life was to accept, admire, adapt to, and appreciate their husbands. Through submission, they could achieve the fullest possible life. In one assignment, women were instructed to write down a list of things they liked about their husbands and a second list of their husbands' faults. They were then told to throw the second list away.

In another exercise, each woman was told to practice telling her husband she loved his body. "Practice," Morgan instructed, "until it comes out naturally."[44] For another homework assignment, the women were told to surprise their husbands with sex. "For a change tonight," Morgan wrote, "place a lighted candle on the floor, and seduce him under the dining-room table. Or lead him to the sofa. How about the hammock? Or in the garden? Even if you can't actually follow through, at least the suggestion is exciting. He may say, 'We don't have a hammock.' You can reply, 'Oh, darling, I forgot!'"[45] Other evangelical books about sex followed, including *What Wives Wish Their Husbands Knew about Sex*, by James Dobson, in 1975, and *The Act of Marriage*, coauthored by Tim and Beverly LaHaye, in 1976.

Some scholars have seen this flurry of literature as an attempt to make sex "safe" for conservative Christians and allow them to participate in some way in the broader cultural revolution that was happening in America.[46] But the books notably did not say that it was possible to achieve sexual satisfaction and still be a good Christian. They said sexual satisfaction was attained uniquely through belief. They argued that belief in Jesus and the Bible was directly, causally connected to complete personal fulfillment. They held up an ideal of abundant life that was also everyday life. "Normal" life, lived in the white, middle-class suburbs of America.

The philosopher Charles Taylor talks about this as an "immanent frame." He argues that in Western history there has been "a revision downward of God's purposes for us" so that now there are "no final goals beyond human flourishing, nor any allegiance to anything else beyond this flourishing."[47] People seek spiritual fullness not in transcendence over self but in the realization of their best selves, and they want that to happen not in some time beyond time but in the here and now, the day-to-day, which is to say, in "immanent" reality. Instead of eternity, or the glory of God, or absorption into Being itself, "fullness" is thought of as a very individual, very human thing. Whether or not that's an accurate account of Western history and "secularity" writ large, it describes the sensibility of the 1970s Christian bookstore pretty well.[48] Love Jesus, the books promised, read the Bible, and you will have abundant life in the master bedroom of your tract home.

Some of the most popular books were testimonials to God's transforming power, such as Merlin Carothers's *Prison to Praise*, Chuck Colson's *Born Again*, and Joni Eareckson Tada's *Joni*. Other popular books told readers how to have the best children, such as James Dobson's *Dare to Discipline* and Larry Christenson's *Christian Family*. And there were books about how you could understand the chaos of current events through Scripture, and be assured of your own safety in the dark days ahead, like Hal Lindsey's *Late, Great Planet Earth*.

As these books created a community and a conversation, the central question readers were invited to consider, again and again, was how to achieve abundant life. How to flourish. Oke's book, a novel, was a powerful addition to this conversation. The fiction invited readers to imagine the experience of spiritual fullness as falling in love, and feeling safe, and knowing someone has the best plans for you.

Leaving to Love, Learning to Believe

Love Comes Softly starts when nineteen-year-old pioneer Martha "Marty" Claridge is forced by circumstance to marry a stranger. Her husband, Clem—"strong, adventurous, boyish Clem"—has died in an accident as they trekked west to claim free farmland on the open frontier.[49] Their wagon broke down. A horse ran away.

Then the other horse fell and killed Clem, leaving Marty a pregnant widow with winter coming on.

"This was the West," she thinks. "Things were hard out here" (17).

Marty has only just buried her husband, Clem, when a man introduces himself. "My name be Clark Davis," he says, in the frontier dialect unique to the novel, "an' it 'pears to me thet you an' me be in need of one another" (19). The proposal shocks Marty. "I'd rather die than marry you," she thinks, "or any man" (20). Clark explains, however, that this will be a practical arrangement. It is a trade: She needs someone to provide for her and a place to live, at least until spring comes and she can return east. He needs someone to take of his daughter, "a little 'un, not much more'n a mite," since his wife has died (19). They can help each other out.

It is not clear why marriage is necessary for the arrangement. It's not an issue of morality. Clark is not suggesting they have sex. They will not share a bed or even a room. Clark commits to sleep in a lean-to, outside the cabin, giving what was his and his wife's bedroom to Marty and his daughter, Missie. He is asking Marty "jest to be Missie's mama," he says. "Nothin' more." The marriage is perhaps thought of as an issue of propriety, necessary because people would think they were living "as man and wife" if they were living together in the small frontier cabin. But that's not explained. The marriage is just described in the novel as "the only sensible thing to do" (24). Marty is forced to agree, and this sets up the major conflict in the novel, the conflict between her life situation and her heart's desire.

She hates the idea of marrying Clark, but she also accepts that this is how it has to be. She does need help. The wagon she and her husband were driving is broken down. One of their horses is lost, the other dead. She has no shelter for the winter. She doesn't have enough money to pay for help. Also, she's pregnant. The facts of the situation compel her to accept help on whatever terms it's offered. She agrees to Clark's proposal, but it's really not a choice. She doesn't love this man. Nor does she expect to.

The romance novel heroine does not even believe she can find love. She loved her late husband, who "had captured her heart and her hand," but tragedy has taken that from her. Now there's just life. Just the West. "I hate this country!" she says. "I hate it! I hate him!" (21). She feels like she is forced to give up a dream, to give up her desire for a good life, the desire to be personally fulfilled. The thought of it almost overwhelms her. She tries not to think about it. "She couldn't face too far into the future," Oke explains, because "she was sure if she let her mind focus on the weeks and months ahead of her in this tiny cabin with a husband she had not chosen and a child who was not hers, she'd break under the weight of it all" (70). Marty thinks she will have to settle. She will have to accept that this is life, day after day without love.

Marty goes about her life with this fear, doing chores. They are mundane tasks, described in extensive detail. She cooks, cleans, and sews. The story does not skim over these activities but dwells on them. The chores are not incidental; they are not a device to add realistic detail to help readers identify with the put-upon heroine, struggling in a strange pioneer cabin on an unnamed Western prairie. They are important. Marty thinks they are important, and the novel presents them that way too.

The first morning she makes coffee, which she is good at. Then she struggles with breakfast. The struggle is rendered in detail. It takes two pages for the author to describe how the heroine finds the eggs, milk, and bacon, which are stored outside in a kind of root cellar, a pioneer cooler accessible via a rope and pulley. Then Marty tries to dress Missie. This takes four pages. First she has to find the clothes, and Missie starts screaming. Breakfast starts to burn because the wood stove is too hot, and then there's a spill, and Marty doesn't know where to find a rag in this strange kitchen. She burns her finger. Then she goes back to fighting with the crying, kicking child, who doesn't want to get dressed. Marty finally gets her clothed. She calms the girl down, rocking her and whispering to her, and then cleans her face and combs her hair. Breakfast is ready, eventually, but only because Clark finishes the cooking while Marty struggles with Missie. A pioneer wife's normal morning routine is too much for Marty to handle on her own. This is the horizon of her life, and the realm in which the novel imagines she will find, or not find, her own flourishing.

The first signs of hope come for Marty with hints that Clark cares for her. He wants something better for her. In one early scene, he worries that she doesn't have a bonnet to protect her from the sun. What did he care about the hot sun on her head? Marty wonders (23). But he does. Later, Marty expects him to be mad when she makes a mistake while doing the chores. He's not. In fact, he seems to assume she's doing her best, and to trust her (64). In another scene, Clark urges Marty not to work too hard. She has thrown herself into the chores, learning how to cook and clean, struggling to care for the child. He encourages her to take a break (64). Clark is even sensitive when he eventually learns Marty is pregnant with her late husband's child. He immediately offers to raise the child as his own. He also says, without prompting, that since it is important to Marty, he will make it clear to people that the child is her first husband's, not his, even as he provides for the baby. Clark, it turns out, is gentle, thoughtful, and kind.

Marty doesn't immediately see this. Or perhaps she doesn't understand what she sees. At first, she describes Clark as a "cold, miserable man" (21). She softens a bit when he is not harsh with her, and she remembers he has also lost a spouse. She stops being angry at him. Still, though, he sees him as "a stranger to avoid whenever she could" (97). She softens a bit more when they have the conversation about the coming child. When Clark makes it clear he understands about the baby, and how the child's paternity is important to her, Marty notes that she is still trying to "sort out this man" (127).

She doesn't know exactly what to think. She starts to reconsider, thinking her initial judgment might have been too severe.

The reader can see what Marty does not: Clark cares for her. He does not want her to accept the death of her dreams and the deadening of desire. He wants what's best for her. He wants her to thrive and be happy.

The novel suggests that Clark feels this way because of his belief. He extends grace to Marty because he has, as he understands it, received grace from God. He wants what is best for her because God wants what is best for her. She should have what she wants, because that is God's greatest desire, that people flourish.

This is expressed in a speech Clark gives Marty the first morning. Clark starts out just explaining where things are, so Marty can find what she needs to do the chores. There are vegetables in the root cellar. Some canned goods. They are low on fresh meat, but there's pork in the smokehouse, and there will be more meat when the weather turns cold and he can hunt. There are fish, too, in the nearby creek, and an orchard of young fruit trees that might bear fruit next year. "I'm a tellin' ya this," Clark says, "so's ya be knowing the lay o' the land, so to speak." He doesn't mean just the physical lay of the land, though. All this, he says, is God's blessing. God has provided. That means, he explains, "ya don't need to apologize for askin' fer what ya be needin'" (43). Clark is, in part, making a theological point. He believes that God takes care of him. He believes that, because he has a right relationship with God, God is his shepherd and cares for him.

Clark, Marty will soon learn, has a very personal relationship with God.

Clark is an unusual hero in the romance novel genre. English professor Pamala Regis writes in *A Natural History of the Romance Novel* that heroes in twentieth-century romances tend to fall into two types. The first is "sentimental." These male characters are wounded, either physically, psychologically, or emotionally, and need to be healed by the heroine. The other type is the "dangerous hero." The dangerous heroes were especially popular in the 1970s, though they can be found throughout the genre. These characters are portrayed as wild men who need to be tamed by the heroine's love.[50] These men can sometimes seem like they should be the villain. More than one such "hero" rapes the heroine.[51] Clark might initially be perceived as a "dangerous hero." The threat of danger is certainly present in the first pages of Oke's depiction, but the heroine quickly learns he is not that sort of man. But neither is he the "sentimental" type. The fiction hints at his wounds—he is a recent widower, after all. But the truest thing about Clark turns out to be neither his wounds nor his danger but his relationship to God. He loves God and only wants the heroine to trust that he and God want the best for her.

Slowly, as Marty makes meals and cleans and sews, she realizes the kind of man this man is. She starts to trust him. She starts to believe again and feel like herself again, and she starts to imagine that she might be able to have a fulfilled life. She is awakening to love, and at the same time developing her own relationship with God.

When the story starts, Marty is almost entirely unfamiliar with Christianity. She has never been to church, "apart from marryin' an' buryin'" (Oke, 30). She has never heard a prayer outside of church, and she actually doesn't think she has ever known anyone who has ever said such a prayer. She hasn't read the Bible. She believes in God, but just in the sense of intellectually agreeing that God exists. When she suffers, God feels aloof and very far away.

There is a little organized religion on the novel's imagined prairie, but not much. There are no churches and no regularly scheduled religious services. A traveling preacher—a circuit rider, perhaps—comes through, but only on occasion. Marty has only a vague impression of him, even after he buries her husband and performs her wedding. The reader, likewise, is given no clear picture. Even his name is uncertain. At the beginning of the novel, he is "Pastor Magnuson" (17). Later, he is "Pastor Simmons" (209). The novel does not note that the name has changed but is explicit that it is the same man (207). It would seem to be a mistake in continuity, an editing error, but if no one caught the mistake, it's because it doesn't really matter. The name is not important. The minister is not essential to the character's new religious experience. To Marty and to the novel, the minister is merely a functionary. He just "spoke the words that were fitting for the occasion" (17).

The only hint that belief might be something more than that solemnizing formality comes from the one personal thing the minister does when he buries Marty's first husband. Before he leaves and continues on his circuit, he turns to Marty and, "in a simple, straightforward manner," takes her hands in his and wishes God to be "very near her in the coming months" (25). Marty has no response. She's not even sure what that would mean.

Even basic Christian ideas confuse Marty at first. She's apparently never heard Psalm 23. When she does hear it, "Marty's mind kept puzzling over the Scripture passage" and struggles to grasp the meaning of the central metaphor: "*How could the Lord be a shepherd?*" (105). She wonders too about the life application. Can anyone just take the words of the psalmist and make them her own? When Clark reads them aloud, is he also saying them for himself? Could she take them for herself? Marty notes that "Bible reading hadn't been a part of her upbringing" (105).

Marty is introduced to Christianity through Clark. For him, the most important thing about this belief is that it brings him comfort. He doesn't talk about Christianity in terms of intellectual assent to ideas. He has no interest in proving that God exists or in constructing a worldview. He also talks about it as an almost entirely individualized thing: a personal relationship. And the result of that relationship is his own flourishing. Clark never mentions eternity or God's transcendent purposes. For Clark, belief is personal and relevant right now, in this world. Everything, for him, fits in that immanent frame.

This is apparent in Clark's prayers. He prays a lot, and Marty is initially shocked by this. The first day in his home, when he prays before eating, she sits "wide-eyed looking at this man before her, who spoke, eyes closed, to a God she did not see or know—and him not even a preacher" (30). It's not just that he is peculiarly devout, he is also so familiar with God. He addresses God as father and assumes God is interested in the details of his daily life. He prays about the weather and the livestock. He compliments his new wife's hard work. He tells God how he's feeling.

Clark also appeals to the Bible regularly—but just to a few, specific passages. These invariably emphasize the idea that God cares for people personally. Clark reads Psalm 23 several times. He leans heavily on the idea that when bad things happen, that can be understood as God's rod and staff, intended ultimately for his comfort. Clark also reads from Psalm 121, which says, "I will lift mine eyes unto the hills, from whence cometh my help" (41). For Clark, this is the point. As he understands the Bible, the message of the book is that God, who runs the whole world, cares about him and the apparently mundane details of his life.

Marty starts to refer to God as "Clark's God." It's not a phrase Clark would disagree with. As the novel imagines it, God does, in a sense, belong to him. Clark, for example, consistently links God with his own prosperity. In his four years in the West, he has done well. He has chickens, pigs, cows, a vegetable garden, and grain fields, and they've all thrived. Clark explains this by saying "we have us real good land and the Lord be blessin' it" (43). Clark does not understand his own life to be part of some larger, divine plan. Rather, he understands the divine plan to be oriented around his own flourishing. He has a personal relationship with God, and God, in an important way, belongs to him.

There are a few statements about God's glory that could be

seen as speaking of transcendence. The character of God is always articulated in immanent terms, though. Clark speaks of the goodness of God, for example, but not in an ontological sense, where God is imagined as all-good or absolutely good. Rather, Clark talks about God being good in the context of God providing. "Thank ya fer this food ya provide," he prays in one scene, "by yer goodness" (30). God is the Almighty, but that almightiness is understood anthropocentrically.

Clark does think that God is, in some sense, beyond human comprehension. What that means for him, however, is that humans do not always know how God's actions will result in human flourishing. They just have to trust that it will. When a storm comes and cancels plans for a Christmas party, Clark prays, "sometimes, Lord, we be puzzlin' 'bout your ways." Then, however, he suggests that God sent the storm at that time so that none of the neighbors would be caught outside. Clark thanks God for this. The puzzle is thus solved. Clark can't know, definitively, that that was God's purpose in sending the storm, but it's a good enough explanation for him. Similarly, when his prayers for "an extray cow or two" go unanswered, Clark says this is because God knows it's better for him not to have what he asked for than to have what he asked for (189). There is a higher purpose, but it relates directly to him.

With more serious tragedies, this trust that God always and only acts in the best interest of the believer can be more difficult. The problems of human suffering can, of course, cause people to have serious questions about belief. For Clark, this isn't what happens, though. He trusts. When Clark's barn burns down, for example, there's not an obvious way this will contribute to the family's flourishing. He nevertheless understands it as an opportunity to trust that God intends this for his benefit. How is a mystery, to him, but there's no question that that is the outcome of what God did and does. He reaches for his Bible and rereads Psalm 23 to affirm this (196).

Oke's Theology of Suffering

Clark's theology was Oke's own, born out of her experiences of suffering and flourishing, and the doctrines that carried her through. She discovered this faith at age ten, when she responded to an altar call at a Christian summer camp at Gull Lake. She was Janette Steeves then, the child of farmers on the Alberta prairie. In 1945, Janette was invited to an evangelistic summer camp for children. Her parents weren't churchgoers, but they let her go, and it changed her life.

The camp was run by the Missionary Church, a denomination of Mennonites who had embraced revivalism. One thing that set the Missionary Church apart in western Canada was its women ministers. On the "needy prairies," the church authorized at least two dozen ministering sisters to organize revivals, preach, and plant churches. The church in nearby Hoadley, Alberta, for example, was founded by Pearl Reist. In the middle of the Great Depression, thirty-eight-year-old Reist took over a pool hall, built a pulpit out of wooden crates and pews out of nail kegs, and began to preach. Eleven years later, the church was sponsoring farm children for a summer camp at an Alberta lake.[52] The evangelist, in the summer of 1945, was another ministering sister named Beatrice Speerman Hedegaard.

Hedegaard preached to the prairie children about yielding their lives to Christ. It wasn't enough to be good, she said. It wasn't enough to read Bible stories. It wasn't enough to believe God existed. It wasn't enough to say that Jesus died for your sins. To really believe, you needed to turn everything over to Jesus and truly, totally give your life to God. If you did, you would have the best life. You should submit yourself to God because God loved you and had a plan for your life.

This theology is called "higher life" or Keswick (pronounced "kezzick") theology, named after a camp in the Lake District of England.[53] Sometimes it is summarized with the slogan "let go and let God." The idea is not that if you trust God and have faith you will get whatever you want, but that if you trust God and have faith God will give you what is best for you. You will flourish in the immanent frame and have abundant life in your regular, normal day-to-day. This theology does not promise a life free from pain and sorrow, but rather that God will carry you through and comfort you.

As Oke would later describe it, characterizing her own books, "It isn't that God protects us from all these tough things in life— What I want to emphasize is the fact that he's there to help us through those things. . . . He's holding you steady. He's going to see you through."[54] If you give your life to Jesus, Oke believed, you can know how much he loves you, and wants the best for you, and his love can comfort you when life is hard. What you have to do is yield to his love.

Young Janette sat through an altar call every night, her heart beating hard, her palms sweaty, trying to decide whether she would yield. The children were invited to come forward if they would submit to God, and Steeves wanted to go forward. She felt a longing that almost pulled her out of her seat, she wanted to go forward so bad. But she was afraid she'd be embarrassed in front of all the other children.

Finally, one night, Hedegaard didn't give an altar call. Instead of asking people to come forward, she told the children if they wanted to give their lives to Jesus, they should just raise their hands. Steeves's hand went up. Then Hedegaard said, if your hand was up, you should come forward.

As she described the moment more than forty years later, Oke remembered that she felt free of shame. She had been worried about being embarrassed, about walking to the front and standing in front of the other kids. She wasn't, though. She felt free from shame and from the fear of shame. It was just a "wonderful realization of forgiveness."[55]

This became the core idea of how Oke understood belief. She thought of it as an act of submission. You should submit to God and trust God. "God's way is the best way," as one of her favorite hymns put it. "God's way is the right way / I'll trust in Him always / He knoweth the best."[56] If you believed, you could fully submit, and if you submitted, Oke thought, God would give you abundant life. In your day-to-day experience, in the mundane details, you would be triumphant and could live a "higher life."

Oke didn't think you yielded just once, though. You surrendered all your life to God: through your successes and your suffering. She would return to that hymn, singing, "God's way is the best way," when her life was really hard and she needed to recommit herself to trusting God. She sang it, for example, when she was twenty-two and had a miscarriage alone in an apartment very far from her family.

That happened right after Janette married Edward Oke in 1956 and they moved south to Mishawaka, Indiana, so Edward could finish his BA there and then get some seminary training in the Missionary Church. There was one mishap on the way down when they got a flat tire. The shoulder of the road was soft and the jack wouldn't lift up their car, packed full of what they owned. It was dark and scary, on the side of the road, but then they got help and it was okay. They laughed about how scared they had been. They were young. They loved each other. It was an adventure.

In Mishawaka, Edward was busy at school. He also got a job, as an assistant minister at Beulah Missionary Church in nearby Elkhart, so he always had to drive over there. Oke stayed in their $65-a-month apartment most days. She unpacked their things. She made it their home. She got pregnant. Then there was a miscarriage, and she couldn't call anyone because Canada was too far away.

Oke laid down and cried. And after a while, she sang:

God's way is the best way.
God's way is the right way.
I'll trust in Him always.
He knoweth the best.[57]

Oke believed that. And she felt better.

Edward finished his BA in the spring of 1958, and the couple moved to Goshen, Indiana, to be closer to Edward's church and so that he could take seminary classes at Goshen College. Oke got a job in the mail room of a manufacturing company. She got involved in the church, teaching Sunday school. There were flashes of pain sometimes, when she thought about the baby she didn't have, surrounded by the children in the church, their chubby cheeks and stubby fingers. But it was okay. She trusted God. Then she got pregnant again.

Her joy was mixed with fear. Maybe she'd miscarry again. She didn't want to lose another baby. She prayed that she wouldn't. She asked God to protect her baby. Please, God. Give her this baby.

Then Oke worried that praying like that wasn't right. She should trust God. So she prayed a different prayer. She surrendered her child to God. She put her trust in him and gave her child to him. The baby was God's baby, given to her as a gift from him. She told God he could take her child if that was his will. She would trust him always.

She gave birth to a son in October 1959. He died before she even got to hold him. The infant had a heart murmur and an enlarged liver, though the pediatricians did not know the underlying cause. The doctors spent hours trying to save the child but couldn't. The news was shattering. Later she recalled thinking, over and over, "I didn't even get to hold him. I didn't even get to hold him."[58] After she got home from the hospital, Oke spent days looking at the empty crib in their apartment, just crying.

She said to God, "I know that I said you could take him—but I didn't promise not to cry."[59]

Eighteen years later, surrounded by her happy family, including four healthy and growing children, she still believed that God's way was the best way. That's what she was writing in her novel—a story about human love, and divine love, and how important it was to trust God through suffering.

"Each struggle Clark and Marty worked through," Oke wrote, "I struggled through with them. Each triumph they experienced was my own. Each truth about the faithfulness of the God they served was a wonderful reminder to me" (10).

A World of Tragedy

There is a lot of tragedy in *Love Comes Softly*. There are the tragedy that serves as the inciting incident of the novel and the tragedies that provide pivotal plot points, such as the barn fire. But the romance goes further in its depiction of tragedy. Almost every minor character is shown to have suffered. The novel imagines a world in which suffering is always a reality but belief helps people through the struggle.

After Marty has her baby, a stream of pioneer women comes to visit. These are new characters, introduced three-quarters of the way through the story. As the women come through the cabin, the world of the novel expands. As it expands, it shows readers that Marty's tragedy is not unique. Every woman bears these burdens. Everyone goes through trials. Some, however, share their struggles with Jesus and have the assurance that their struggles will work out for good.

The first to visit is a woman named Wendy Marshall. Marshall is "small and young, with blond hair that at one time must have been very pretty" (175). She smiles but still seems sad. At first it is just a hint. The protagonist intuits the sadness in the woman's eyes. Then the sadness rises up and overwhelms her. Marshall peeks in at the sleeping baby boy. She sees "the soft pink baby face, with lashes as fine as dandelion silk on his cheek," and she can't stand it (176). She leaves the room and goes and stands at the cabin window and cries. Marshall apologizes to Marty, confessing that she had three children of her own, but they all died.

"It's this wretched country," Marshall says. "If I'd stayed back east where I'd belong, things would have been different. I would have my family—my Jodi and Esther and Josiah. It's this horrible place" (177).

Lost children are not the only kind of tragedy the women in the world of *Love Comes Softly* suffer, either. Another character who comes to visit Marty and the new baby is burdened by poverty. She comes on the scene an "ill-clad stranger, with two equally ill-clad children" (180). The woman mumbles her name and the names of her children and doesn't make eye contact—too ashamed, it would seem, to be polite company.

Marty later learns the woman's husband is, as one neighbor puts it, "one lazy good-fer-nothin'" (184). Jedd Larson shirks work. He's generally irresponsible. He will, however, gladly help himself to other people's generosity. People look at Mrs. Larson—readers never learn her first name—and they either judge her or pity her. She can't stand it. But she doesn't have a choice.

Another woman's burden is more literal: she is overweight. Marty puts it politely, noting that Maude Watley is "rather stout," but it is clear that this is not a matter of a few spare pounds. Watley can barely walk. She doesn't walk into the bedroom of the cabin to see the baby; instead, she asks that the baby be brought to her. When it's time to leave, she doesn't walk to the wagon but waits until it is pulled up to the front door. In the meantime, she eats "several helpings of cookies and loaf cake" (183). A neighbor gossips that Watley actually used to be a "dance-hall girl" before she was married (185). The history of what happened in the intervening years is cryptic, but the suffering is plain.

Perhaps the starkest tragedy to befall one of the novel's minor characters is what happens to Laura Graham. Graham is the second daughter of one of the neighbors and is seventeen years old. She is barely mentioned until the last thirty pages, and then her story, her tragedy, is the cap on all the novel's tragedies.

It starts when Graham gets pregnant before she is married. No one even knew she was seeing anyone, but Graham, it turns out, has been secretly spending time with a bachelor named Milt Conners. And she got pregnant.

Her parents are upset and perhaps also scandalized, but Graham stoutly insists that she loves Milt and is going to marry him, "come what may" (205).

She does marry him, and it seems, for a moment, that tragedy may be averted. The young woman does not seem to carry "the glow that a new bride should," but she does seem determined to make it work. She's committed to her marriage, even if Conners does have a deserved reputation for being wild. The women at the wedding hope her love might make her husband a better man (205, 211). Conners, for his part, looks "rather careless in demeanor and attire" but remembers to trim his beard before the big day (211).

Things do not get better. Graham withdraws from the community. She refuses even small, neighborly favors. There are signs of spousal abuse: she carries a bruise on her cheek. Then it gets worse.

Clark brings Marty the news: "It's Laura. They done found her in the crik over by the Conners' cabin."

"Is she . . . is she . . . ?"

"She be dead, Marty" (222).

Marty is there when the young pregnant woman is pulled from the water. Graham's mother holds the frail corpse in her arms, rocks back and forth, and cries. Then she wipes her tears, squares her shoulders, and begins preparing for the funeral.

Everyone suffers in *Love Comes Softly*. Tragedy is a fact of life. The novel does not invite readers to imagine that belief changes that. It does suggest that belief helps. Belief comforts. Further, the novel imagines that the context of belief is this context of human suffering, and that belief is important because it is relevant to the kinds of tragedies these women endure. Put another way, in the world of *Love Comes Softly*, belief brings the reassurance that the meaning of suffering is immanent. God works all things together for the good of those who love him, and not in abstract, transcendent terms.

All of this appeals to Marty, but she is slow to submit.

Her first step is just thinking it would be nice to have that sense of divine assurance. It sounds nice. She thinks the idea of "God's love, for me!" and the promise of abundant life are really attractive. But she's not immediately ready to believe.

She hears Clark reading from Psalm 121, and she wishes she had help coming from the hills (41). She returns to the thought again, a short time later. While doing more chores, Marty sees the mountains to the west. "Far beyond the rolling hills," Oke writes, "blue mountains rose in majesty. Was it from those peaks that Clark was seeking the help of his God?" (47). The idea doesn't seem crazy to her. She's drawn to the thought of a God who cares about her like that.

Before long, Marty finds herself wanting to pray (61). The thing she wants to pray about is notably not a matter of ultimate reality. It's a mundane detail. In the process of doing her chores, Marty had washed the cabin walls, including the chinking holding the logs together. This seems to have been a mistake. The hard white plaster turns muddy (64). Pieces fall from the wall. It turns out not to be serious—Clark fixes it easily—but that's the point. Marty is not interested in a God who would only care about serious, heavenly things. She's drawn to the comfort of a God who would care about little details that didn't matter, and care just because she was worried.

She hesitates, though. Marty explains this to herself as a knowledge problem. She doesn't know how to pray (61). She thinks because she wasn't raised religious, she may have "missed out on something rather important," and so now lacks the skill of prayer that other people have. This explanation is not quite right, though. While it's true that she lacks knowledge, the novel imagines that this explanation is really an expression of fear. "Marty found herself wondering," Oke writes, "if she dared to approach Clark's God in the direct way that Clark himself did. She felt a longing to do so, but she held back" (105-6). It's emotional, not intellectual. Even when it's a statement about knowledge, it's a statement about desire: "She knew very little about God, and sometimes she caught herself yearning to know more" (105).

Marty does not take the direct approach, at first. Her first prayer in the novel is a tentative whisper. Ma Graham, the Davises' neighbor, comes by to help Marty learn to take care of a pioneer cabin. She teaches her to make bread, gives her a lot of recipes, and offers tips for making it through a frontier winter. She reassures her that everything will be okay. She mentions God, though barely. She acknowledges Marty's mourning in passing, and hints that she has had her own tragedies, in the past. Speaking from that experience, she says time and God heal the heart (74). When Graham leaves, Marty is so moved she is moved to pray. It's only tentative, though. She prays for God to bless Ma Graham for her kindness, but then she couches that request in a conditional: she prays that God would bless the woman "if there truly [is] a God up there somewhere" (67). She's not ready to risk more.

Marty's second prayer is even more tentative. It's not even whispered. It happens on a Sunday—the Lord's Day—and she is stirred by Clark's reading of Psalm 23. As he reads, he stops and explains a few things, offering "words of his own as background or setting to the Scripture" (105). Then he prays. She wants to participate in his prayer but doesn't. At the end, however, Clark says "amen" and his daughter declares "her loud ''men,' too," and Marty is so close to joining them. She mouths the word but doesn't make a sound (106).

Marty turns from prayer to Bible reading. She's inspired by the Christmas story. Clark reads the story aloud on Christmas Day, when he and Missie and Marty are snowed in. He starts with the angel appearing to Mary to tell her she is going to have a child. In the Bible passage, the angel says, "Fear not, Mary: for thou hast found favour with God" (Luke 1:30 KJV). Clark reads on, about the trip to Bethlehem, about the inns where there was no room, and the stable with the manger where the infant was laid. Clark reads about the shepherds and how the angels appear to them and the one says again, "Fear not," and tells them the good news (Luke 2:10).

In the Gospel of Luke, the story leaves Mary pondering these things in her heart. In *Love Comes Softly*, the story has the same effect on Marty. "The story captured Marty's imagination," Oke writes, "as she waited for the birth of her own first child, and she thought of it as she did the dishes" (152). Marty identifies with Mary. She thinks about what she would have done if she had been Mary.

As Marty hears the story, the nativity is about God providing in difficult circumstances. The story, of course, is also about the incarnation. The angel in the gospel says the child will be conceived miraculously by the Holy Ghost and will be the "Son of the Highest." Evangelicals understand Luke 1 and 2 as an account of how God became human. Marty notes that aspect, remarking that the "little baby born in a stable was God's Son" (152). For her, though, this divine parentage is part of the larger message of God's love and concern. The incarnation, in a sense, folds into the story about

God's plan. Marty thinks Mary probably couldn't understand why it was part of God's plan to have God's Son born in a barn. Mary could trust, though, that God would do what was best for the child. Marty can imagine herself like Mary. This means she can imagine herself trusting God.

"*Wouldn't be carin' fer my son to be born in a barn,*" she thinks. "*Still—God did watch over Him, sendin' angels to tell the shepherds an' all. An' the wise men, too, with their rich gifts. Yes, God was carin' 'bout His Son*" (152).

God's plan might look different than one would expect, but you could still trust that God's plan was intended for human good. The incarnation, the nativity, and Marty's marriage of convenience are all part of God's plan, and the plan is fixed firmly in the immanent frame.

Marty ponders these things while attending to the dishes after Christmas dinner. She decides she would like to read the story again, so she sits down and picks up the Bible. She doesn't know how to read the Bible, though, just like she didn't know how to pray. "She wished she knew where to locate the Christmas story," Oke writes, "but as she turned the pages she couldn't find where Clark had read" (153). Marty ends up reading an entirely different portion of Scripture, but the text still turns out to be about how God cares for people. Marty ends up reading Psalms. She read them "one after the other as she sat beside the warm fire." She didn't understand what she was reading, necessarily, but it didn't matter. "Somehow they were comforting," Marty thinks, "even when you didn't understand all of the phrases and ideas" (153).[60]

The Bible comforts her. It assures her that God loves her and encourages her to take an emotional risk and respond to God. As presented in *Love Comes Softly*, this is, in fact, the point of the Bible. Marty phrases the key question this way: "Do ya really think thet God, who runs the whole world like, be knowin' ya?" Clark says yes. He says he believes. He's sure God cares for him. As he explains, "I believe the Bible, and it tells me thet He does" (189).

Marty finally feels that for herself when the snow begins to thaw. After her child is born and she names him after his father, Claridge Luke Davis, after Ma Graham tells her how love sometimes "comes sorta stealin' up on ya gradual like," after the barn burns down and then the neighbors help build a new one, Easter comes (173). The traveling preacher, now known as Pastor Simmons, preaches about Jesus's crucifixion. Marty hears the message. She takes it personally. "She had heard before how cruel men of Christ's day had put him to death with no just cause," Oke writes, "but never before had she realized it had anything at all to do with her" (210). The preacher explains about sins, and how they separate people from God, and how Jesus came to take those sins, the cross serving as a bridge back to God. Marty, sitting on a bench, is moved to tears. "*I didn't know—I jest didn't know thet ya died fer me*," she prays. It's a spontaneous prayer, from her heart. When she realizes the magnitude of what Jesus did, and she knows God will go to any length for her, she responds with this outpouring of emotion, "her heart filled with such a surge of joy" (210). She is unafraid of the emotional risk of belief. She speaks to God directly.

"*I've given myself to be a knowin' Clark's God*," she thinks. And Oke tells readers Marty was "awed by the thought" (210).

The novel's conversion narrative could plausibly have ended there. The story goes on, though, to show how belief works out in Marty's life. At the end of the novel, after her conversion, Marty is confronted with two more tragedies. The first is Laura Graham's death. The girl's tragic end hits Marty particularly hard. She goes to the woods, to the place where Graham died, to think about it and pray.

"She really needed a place to think," Oke writes, "to sort things out." Marty sits by the water, leans against a tree. "I know thet yer good," she says to God. "I know thet ya love me, thet ya died for me; but I don't understand 'bout losin', 'bout the pain thet goes so deep I can't see the end. I don't understand at all" (226). The pain and tragedy are a mystery, but because she has found faith, because she believes, Marty is confident that human suffering can be explained in terms of God's love for her.

This is similar to how the Okes dealt with their loss, after the miscarriage and the child who died in infancy. They understood it as "a growing time." They believed that God, in fact, would use the tragedy in their lives, making it meaningful, in a real and practical way. "They were reminded," Oke's biography says, "that if they planned to serve in the ministry, in years ahead there would doubtlessly be many times when they would be called upon to share the grief of someone in their congregation." That didn't mean it didn't hurt. It didn't mean it wasn't horrible. But the Okes felt that God helped them through the tragedy. In fact, "Janette was thankful that a loving God had cushioned the blow as only He could. He had prepared her heart so there was no bitterness, and he was with her daily, helping her with her sorrow and tears."[61]

Oke puts this belief in the mouth of her protagonist: "*I thank ye, Lord, that ye be teachin' me how to rest in you,*" Marty prays toward the end of the novel. "*Ya be comfortin' me, and I be grateful for it.*"

The novel concludes with Marty in Clark's arms. She didn't even realize it was happening, but now she loves this man. "This man," Oke writes, "who comforted her when she sorrowed, understood her joys, gave her strength when her own strength was spent, shared with her his faith, and introduced her to his God. There was so much she felt. The strange, deep stirring within her—she understood it now" (236). The married couple embrace. She yields to him, "looking deep into his eyes" and "feeling the strength of his body tight against hers" (237). Love, at the end of the narrative, overcomes all obstacles. Submitting to it and trusting it empower one to live triumphantly and abundantly. They live happily ever after, a version of eternity in the here and now.

The Reception of Love Comes Softly

Evangelical publishers weren't publishing novels like this. Oke didn't know that, though, so she sent out her six queries and waited. Sometimes she felt tempted to be proud of her work. She would have the thought "you've done a pretty good job." But then she would address it as the enemy: "You know and I know that is not the truth," she would say. "I've given myself, my imagination, my stories to God."[62]

She finally got a response from one of the publishers. Zondervan, in Michigan, asked to see three sample chapters. But then, after reviewing them, editors wrote Oke to say the romance did not fit the company's "present publishing schedule."[63]

Then she heard from Bethany House. One editor, reading the changes in the market, pushed Bethany House to give the manuscript a chance. Carol Johnson was one of the few female editors in evangelical publishing at the time. She asked for the entire manuscript and then convinced her male colleagues to publish the book.

The risky acquisition quickly paid off. At the Christian booksellers convention in 1979, evangelical retailers snatched up forty-four of the forty-five available sample copies. The last was shrink-wrapped to a bookstand to keep it from disappearing.[64] The booksellers knew there was a market for fiction. Across the country, they stocked the novel, and by the end of 1979, it was one of Bethany House's best sellers.[65] It continued to be a best seller for years to come, selling an average of fifty-five thousand copies a year for twenty years.[66]

On the social cataloguing site GoodReads, about half of the readers of *Love Comes Softly* give the book five out of five stars.

Nearly 30 percent give it four stars. The readers who love it talk about how they identify with the characters and how they thrill to the themes of faith, family, and flourishing. "A simple book about faith and hardship and enduring-serving-life-long love. I really loved this book," wrote one white woman. "The amount of tears were at least doubled due to my pregnant state, yet I felt I could somewhat relate through my own experiences with death."[67]

A mother of three in Indiana reported that she had read the book in one sitting—from 2:00 p.m., overnight, to 9:30 a.m. "My hubby was mad because I wouldn't turn off the light," she said. The book was so moving she couldn't stop reading, and by the end she was thinking in the accent of the characters. "I'm sure my family will mock me shortly," she wrote. "You simply fall in love with the characters."[68]

Most of the readers were churchgoing women: white, married, mother of a few children, middle class. The readers who liked it also recommended it to others, not infrequently in terms of encouragement and faith. One reader said Oke's romance "inspires you that even in the time of sadness happiness and love is waiting behind the door waiting for you," and said she would recommend the book to those "who just want to read a lovey dovery novel," but also people in deep need, "anyone who wants to see the sun in the middle of the cloudy winter."[69]

Reading the love story, about human love but also divine, could be a kind of devotional act, according to scholar Lynn S. Neal, who extensively interviewed readers and read about one hundred letters from fans to authors for her study *Romancing God: Evangelical Women and Inspirational Fiction*. The readers devoted to the genre "imagine evangelical romance reading as a devotional practice *through* which to articulate a women's faith and a women's ministry," Neal wrote.[70] They used the novel to narrate their own religious experience, to center women's experiences of the world, and to think about their relationship with God. They experienced pleasure reading the books, which is a normal part of the fiction-reading experience, but with Christian romance novels, Neal found, they described that pleasure as spiritual fullness and took the fiction as an opportunity to reflect on God's love for them and God's desire for them to live their best lives.

"It uplifts me spiritually and gives me a boost, you know, closer to God and to live that way," one woman told Neal. "I do feel that I get closer to God out of reading them."[71]

It would be a mistake, though, to think that everyone read Oke's book and liked it. The poet LaDonna Witmer read the books as a kid because her mother had all of Oke's books, and she had nothing else to do. "Sometimes you read something knowing it's not going to be great but you read it anyway because it's better than being bored," Witmer wrote in her GoodReads review. "It was better than the back of a cereal box."[72] She gave the book two stars.

Some readers were not bored but found the genre itself to be dangerous because of the way it drew them in. One young woman wrote that she was too focused on her feelings and emotions already, because of her "romantic personality," and Christian romance novels made it worse. "I had a 'perfect' picture of love and romance," she said, "complete with fluttery feelings and dizzying emotions. I was occupied with the longing to be 'swept off my feet' by the handsome prince of my dreams." The fiction's emphasis on the comparison between a man's love for a woman and God's love for a woman—the *perfect* perfect love—didn't help matters, for this reader. "My very attraction toward these things was exactly the encouragement I should have avoided," she wrote, after rejecting the fiction completely. "Instead of allowing my focus to rest on finding a perfect, ideal, romantic relationship, I should have instead turned my eyes and heart to seek God's will for me, and my future husband."[73]

A lot of people were annoyed by less serious things: the way the characters spoke or the fact that the plot was too predictable.

But critiques of the quality of the writing were also frequently connected to theological shortcoming. "It's not the most well-written," wrote a woman from Texas. "The Christian doctrine taught in it is pretty generic. It doesn't always fit what I believe, but no big deal." She ended up recommending the novel to a friend anyway.[74] On GoodReads, about 1 percent of the people who took the time to rate the book gave it only one star. Another 3 percent gave it two.

Sometimes the most serious critiques had a way of wrapping around to focus on the concern most central to Oke's fiction—how people could experience God's love in their daily lives. In *Christianity Today*, author Elizabeth Cody Newenhuyse worried about whether the escapist aspects of Christian romance novels drew the imagination to the past, making it seem as if the prairie in the olden days was the only place faith could really be felt fully.

"After a hard day, when the kids are tucked in bed and you have a little time for yourself, it's comforting to curl up with one of these fictional friends," Newenhuyse wrote. "But why are these historical stories so comforting? . . . Is there something about the world of fax machines and malls that makes Christianity seem out of sync with the times?"

But in the Christian bookstores in the suburbs across America, readers weren't being pulled away from the question of their religion's place in their lives, but to it, again and again. Oke asked them to imagine what it was like to flourish in your everyday life, to trust God and know God's love even while doing chores, even while struggling through real hardship.

"We live in a hurting, confused world that is searching for answers and purpose," Oke said in an interview with Christian book.com. "My hope is that my books . . . will show readers that a personal faith in God and the fellowship of family and selected friends will bring harmony and inner peace to their lives."[75]

Soon Oke had a second novel asking the same question in a slightly different way, and many of her readers themselves became writers, contributing to this ongoing conversation about what it meant to have a relationship with Jesus in everyday life. Other publishers saw the success of *Love Comes Softly* and agreed to publish these romance novels inspired by Oke, imitating Oke, and iterating her ideas about spiritual fullness. By the mid-1980s, Christian bookstores were full to overflowing with this fiction that intended, as an advertisement for two Zondervan romance sagas put it in 1984, to "capture the imagination . . . while speaking to the heart." Or, as another ad explained: "Our faith is inspired when we read of these people whose lives were in many ways more difficult than our own, yet who persevered and overcame hardships triumphantly."[76]

That was exactly what Oke felt, in the station wagon with her family going on vacation in 1977. That was the idea that shaped her dream of a novel, and the discourse that followed and the community that was organized around it: What does it meant to flourish in your life? What does it mean to know God really loves you? What does it mean to accept that, right now?

2

Spiritual Warfare in Everyday America

Frank Peretti's *This Present Darkness*

There was no room on the market for Frank Peretti. Peretti was trying to find a publisher for his evangelical horror novel *The Heavenlies*. It imagined a small, idyllic American town taken over by an occult conspiracy. Demons skittered around in the shadows. No one could see them, but a few praying Christians could sense they were there. "It was amazing how well the demons could hide," a struggling pastor reflects in the novel, even though the pastor sometimes doubted their existence.[1] In Peretti's story, the only thing that can stop these demons is belief. The pastor has to somehow rally the apathetic, lukewarm Christians to see the true dimensions of their spiritual struggle. He has to show them, somehow, that the daily cultural practice of belief is a spiritual battle with the principalities and powers of darkness.

Peretti himself was inspired the write the novel after losing a few such battles. He was a thirty-three-year-old ex-minister, recently resigned from a pastoral position at an Assemblies of God church. He was living in a twenty-five-foot travel trailer parked on Vashon Island, in Puget Sound in Washington State, writing the novel between shifts at the ski-equipment factory job he took to make ends meet. His was not a story of spiritual fullness achieved in America's suburbs, but one of conflict and desperate prayers. But that's not how belief was imagined in evangelical bookstores in the early 1980s.

Evangelical fiction was a booming business after Janette Oke's success. Each of the many family Christian bookstores across suburban America carried dozens of new Christian novels every year. Even secular booksellers saw financial opportunities in the new evangelical market. B. Dalton, for example, a chain with stores in more than seven hundred malls, was experimenting with stock from at least four evangelical publishers and advertising to white, middle-class evangelical book buyers in *Christianity Today*. "People who know Christian books," one ad said in 1984, "know B. Dalton."[2]

People who knew Christian books also knew evangelicals wouldn't buy Peretti's novel. He sent the 376-page manuscript to an evangelical publisher and got rejected. He sent it out again, got rejected again. He sent it out three times, four, a dozen. No one was interested.

Evangelicals liked romance novels. Peretti's fiction was part of the horror tradition H. P. Lovecraft called the "spectrally macabre." This was horror that imagines a world just like the readers' everyday reality but then disrupts that mimetic representation with otherworldly and occult forces. Lovecraft, one of the most significant horror writers in the twentieth century, said Americans liked horror with a supernatural touch. It spoke to those who were depressed, despairing, and disenchanted. It gave their lives a shiver of the numinous.[3]

In the early 1980s, stories of cultural subversion and behind-the-scenes subterfuge were quite popular in the general market. Mostly, these were Cold War stories. Spy novels by John le Carré, Robert Ludlum, Ken Follett, and Frederick Forsyth regularly earned the top spot on the *New York Times* best-seller list. Americans also liked stories about occult-ish forces scratching at the edges of realism. Stephen King built a career out of this. He had a major success with his 1976 novel *'Salem's Lot*, about supernatural evil taking over an iconic American town.[4] King's subsequent fiction frequently played with the idea of "spectral" forces at work unseen in everyday life. His stories had plots involving a tentacled monster that moves in an unnatural mist (*The Mist*, 1980); a seemingly possessed dog (*Cujo*, 1981); resurrected corpses (*Pet Sematary*, 1983); a demonic truck ("Uncle Otto's Truck," 1984); a gypsy curse (*Thinner*, 1984); a murderous witch possessed by Hastru, a malevolent god from the fictional Cthulhu Mythos created by Lovecraft ("Gramma," 1984); and a supernatural force that takes the form of a predatory clown to lure children to their doom (*It*, 1986). His work was so popular that when one marketing survey asked readers what they would want to read if marooned on a desert island, King's fiction ranked second behind the King James Bible.[5]

But evangelical publishers weren't interested in supernatural horror.

Except brothers Jan and Lane Dennis.

The Dennises read *The Heavenlies* and felt a shiver of recognition. The novel articulated something they believed about belief. Evangelical belief, they thought, should compel conflict. Evangelicals should think about reality differently. Christianity—rightly understood—was a worldview irreconcilably at odds with every other worldview, and true Christianity should lead to cultural clashes.

The Dennis brothers started their publishing company, Crossway, in 1979, a few years before Peretti started writing. Crossway was part of the '70s boom of evangelical publishing houses, but the Dennises also had a history in the business. Their parents were gospel-tract publishers. Clyde and Muriel Dennis started Good News Publishing in 1938. According to the family legend, they began with two hundred pounds of paper they bought for twenty dollars. They printed a first run of forty thousand tracts, sent them to six hundred Christian evangelists, and the Dennis family was in business. They published 50 million tracts during World War II. By the mid-1960s, the Wheaton, Illinois, company was distributing more than 12 million per year. With Crossway, the sons expanded the business into book publishing.[6]

The company was committed to evangelism. Its mission was to "bring men, women, and children to Christ as their Lord and Savior." It also had an expansive sense of what Christ's Lordship meant. Salvation was not just a personal thing, concerning the soul or individual flourishing. Jesus, according to the 1979 mission statement, was king, with dominion "in every area of life." Conceived that way, a fundamental claim of evangelicalism was that anything not in submission to Christ was treason. Christ had a claim over everything. That claim could cause and should cause conflict between those who recognized its authority and those who didn't.

Crossway, from the beginning, decided to specialize in the literature of the Religious Right, promoting the politics of cultural conflict. One of the first books the brothers published was *Whatever Happened to the Human Race?* by C. Everett Koop, the surgeon in chief at the Children's Hospital of Philadelphia, and Francis Schaeffer, a missionary to Switzerland. The book warned Christians about abortion, infanticide, and euthanasia. There was a struggle going on for America's soul, and innocent lives were at stake. In a publisher's preface, the Dennises argued these were not isolated issues about which people happened to disagree. The real disagreement was over "our most basic beliefs about God and man."

"Ideas have consequences," the Dennises wrote, "and abortion, infanticide, and euthanasia are the logical consequences of several powerful ideas. . . . These ideas have taken root in American society."[7]

Crossway went on to publish a slew of nonfiction titles advocating Christian cultural engagement. But the Dennises weren't publishing any fiction. The market was dominated by novels imagining belief as the key to human flourishing, and the Dennis brothers didn't care for prairie romances. They didn't identify with female characters who discovered love and their best selves. *The Heavenlies*, though, presented a version of evangelical belief they could identify with. Peretti had written a book they thought their readers might like.

"He has written a book," Jan Dennis said, "for the so-called moral majority. They can hold this up and say, 'This is how I see the world.'"[8]

The Worldview Thinking of Francis Schaeffer

It's no accident the Dennises felt such an affinity for Peretti. The publishers and the novelist were all deeply influenced by the "worldview" thinking of Francis Schaeffer.

A lot of evangelicals were. Schaeffer made a compelling theological case for cultural engagement at a time when many conservative Protestants felt a great need for that argument. They felt they had retreated from the public sphere and disengaged from public life. A number of historians—notably Daniel K. Williams and Matthew Avery Sutton—have shown they were wrong about this. Conservative Protestants actually hadn't disengaged from public life.[9] They had always been politically active. They were an important group of voters in every presidential election in the twentieth century, from the election of William McKinley to that of George W. Bush. Even after the embarrassment of the Scopes monkey trial in 1925, self-identified "fundamentalists" continued their outspoken support for prohibition and opposition to "wet" candidates.[10] In the 1940s, when theologian Carl F. H. Henry was writing about the problem of conservative Christians' cultural withdrawal, Harry Truman's presidential campaign was worrying about how to win their votes.[11] Nevertheless, by the 1970s, many of the shoppers at suburban Christian bookstores conceived of themselves as marginalized, and they worried they had abandoned the public sphere. Schaeffer was one of the leading articulators of why engagement was theologically important, even necessary, for evangelical Christians.[12]

Schaeffer was a conservative Presbyterian from Pennsylvania who established a mission called L'Abri in Huemoz, Switzerland, in 1955. He didn't speak French, so he couldn't reach the local Swiss with the gospel, but he and his wife, Edith, ministered to wayward American youth and European university students on holiday.[13] To engage these educated young people, Schaeffer found it was best not to start with theology or the Bible. It was more effective to start with cultural criticism: talking about and then challenging the ideas of contemporary art, music, and philosophy. He discussed everything from *Phänomenologie des Geistes* to *Sgt. Pepper's Lonely Hearts Club Band*. In every modern work of art and thought, Schaeffer claimed, one could discover a cry of despair. More, he argued, modern people should despair. Despair wasn't wrong. Despair was the only logical conclusion for a worldview that did not start from Christian presuppositions about the reality of God and the nature of truth.

The evangelical worldview, in Schaeffer's account, started with the foundational, prerational assumption—or presupposition—of God's existence. That idea, then, entailed ideas of objective reality and absolute truth, which served as the basis for rational thought. The "antithesis," a word Schaeffer used to mean an irreconcilable opposite, was secular humanism. Secular humanism was the predominant worldview in Europe and America, according to Schaeffer, as seen in Hegel and the Beatles, but also in *Time* magazine, Ingmar Bergman, Woody Allen, and Marcel Duchamp. Secular humanism first took hold in philosophy and then filtered down through art, music, general culture, and finally contemporary theology, which led to the apostasy of the "modernist" side of the modernist-fundamentalist divide in American Protestantism in the 1930s.[14] Humanism was antithetical to Christianity because it started with a theory of knowledge—an epistemology—grounded in human experience rather than in God's existence. In this system of thought, "men and women, beginning absolutely by themselves, try rationally to build out from themselves, having only Man as their integration point, to find all knowledge, meaning and value."[15]

In his arguments for the philosophical foundation of Christian belief, Schaeffer would grant that secular humanism's approach to knowledge seemed promising at first. Many were originally very optimistic about what they could know and how certain they could be of what they knew, working only with knowledge that was available to all equally. But without God to guarantee the absolute quality of truth—without revelation—that approach to knowledge was ultimately unsustainable. The rationalist project would collapse into antirationalism. When men and women try to think "absolutely by themselves," they can't really know anything, because their knowledge isn't objective. "We can see it in the drug addict—he has often lost the distinction between reality and fantasy," Schaeffer wrote. "But the scientist can be in the same place. If he loses the epistemological base, he, too, is in a serious position. What does science mean once you are no longer sure of the objectivity of the thing, or you are no longer on an epistemological base which gives the certainty of a correlation between the subject and the object, or a clear base for the difference between reality and fantasy?"[16] Secular humanists ended up, inevitably, in the existentialist despair the philosopher Jean-Paul Sartre imagined as subjectivist hell in his play *No Exit.*

"It was as though the rationalist suddenly realized that he was trapped in a large round room with no doors and no windows, nothing but complete darkness," Schaeffer wrote. "From the middle of the room he would feel his ways to the walls and begin to look for an exit. He would go round the circumference, and then the terrifying truth would dawn on him that there was no exit, no exit at all!"[17]

Not all secular humanists experienced this existential crisis, of course. Schaeffer thought this was because people were inconsistent and didn't have the courage to face the self-referential incoherence of their ideas. With apologetics, Schaeffer argued, the evangelical should push secular humanists toward the crisis. "We ought not try first to move a man away from the logical conclusion of his position but towards it," he wrote.[18] That apologetic could be cruel. Schaeffer said it might even drive someone to suicide. So be it.[19] In their screams of horror, souls might be saved. Most people would recoil from the logical conclusion of their secular humanist presuppositions and choose, instead, to embrace the founding propositional claims of Christian belief: There is a God, "He is there and He is not silent. . . . He has spoken and told us what He is and that He existed before all else."[20] Christ is Lord, with dominion over all creation.

Schaeffer's grasp on the art and philosophy he critiqued was pretty tenuous. He lifted terms like "secular humanism," "antithesis," and "Weltanschauung" out of context. He used them in his own idiosyncratic ways. He often critiqued authors without seeming to have read them closely. His biographer thinks he probably hadn't read them at all. "While there can be no certainty on this point, it is highly unlikely that Schaeffer ever actually read Hegel, Kant, Kierkegaard, and the other modern thinkers he would later critique," historian Barry Hankins writes. "Schaeffer was a voracious reader of magazines and the Bible, but some who lived at L'Abri and knew him well say they never saw him read a book. It appears highly likely, therefore, that Schaeffer learned western intellectual history from students who had dropped out of European universities."[21] Whether this is true or not, it does not seem that Schaeffer could explain the basic ideas of the thinkers and artists he discussed, or basic differences between them. He didn't think the differences really mattered. For him, Paul Gauguin's 1897 post-impressionistic painting *Where Do We Come From? What Are We?*

Where Are We Going? had the same message as Woody Allen's 1977 romantic comedy *Annie Hall*.[22] Nuance was obfuscation.

Schaeffer argued that it was the larger commonalities that spoke to the spirit of the age and "the struggle of modern man."[23] As one defender put it, to understand Schaeffer, you had to understand that he spoke "in italics."[24]

It's worth noting, however, that there were also more mainstream voices who also thought modern, secular society was beset with foundational problems. The sociologist Max Weber, for example, said there was a basic epistemological conflict in liberal democracies. How can we decide questions of value without appealing to arguments of authority or special revelation—or just resorting to force? Any rational discussion of values relies on epistemological foundations that are, themselves, resting on normative judgments (such as the claim that inconsistency is bad). Conflicts of epistemological values thus cannot be resolved rationally. Weber calls this clash of absolute claims a kind of "war of the gods"—spiritual warfare.[25]

In the same year Schaeffer went to Switzerland, 1955, the public intellectual Walter Lippmann published *The Public Philosophy*, raising the same concerns about the fragile foundation of the Western social order. Lippmann, no conservative, was skeptical of mainstream liberalism's belief that liberty and democracy were possible without a commonly shared criterion for determining what was good. Modern pluralism, he said, undercut the idea of natural law, a morality that is universally available and obvious to everyone. As a result, Lippmann wrote, "the great frame of reference to the rational order was missing" from conversations about public policy. That meant a "dissolution of public, general, objective criteria of the true and the false, the right and the wrong."[26] Liberal society was disinherited from its Christian past, the masses unmoored without "belief and faith that they can live by."[27] Lippmann feared that democratic society would be overwhelmed by totalitarianism—with its more rational appeals to ethnic nationalism and violence—unless it could be reinvigorated with new philosophic arguments.

The most serious attempt to provide new philosophical foundations for pluralist democracy was probably the work of German philosopher Jürgen Habermas. Habermas argues that people with radically different values share, nonetheless, civil discourse, a neutral space where the "war of the gods" could be worked out in calm, rational conversation.

To Schaeffer, of course, this is nonsense. This can only be another example of the incoherence at the bottom of the modern, secular order. Human reasoning can't start with a foundation of human reasoning—or it can, but that inevitably leads to disorientation, irrationalism, and despair. Thus the claim of secular neutrality—grounded, Habermas would say, in the common presuppositions implicit in public conversation—is always a lie. It's a trick. It is an act of rebellion, actually, against the God who is God over all.

"There are no neutral facts," Schaeffer said. "For facts are God's facts."[28]

There is thus no common ground between the evangelical Christian and the secular humanist, except inasmuch as humanists are being inconsistent with their own rejection of absolute truth or Christians are being tricked into surrendering the key claims of Christian belief or withdrawing from the public square.

Too often, Schaeffer said, that is precisely what happened. Christians had retreated. They had stopped speaking boldly. They needed to be reawakened to the true dimensions of their spiritual struggle and the irreconcilability of different worldviews. They had to see how their Christian belief called them into cultural conflict.

Schaeffer's Influence

After a decade of engaging English-speaking youth at L'Abri, Schaeffer took to the American evangelical lecture circuit to make the case for this sort of apologetic engagement. His first talk was at Harold J. Ockenga's church in Boston in 1964.[29] The next year, Schaeffer gave a weeklong series of lectures at Wheaton College.[30] In 1968, as his previous lectures were edited into book form and published under the titles *The God Who Is There* and *Escape from Reason*, he embarked on a fourteen-city US tour.

Schaeffer's message of clashing worldviews and antithetical presuppositions had significant impact on American evangelicals. It convinced many to take culture seriously and to engage with it critically. It convinced them such engagements and conflicts were not just good but were necessary, because of the nature of belief. As historian George Marsden writes, "Schaeffer provided what became the most influential analysis of what he believed was the larger issue at the heart of the new culture wars. The choice for America, he proclaimed, was simply between a return to Christianity or a takeover by secular humanism and eventually authoritarianism."[31] Many conservative Protestants felt they faced a choice between shunning and separating from the wider American culture and engaging the culture and waging culture war. Schaeffer, as his biographer explains, "was the most popular and influential American evangelical of his time in reshaping evangelical attitudes towards culture, helping to move evangelicals from separatism to engagement."[32]

Many young white evangelicals were changed by Schaeffer's lectures, but one especially notable case was Lane Dennis. In 1965, Dennis was working at his father's tract-publishing company in Wheaton, serving as the production manager in the printing division.[33] Dennis attended a Schaeffer lecture at nearby Wheaton College and "began, for the first time, to find a way to understand the flow of life in history and philosophy," according to the authorized history of the family's publishing company.[34] Dennis "learned from Dr. Schaeffer how to integrate these new understandings into such diverse realities as everyday business and social upheaval in the 1960s."[35] It was because of this new understanding that Dennis started Crossway with his brother Jan.

Crossway published Schaeffer's books, starting with *Whatever Happened to the Human Race?* in 1979 and *The Christian Manifesto* in 1982. The Dennis brothers published *The Complete Works of Francis Schaeffer: A Christian World View* in five volumes, starting a few years before Schaeffer died in 1984. With a mission inspired by Schaeffer, they published a whole list of books that were important to the formation of the Religious Right in the 1980s. A brief catalogue shows how Christianity was being conceptualized as necessary worldview conflict: *A Time for Anger: The Myth of Neutrality*, by Franky Schaeffer (Francis's son), was published in 1982. *The Stealing of America*, by John Whitehead, came out in 1983. *Who Speaks for God?*, by Charles Colson, came out in 1985. *The Way Home: Escape from Feminism, Back to Reality*, by Mary Pride, was released the same year, followed by *The Child Abuse Industry*, also by Pride, in 1986. *Dark Secrets of the New Age: Satan's Plan for a One World Religion*, by Texe Marrs, was published in 1987; *Prodigal Press: The Anti-Christian Bias of the American News Media*, by Marvin Olasky, and *Beyond Good Intentions: A Biblical View of Politics*, by Doug Bandow, were both published in 1988.

Another young Christian who was notably influenced by Schaeffer was Frank Peretti. It isn't clear exactly when Peretti first encountered Schaeffer, but he has regularly cited him as one of his biggest influences.[36] Peretti was seized, especially, by Schaeffer's image of humanist confusion. Peretti turned the example of the disoriented man in a featureless room with no exit into a talk he gave a number of times on the evangelical lecture circuit. The talk was broadcast widely on evangelical radio stations by Focus on the

Family.[37] Peretti reprised the speech as late as 2005 in an invited address at Liberty University, the Virginia school founded and at that time run by Religious Right leader Jerry Falwell.[38]

"Imagine a really really big room," Peretti said in the talk, "but this a featureless room. There is nothing in this room. It's dark in this room. There aren't even any corners in this room. It's a round room. I'm groping about, trying to find where I am. You need to have some point of reference to tell you where you are."

On stage, Peretti acted out the problem of being lost in this space without fixed references. Waving his arms and walking with exaggerated steps through the imaginary formless void, Peretti finally found what, in his performance, stood for a moral absolute: a chair. From the fixed point of the chair, he could measure and explore the space. The chair could serve as the basis for knowledge as long as, like absolute truth, it didn't move.

"In order for a fixed point of reference to be any good," Peretti said, "it has to be separate from you, and it can't move. . . . This is the essence of Christian thought, is that we do have a fixed point of reference by which we measure Right, Wrong, True, False, Good, Evil, all those big absolutes."[39]

Peretti was captured by Schaeffer's idea that Christians needed to be awakened to the true conflict taking place around them. With his novel, he wanted to dramatize what Schaeffer had argued, the idea that faithful Christians needed to look again at the world around them, and this time really see, really feel, the call to struggle. Schaeffer ended one of his 1968 lectures intoning, "There is death in the city; there is death in the city; there is death in the city." In the book version, published from transcripts made by students from InterVarsity Christian Fellowship, this is slightly modified. Edited, Schaeffer says, "Because man has turned from God, there are hungers on every side; there is death in the *polis*, there is death in the city!"[40] That was the story Peretti wanted to tell.

Peretti imagined a pastor—like himself, burnt out by the work of being a pastor—walking into the center of a small American town to directly address the death in the city. He would have a supernatural confrontation. The pastor would go and sit on a public bench, in the public sphere, the secular space. He would say, "I'm here, Satan."[41]

Peretti didn't imagine the pastor actually seeing Satan or any of Satan's minions in the bustling business district in the bright of day. The pastor would see only the town center. He would think about how he was failing to reach this town with the gospel, failing as a minister. He would be overwhelmed by church politics—his little community church divided against itself, planning a congregational vote over whether to keep him as pastor. The pastor—call him Hank Busche—would feel like he just had no strength left. Peretti imagined that the hero had been told he was going to lose that vote and lose his church. But he would know church politics wasn't the real issue. And the town that was losing its Judeo-Christian moorings wouldn't be the real issue either. Behind the facade of the town that ignores him and the facade of church divisions, the pastor would know the real issue was spiritual.

Peretti wrote this down, describing his hero, Busche, going to a public square to sit on a city bench. Imagining the pastor's thoughts, Peretti wrote, "I can't see you, and maybe you can move faster than I can, but I'm still here, and by the grace of God and the power of the Holy Spirit I intend to be a thorn in your side until one of us has had enough!"[42]

The Dennises didn't know if this would sell. Probably not, actually. Fourteen publishers had rejected the manuscript. Crossway didn't have any expertise in that part of the market. But they liked the idea of *The Heavenlies*. They had been talking about publishing fiction inspired by Schaeffer, looking for novelists who, they thought, "could write well only about the confusion and chaos they experienced in their own lives and saw reflected in the wider culture . . . below the line of despair, as Francis Schaeffer so aptly put it."[43] Peretti fit the bill.

Crossway accepted *The Heavenlies* for publication but changed the title to *This Present Darkness*. The new name was inspired in part by C. S. Lewis's title *That Hideous Strength* and in part by the Revised Standard Version translation of Ephesians 6:12, where the apostle Paul says, "We are not contending against flesh and blood, but against the principalities, against the powers, against the world rulers of this present darkness." The Dennises published the book in 1986.[44] It was stocked in more than five thousand evangelical bookstores across the country.[45]

Political Conflict

This Present Darkness is a novel of belief imagined as worldview conflict in a small American town. As Peretti presents it, there are three levels of conflict: a struggle for social control of the town; a conflict over political spaces and the shape of public discourse; and most importantly, a conflict over the hearts and minds of individuals in the town. It's a battle for society, a battle against false neutrality, and a battle for souls.

On the first level, *This Present Darkness* is the story of the fictional small town of Ashton and how the town's civic leaders are all part of a secret New Age, neo-pagan group. The faculty of the local liberal arts college, the law-enforcement officers, city council members, and liberal ministers, "a cross section of Ashton's best," have formed a local branch of the Universal Consciousness Society.[46] They are working toward a sort of New Age *parousia*, a coming of the Universal Mind, in which "all the inhabitants of the world will make a giant evolutionary leap and meld into one global brain, one transcending consciousness" (254).

The Universal Consciousness Society is backed by a global corporation, the Omni Corporation. The Omni Corporation is secretive and powerful, with controlling interests on every level of the global economy, from oil production to banks to retail outlets (277–78). The Omni Corporation has significant political influence, nationally and internationally (280, 222). All the world systems are being quietly taken over.

But this is not just the work of a new religious movement or a conglomerate of the global economy. It is ultimately spiritual. As one character warns, "You have no idea who you're really dealing with. There are forces at work in that town—." He clarifies: "political, social . . . spiritual too" (86). The conspiracy is really the work of a demonic lord known as the Strongman. The Strongman is an intimate of Satan himself and commands an army of lesser demons. He is "a vicious global tyrant responsible over the centuries for resisting the plans of the living God and establishing Lucifer's kingdom on earth" (176, 432–33). His plan, as the novel starts, includes taking over Whitmore College, the fictional school at the center of Ashton, and then Ashton. He will turn the town into a beachhead for a New World Order (471). At the start of the novel, the demons have infiltrated, preparing for this takeover.

The demons inhabit physical space in this fictional world and are described by Peretti in visceral, fleshy terms. Many have thick, leathery hides. They have talons and yellow eyes and speak in gargling voices. The Strongman looks like "a monstrous, overweight vulture." He resides at the center of a violent, churning swarm of gargoyle-looking things. Individual demons often have particular features fitting specific tasks of torture. One has "knuckles honed into spikelike protrusions," while another is "like a slimy black leech" (56, 43).

At the same time, the demons are not corporal beings. They can't be perceived directly by the people of Ashton. They are invisible, ghostly presences, immaterial and yet interacting with the world. One demon is described as a "breach torn in space," a shadow with "an animated, creaturelike shape" that "crawled, quivered, moved along the street" (4). Another is "an eerie projection in midair, a glowing painting on black velvet" (68). These hideous beings are all over the town, and yet the town doesn't appear any different than normal. Ashton looks, Peretti writes, "like the background for every Norman Rockwell painting" (3).

Regular people in the town know something is wrong but can't quite identify what. "People around here are starting to act weird," one notes (142). Maybe it's the newcomers? There's been an influx of new residents, and they "all seemed to have a very unique rapport with each other—their own lingo, their own inside secrets, their own ideas of reality" (212).

The leader of the secret group of human conspirators is named Juleen Langstrat. She is Whitmore College's professor of psychology of the self. She teaches classes such as "Pathway to Your Inner Light," "Introduction to God and Goddess Consciousness and the Craft," and "How to Enjoy the Present by Experiencing Past and Future Lives" (122). Outside the classroom, she leads Ashton's elite in the experimental spiritual practices of the Universal Consciousness Society—worshiping demons through meditation aimed at achieving the universal mind. She leads the group in a chant of the name of the demon Rafar, the Strongman's deputy devil, an ancient prince of Babylon. These secret religious sessions are aimed at achieving political power. "Our purpose here," Langstrat says to one gathering, "is to combine our psychic energies to assure the success of today's venture. Our long awaited goal will soon by realized: The Whitmore College campus, and afterward the whole town of Ashton, are going to become part of the New World Order" (471).

The takeover effort is effected through practical measures, in addition to these combined psychic energies. Peretti describes how a growing number of Ashton's businesses are secretly controlled by the Omni Corporation. The town's small-business owners are converted, one by one, and sign ownership over to the conspiracy. Or, if they refuse to be converted to the New Age movement, they are forced to sell. The small-business owners find themselves hit, for example, by bills for taxes they have already paid. Their protests go unheard and unheeded, and the property is seized and put up for auction, only to be bought by a representative of the Omni Corporation.

Civic leaders are, likewise, either brought in or forced out. This includes elected officials and those on every level of the judicial system, but also the town's pastors, the man who runs the local newspaper, and the college's administration. Some who attempt to stand against the conspiracy are set up on charges of child molestation. Others are falsely accused of rape and extramarital affairs. They are hounded by rumors that destroy their reputations or mental health, or both. One by one, they fall (284–85). Each is replaced by an associate of the Universal Consciousness Society. The conspirators then use their positions to further the occult plan. The college's new administrators, for example, steer the school into financial ruin, so that it seems legitimate to privatize the college, selling it to the Omni Corporation.

"Let the Devil have that town!" one beleaguered character says. "If he wants it so bad, let him have it" (284).

All this is about as subtle as *Pilgrim's Progress*. It's a thinly veiled allegory for the social concerns of the Religious Right, who feel like they're losing control of America. It's the anxieties of conservative white Protestant men translated into a fantasy of cosmic struggle. Their fears—from feminists in higher education to the displacement of the patriarchal father to the possibility of consequences following accusations of sexual misconduct—are strung together into a narrative. It's true Peretti also seems concerned about things like global capitalism, which was not an agenda item for the Religious Right, but that may be the author's idiosyncrasy. Mostly, the "spectrally macabre" plot to take over the town can be neatly mapped onto the Religious Right narrative of cultural subversion and the "stealing of America."

This Present Darkness also does something more subtle, however. It doesn't just reimagine cultural conflict as cosmic battle. On a second level, it reimagines the space where that conflict happens. It focuses on the shape of the space where debate occurs and not just on the content of the debate itself. The novel remaps the relationship between metaphysical commitments and political discourse, and invites readers to imagine that the supposedly secular sphere is always shivering with the numinous.

As the journalist Daniel Radosh points out, *This Present Darkness* is not really a novel about politics, in the normal sense of disagreement over public policy. The novel rather tells the story of evangelicals awakening to the truth that there is no common ground in a culture war. "Common ground will never be possible," Radosh writes, speaking on behalf of the secular side of the struggle, "because they don't object to specific ideas that can be reframed or adjusted. We want to persuade them, reason with them, listen to them, and accommodate them. They want to save us. It's not even the same playing field."[47]

Peretti's characters "come to this revelation—'it's not even the same playing field'—again and again." They model the realization for readers. In one example of this, the people from an evangelical Bible church gather at "a modern log cabin on the outskirts of town" (264). They are brought together by their concerns for the town, including the curriculum at the college. They gather like groups of politicized evangelicals gathered in the late 1970s and early '80s. They are, as *Christianity Today* described the nascent Religious Right in 1979, "concerned about the nation's moral drift and its impact on their families, but unorganized and unable to stop the decline."[48] One man, in this fictional meeting, reflects on the changes in Ashton. The college has changed. The city government has changed. The civic leaders are more hostile to conservative Christians than they used to be. Then another man makes the argument that the real reason for the town's transformation is that evangelicals have allowed themselves to be marginalized. "The problem is we've all just sat to the side and let it happen," he says. "It's time we got concerned and scared." Here, importantly, the act of getting concerned is not simple political mobilization. The answer isn't a get-out-the-vote campaign. Rather, the characters realize the political sphere is not as they thought it was. They're trying to fight a conspiracy, and more specifically, a spiritual conspiracy. "It's time we got concerned and scared," the man says, but continues, "and on our knees to see that the Lord does something about it" (265). At the climax of the scene, the group decides to pray.

This Present Darkness emphasizes the importance of prayer. In an early scene, the novel's hero, Hank Busche, is shown praying. He is "kneeling in earnest prayer, his head resting on the hard wooden bench, and his hands clenched with fervency." He is observed by an angel, who interprets the scene. When compared to the challenges he faces, the pastor might seem insignificant, the angel observes. But his prayer is "not so insignificant" (6). Prayer might seem marginal to public matters, completely separated from the public sphere, and private. But it's not.

The relationship between politics and prayer can seem a non sequitur. The novel invites readers to imagine otherwise. The character Edith Duster, for example, brings up angels at seemingly odd moments. Duster is an older woman, a former missionary to China, now retired, who is greatly respected by the minister and others in the church. The pastor goes to her to discuss the impending congregational vote, which will likely go against him. "That church can't possibly survive if half the congregation removes its support," he says. The older woman replies, "Oh, but I've had dreams of angels lately" (146). The reader might see this as a sign of the woman's senility or, at least, her disengagement from practical issues. But the novel presents this as the right response.

It is this right relationship between "private" prayer and "public" matters that Busche asserts in his prayer on the city bench.

The site is important. He addresses the supernatural in public. Not in a church. Not in the quiet of a minister's study. Not in a private home. In doing so, he rejects the idea that the sacred can be walled off and set apart from the hustle of the ordinary world. He rejects the "neutrality" of the secular space, seeing it instead as a space in rebellion against Christ's claims of dominion. The reader follows Peretti's pastor as he breaks down the divisions of public and private, secular and sacred, overcoming the illusion that these walls really exist (88).

Later, angels wake Duster from sleep to tell her the pastor has been arrested on false charges. He has been accused of a rape he didn't commit, framed by occult forces, human and supernatural. The elderly woman is told this news and told it is urgent she respond—by praying. An angel explains, "We are going into battle for the town of Ashton. The victory rests on the prayers of the saints of God" (401). The woman gets out of bed and kneels to pray. "She prayed," Peretti writes. "She prayed. She prayed" (402). This is shown to have an immediate effect, as the novel pulls back to look at Ashton from above, quiet in the predawn hours. The omniscient gaze then turns to the sky, where angel warriors are rallied to arms by the old missionary's intercession.

As religious studies scholar Jason C. Bivins argues, "Peretti's fiction has energetically identified tools of Satanic machinations, frequently naming long-standing sources of evangelical concern." This, however, is not a simple matter of judging particular policy positions as demonic. What's going on is more a matter, Bivins says, of "boundary negotiation." The fiction is inviting readers to imagine the political as spiritual and staging a drama where the "antithesis" of worldviews, the irreconcilable conflict over supposedly neutral space, can be experienced. "Such narratives," Bivins writes, "remap the world."[49]

This remapping explains one of the more peculiar aspects of the evangelical horror novel: its many, many meetings. *This Pres-*

ent Darkness can actually be thought of as a novel about meetings. There are government meetings, business meetings, college meetings, church meetings, prayer meetings, family meetings, and more. People meet for counseling and spiritual guidance, to gather information and to convey it, to perpetrate conspiracy and plot exposure. And those are only the human meetings: *This Present Darkness* is also fascinated by the concept of supernatural meetings and spends not a little time describing the organizational structure and rules of order for the meetings of both angels and demons. The demons are shown as obsessed with respect and decorum (58). The hierarchies are enforced with sudden violence, as superiors humiliate their underlings at will (62). Angels, on the other hand, have orderly and productive meetings. They trust each other, can disagree without threatening anyone's status, and aim toward consensus and unity. At the end of each meeting, the angels rededicate themselves to their mission in unison, "For the saints of God and for the Lamb!" (56).

The variety of meetings alone is a challenge to a normative vision of what a meeting should be. The space that structures discourse is not always the same. Meetings do not always operate according to the same rules, and since the communicative practice is different in different meetings, one cannot easily deduce pragmatic, self-grounding principles of communication, such as publicness, in the way that Habermas might suppose. Instead, as imagined in *This Present Darkness*, meetings come in all shapes, and they are not only the site of conflict but also the subject of it.

The first meeting in *This Present Darkness*, for example, takes place in the shadows. At first sight, the meeting is not obviously a meeting but looks like "some shadows moving stealthily" (3). It's a secret gathering of conspirators. But the secret meeting is also oddly public. It is at a carnival. The conspirators gather at the dark edge of warm summer night of "roaming, cotton candied masses."

They are behind a booth where teenagers throw darts at balloons to win prizes. It is never explained why the conspirators meet here, but presumably, on the level of plot, it is the very publicness of the place that allows it to be inconspicuous. Carnivals, of course, also have a long literary tradition, including in John Bunyan's *Pilgrim's Progress* and François Rabelais's *Gargantua and Pantagruel*. They are literary sites of inversion and subversion, where the social order is turned upside down. Literary critic Mikhail Bakhtin famously argued that for Rabelais, the carnival was internal to the religious, medieval regime, and also a hidden polemic against it. With the carnival, Bakhtin wrote, Rabelais sought "to purge the spatial and temporal world of those remnants of transcendent worldview still present in it."[50] Peretti's villains are similarly at war with the transcendent order, their scheming masked by the deceptive secularity of the spatial and temporal world.

With the carnival, the novel challenges simple ideas of "public" and "private." The carnival is in the middle of the town, put on by the town, and open to all. Yet it is operated by private contractors and is also on private property, a vacant lot owned by a private individual (1). The meeting, likewise, is private because it is public, and its publicness is a lie. Readers can't trust the normal, neat division of space.

A young reporter, guided by angels, takes a picture of the secret meeting. The shadows are lit up by the flash of her camera. The conspiracy is documented and brought out into the open (3). The reporter is reprimanded and told "this is a private meeting" (18). She recognizes two of the people: the police chief and a leading liberal minister. The other three she doesn't know. A short time later, she is arrested on charges of prostitution. She is convinced the arrest is retaliation for exposing the meeting, part of a cover-up (16).

On the other hand, the new editor of the Ashton newspaper, Marshall Hogan, initially assumes the whole thing is a mistake. However, when the police chief and the liberal minister both deny being at the meeting and at the carnival, and even deny knowing each other, the editor reacts, like his reporter, by trying to uncover the secret and make it public. He quickly catches the two men in a lie, proving they do know each other (95). The film that would have documented the meeting is destroyed by the police without explanation, further convincing the editor something nefarious is going on (80).

As reporter and editor begin to piece things together, figuring out who knows who and what their connections are, the editor pauses to ask whether this information they're gathering is rightly public or private. Are they "blurring the lines" (107)? Where are the lines? They don't decide the question but choose to take an aggressive position, contesting the claims of privacy and committing themselves to making these things public.

"If it's a stone," the editor says, "turn it over" (107).

The editor comes to this position at least in part because he is aggravated by another meeting where publicness is contested. This is the meeting of a college class. The editor's daughter—"a beautiful redhead . . . nothing but potential"—is a freshman enrolled in several classes taught "by Langstrat, the leading New World Order conspirator" (39). Hogan is working at the small-town newspaper in part to slow down and be a better father to his daughter, so, in one early scene in the novel, he goes to Whitmore College to pick up his daughter after work. The school is presented as an idyllic space, an ideal institution of higher learning. "The campus looked like most American campuses," Peretti writes. "It was everything a college should be." There are wide lawns with sophomores throwing Frisbees, long brick walkways, and elm-lined streets. The oldest lecture halls are red brick with white pillars, and the newer psychology building is "patterned after some European cathedral with towers and archways" (40). This secular temple of knowledge is not clearly secular, however, in the sense of being public. The college at the center of the town is, in fact, privately endowed. Immediately on entering the psychology building, the editor wonders if he was wrong to assume he would be welcome there.

When Hogan finds the room where Langstrat is teaching, he knows, intuitively, that the rules of discourse in this space do not allow him to engage or to question what is being said. Privately, he is very critical of the lecture, which he describes as a "funny conglomeration of sixty-four dollar words which impress people with your academic prowess but can't get you a paying job" (41). He decides, nonetheless, that he would like to quietly listen in the back of the lecture hall while he waits for his daughter, if for no other reason than to understand what she is being taught. "Then it happened," Peretti writes. "Some kind of radar in the professor's head must have clicked on. She honed in on Marshall sitting there and simply would not look away from him" (42). Hogan is kicked out. It's not immediately clear why. The rules of the space, the pragmatic presuppositions on which it operates, are mysterious to the newspaper editor. He knows that he has violated some norm, but not what that norm is. "So who stole all the 'No Parents Allowed' signs?" Hogan asks his daughter. "How was I to know that she didn't want me in there? And just what's so all-fired precious and secret that she doesn't want any outsiders to hear it?" (45). The professor, of course, is leading a local effort in a neo-pagan conspiracy to establish a New World Order. And conspiracies depend on keeping secret meetings from becoming public.

The novel is not just staging cultural conflicts, it is inviting readers to see how the staging itself is part of the cultural conflict. The first political fight is always about the rules of political fights. *This Present Darkness* returns again and again to the conflict of what is allowed in meetings and who is allowed in meetings. The first pragmatic principle of the public sphere, its publicness, is shown to be suspect. *This Present Darkness* argues that "neutral space" and the Habermasian ideal of secular discourse have to be contested.

The novel climaxes with a contest over a meeting. The struggling pastor and the newspaper editor lead a group of renewed and remobilized Christians to the college. There's a meeting taking place, somewhere in the bowels of the institution. There, the occult forces are attempting to take over the college. The "fired up saints" don't go into the meeting, though. They stay outside and pray (505, 476). The newspaper editor and the pastor go into the administration building and find the conference room where the board of regents is meeting with the head of the Omni Corporation and a team of lawyers to complete the secret sale of the school to the Universal Consciousness Society.

Hogan bursts in, interrupting, and shocking the gathered conspirators.

"How did you get here?" they ask.

Hogan responds literally: "I took the elevator!" (481).

His presence in the room, like the novel's opening camera flash, makes the conspiracy public. The secret is revealed, the meeting exposed. The pastor follows the editor and, in this now-public space, immediately addresses the demonic forces, which are described for the reader in the same way that everything else is described. They are as real as the lawyers, from the prospective of the novel, even though, from the perspective of the human characters in the room, the spirits are invisible. For them, the demons still hide behind the facade of the secular. The novel, however, presents the demons as facts. And the prayerful pastor, Peretti writes, now "knew whom he faced" (482). The meeting becomes an exorcism.

Fight for a Soul

There is also a third level of conflict in *This Present Darkness*. Active Christian belief, as imagined by the novel, compels political

79

conflict and clashes over the shape of public space. But it is ultimately a spiritual battle for souls. The satanic conspiracy is trying to seduce innocent minds away from the truth—innocent minds like Sandy Hogan's.

Sandy Hogan is only one of a number of characters deceived by occult forces in *This Present Darkness*. Her story is presented as representative, though, and is more fully told than that of the others.

She starts as a girl defined, most of all, by her rocky relationship with her father, the newspaper editor (39). Maybe she's just strong-willed. Maybe it's a rebellious phase. Or maybe, Peretti nudges the reader, something darker is going on.

Hogan has been raised on a very liberal form of Christianity. At church, she has learned to look within herself for the truth. "Each person must find his own way, his own truth," the liberal minister of Ashton preaches. "What had remained in the darkness of tradition and ignorance, we find now revealed within ourselves . . . we are inherently divine in our very essence, and have within ourselves the capacity for good, the potential to become, as it were, gods" (92, 171). She just needs to find herself.

Hogan gets this same lesson at college in Langstrat's self-discovery courses (234). Isn't college supposed to be a time of self-discovery? Langstrat starts with the modernist epistemology of René Descartes and his "simple ontological formula, 'I think, therefore I am,'" and then veers off in a mystical, New Age direction (41). The self is the ultimate guide, the ultimate authority, the ultimate source of knowledge. The slippery slope, as Schaeffer predicted, goes from modernist epistemology to irrationalist mysticism.

Hogan's education continues outside the classroom. An older student encourages her to "tune in" to the universe. She tells him she's been a little confused by all the different stuff she's learning, and he says the only way to find peace is to stop worrying about who's right and who's wrong. She should give up the idea that opposites are irreconcilable and embrace, instead, the oneness of everything. "The peace, the unity, the wholeness are really there," the boy says. "Once you stop listening to the lies your mind's been telling you, you'll see very clearly that God is big enough for everybody and *in* everybody" (155–56). Hogan, like the town, finds this foreign at first. She says, "I'm from the old Judeo-Christian school of thought, you know" (154). Nevertheless, she values an open mind and tries to "tune in" to a truth beyond the antithetical.

The novel at that point pulls back, giving the reader the spiritual perspective of what's really happening: "Meanwhile," Peretti writes, "with very gentle, very subtle combing motions of his talons, Deception stood behind Sandy, stroking her red hair and speaking sweet words of comfort to her mind" (157).

The next step in Hogan's demonic seduction is a private therapy session in Langstrat's home. Hogan is taught to meditate. She learns to explore other levels of consciousness, to sink within herself to "the deeper level where true psychic ability and experience could be found." In that process, she is connected to a spirit guide named Madaline. Visualized as a young girl with cascading blonde hair and dressed in shimmering white linen, the spirit guide tells Hogan she has lived many lives, and each life is "simply a step upward." Madaline takes Hogan's hand and leads her into the illusion of paradise (331). The girl with the concerned father and the formerly Judeo-Christian worldview thus willingly accepts a demon into herself.

As the novel goes on, Hogan follows her spirit guide deeper and deeper in her meditative practice, seeking spiritual fulfillment, higher consciousness, and self-realization (465). Then she's brought to a special meeting of the Universal Consciousness Society, in a room at the town college, at the same time the regents are meeting to sign the school over to the Omni Corporation. Hogan, surrounded by New Age conspirators, meditates herself into a trance. She follows her spirit guide into the darkness. Suddenly, there are chains locked to her wrist (491). Madaline gives the girl a knife and tells her to set herself free. "These chains are the chains of life," the demon says, "they are a prison of evil, of the lying mind, of illusion! Free your true self!" Around the girl, in the waking world, the devotees of experimental neo-paganism chant the name of the demon Rafar. Someone puts a knife in her entranced hand (498). If she cuts her chains in the trance, she will slice her wrists in real life.

In the depths of her darkness, Hogan hesitates. She senses something is wrong. There is yet, Peretti writes, a "last remaining shred of her old, discarded Christian heritage still holding her" (465). There's a flicker of doubt. She hesitates at too easy synthesis of the antithetical. Can it really be right that freedom is slavery, pain is pleasure, and death is life? Can it really be that she is the grounds of her own knowledge and the measure of her own truth? Does it make any sense, this promise of transcendence through self-discovery?

Then she really sees: Madaline is not a beautiful blonde girl but an ugly demon, her skin "soot-black and leathery," her eyes "huge yellow orbs." The demon has the mouth of a lion and drools with desire. Before it's too late, Hogan knows the truth. She knows fear. "From somewhere in the blackness," Peretti writes, "this tunnel, this nothingness, this altered state, this pit of death and deception, she screamed from the depths of her tortured and dying soul" (484).

A girl screaming an unstoppable scream: this was not a prairie romance; this was evangelical horror. The image would be immediately familiar to anyone in suburban America. Perhaps the readers would picture the actress Janet Leigh in the shower scene in *Psycho*, her wet face contorted with terror. Perhaps they'd think of Tina Gray, the protagonist of Wheaton graduate Wes Craven's *Nightmare on Elm Street*, writhing bloody on the ceiling of her teenage bedroom, screaming "run" through desperate gulps of air. Maybe the reader would recall Sally Hardesty, the girl who gets away at the end of *Texas Chainsaw Massacre*, who runs and screams, staggers and falls, but rises to scream again.[51] Hogan's scream is a part of this pop culture tradition. But it also resonates in another way for evangelicals inspired by Schaeffer's apologetics. The scream is the right response to the predicament of "modern man." Her horror is the appropriate reaction to the inevitable end of a life without God. When Hogan screams, she screams for her lost soul.

It's easy to think of belief as purely private, the novel argues. It's something someone does at home, or in church. It's easy to think of belief as pretty passive, a quiet mental affirmation of Christian doctrines. But *This Present Darkness* wants to picture belief as a girl's lungs filled with terror. In the novel, the scream is the true sound of the cost of the conflict of irreconcilable worldviews.

And the scream works. Angels are summoned, weapons drawn, and they go into battle for Hogan's soul. Angels and demons meet in combat. "The light of a million suns exploded into the room with a deafening thunder of wings and the warcries of the Heavenly Host," Peretti writes. "Many demons tried to flee, but were instantly disintegrated by slashing swords. The whole room was one huge, bombastic, brilliant blur" (364). Hogan is loosed from her chains by an angelic sword and comes out of her trance. She feels her body again. She sees light again. She runs from the room as the occultists try to grab her and stop her. In the hall outside she finds her father, coming to meet her, and she runs into his arms.

Outside, in the light of day and on the steps of the college administration building, the Christians are fully awake to the true nature of their conflict. They directly address the demons that have tried to take over their town. "In the name of Jesus," they say together, "we rebuke you" (371). Above them, an angel hears the Christians singing. "It echoed through the heavenlies . . . clearing away the darkness with God's holy light" (372). The pastor—once burnt out but now revitalized—surveys the faithful on the college steps. He says, "Let's pray" (376).

An Evangelical Blockbuster

It took a long time for Peretti to get his novel out into the world. It took him five years to write the first draft, then it got rejected by publisher after publisher. Then it finally came out in 1986, and Peretti had to wait.

He went to work at the ski-equipment factory every day, just like normal, and wondered if anything would happen. "I'd call the publisher every month," Peretti later recalled. "I'd go into the locker room there at the factory, and there's a pay phone on the wall and I'd call the publisher and I'd get the last month's sales figures. And we were doing, oh, 40, 50 copies. I mean, it was just trickling out the door." Sales really weren't good. In the first year, *This Present Darkness* sold fewer than one copy per store that carried the title. No one was interested in evangelical horror, and even if anyone saw the connection to Schaeffer, it didn't matter for fiction sales. "I was thinking," Peretti said, "I'm going to be working in this factory forever."[52]

Then one of those few copies found its way to Amy Grant. Grant was a twenty-six-year-old star of contemporary Christian music when she read *This Present Darkness*. She had had a breakthrough hit with her 1982 album *Age to Age*, winning two Dove Awards and a Grammy. The album went gold, then platinum. It was the first evangelical-market album to sell more than one million copies.[53] Her 1984 album *Straight Ahead* won her another Grammy. Grant performed on that year's awards show. She decided she could be a pop star, not just an evangelical pop star, confined to the market for evangelical music. Her record label,

Word, signed a distribution deal with a secular counterpart, A&M, and Grant was launched into the pop stratosphere. Her 1985 album *Unguarded* broke into *Billboard*'s Top 100, and her concerts started filling larger and larger venues: twelve thousand in New York, fourteen thousand in Texas, more than nineteen thousand in California.[54]

Her music mostly expressed the same ideas as evangelical romance novels. This, her songs said, is what it's like to live out your beliefs in modern American suburbia. Suffering is real. Life is hard. But God wants better for you. If you trust God and surrender to God, you can flourish. You can have your best life. "I could stand here an angry young woman / taking all the pain to heart," Grant sang on "Find a Way," *Unguarded*'s crossover hit single. But: "If our God His Son not sparing / came to rescue you / is there any circumstance / that He can't see you through?"

Her message was like Oke's and fit comfortably in the evangelical bookstore. But Grant's crossover success brought scrutiny and criticism. Mainstream music journalists regularly asked if Grant was too sexy for an evangelical. She wore, they pointed out, a leopard-print jacket on stage. "She is projecting," one music journalist wrote, "a confusingly sexy image for an avowedly spiritual singer."[55] Or maybe she was too wholesome to be a pop star? "She's not pure," an A&M executive reassured one journalist. "It's OK to lust after Amy if you want to."[56]

Grant, defensive, tried to explain that her message wasn't about sex, but Jesus.[57] She wanted to show a kind of evangelical life that was modern and vibrant but different from what non-Christians had. At the same time, conservative evangelicals regularly critiqued her for selling out. One Baptist minister, for example, told his one-thousand-member church not to go to her concerts or listen to her music. Grant's music was an "appeal to the sensual." She once got flowers sent to her dressing room with a note tucked inside that said, "Repent."[58]

And she also had some real problems: Grant's husband, Gary Chapman, had a cocaine addiction he couldn't keep secret. Their marriage was marked by occasional outbursts of jealousy, as Chapman, also a musician, struggled with resentment at being "Mr. Amy Grant." Grant thought of leaving him and at one point even planned to escape to Maine, choosing the state because it was far away. She was so depressed, there were days she couldn't get out of bed.[59] Then Grant got pregnant. Thrilled, she announced it on national TV, only to have a miscarriage a few weeks later.[60]

In her crisis, she found Peretti's novel. There was a devotional group on the tour that would read together, talk, and pray. It included Grant, Chapman, contemporary Christian music star Michael W. Smith, and Smith's wife, Debbie. One of the books they chose to read in 1987 was *This Present Darkness*. The message that true Christianity requires conflict really spoke to them. It moved them to prayer and confession. They felt refreshed and renewed. Behind the scenes of the tour, it started to feel like a spiritual revival.[61]

Grant decided to talk about the book on stage at her sold-out shows, and *This Present Darkness* got an impossible-to-hope-for publicity boost.[62] The effect on sales was immediate. "Amy Grant plugged it and was excited about it," Peretti recalled. "Whoa. 4,000 copies. Well, I called in the next month, 'we sold about 30,000 copies.' And the next month, 'we sold about 60,000 copies.'"[63]

By the end of 1989, evangelical bookstores had sold about 500,000 copies of the book. Crossway wrote up a contract for a sequel, paying Peretti a $10,000 advance—enough that he could quit the ski-equipment factory and become a full-time writer.[64] Preorders came in by the thousands.[65] And *This Present Darkness* kept selling. Before the year was up, it had gone into its twentieth printing.[66] It was an evangelical blockbuster. "People were coming into our stores," write Bruce Bickle and Stan Jantz in the official history of the Christian Booksellers Association, "bleary-eyed after staying up all night to finish the book. They wanted five more copies to give away to friends."[67] Some of those books were given to people who didn't think they liked evangelical fiction, thus growing the market.[68] B. Dalton, the chain of mall bookstores that advertised that it "knew" Christian books, decided to stock Peretti, making his novels the first to demonstrate the crossover potential of evangelical fiction.

In ten years, *This Present Darkness* sold more than two million copies. And it kept selling. In 2006, people bought more than eighteen thousand copies, and *Christianity Today* listed it in the top fifty books that shaped American evangelicals.[69] It remains a strong seller today. Crossway sold about eight thousand new copies per year in 2015, 2016, and 2017.[70]

The novel met a receptive audience. Across the country, white evangelicals embraced the novel's articulation of an oppositional faith. They read the novel and imagined belief as a cultural conflict, and imagined themselves and evangelicals across the land being awakened to a war of antithetical worldviews.

Evangelicals Jim and Jean Daly, for example, read *This Present Darkness* together in their car in 1989. They were moving from Northern California to Southern California, a few years after getting married, and read aloud to each other as they drove. When it got dark, they didn't want to stop, so they read the novel by flashlight.

Peretti articulated for them what they were doing—even why they were moving. In Southern California, Jim had a job as assistant to the president of Focus on the Family, a parachurch organization committed to "defending the family" and "promoting biblical truths."[71] *This Present Darkness* made the connection between evangelical belief and political advocacy. "Because these fundamental truths of the Gospel are so important," Jim Daly explained years later, "we at Focus on the Family have been very intentional about speaking up in the public square and promoting a Christian worldview, something Frank was talking about."[72]

Some of the millions of readers of *This Present Darkness* had a more literal understanding of spiritual struggle. They took Peretti's novel as a kind of manual for spiritual warfare, reading it as an invitation to certain new prayer practices. "In prayer groups across the country," the evangelical *World Magazine* reported, "people were binding demons named after specific sins (Envy, Despair, Lust) and calling on angels to beat down devils in charge of particular cities and nations."[73] There's a lot of anecdotal evidence *This Present Darkness* prompted widespread interest in demonology and spiritual warfare, but there were other sources too. Some of this interest was more closely associated with the classes on "power evangelism" that C. Peter Wagner and John Wimber taught at Fuller Theological Seminary from 1982 to 1985.[74] Some seems more directly influenced by the teachings of charismatic exorcists such as Derek Prince and Don Basham, leaders in the Shepherding Movement.[75] Peretti, however, took the anecdotes seriously. He worried about his responsibility in teaching evangelicals to engage in new prayer practices of "spiritual war." By the 1990s, his novels included an introductory note telling readers "this novel is a creative work of fiction imparting spiritual truth in a symbolic manner, and not an emphatic statement of religious doctrine."[76]

Most readers, though, fully understood the fictionality of Peretti's fiction. They didn't think the novels were didactic, but read them instead as a spiritual provocation, an invitation to imagine the otherworldly and occult forces that might be hiding behind everyday cultural conflict. When readers love *This Present Darkness* enough to post rave reviews on the Internet, they often point out how much they enjoy how the novel, in a Lovecraftian fashion, disrupts mimetic reality with realistic portrayals of the supernatural.

On the social cataloguing site GoodReads, for example, more than half of the seventy-nine thousand people rating the book give it five out of five stars. Many of the positive reviews address its fictionality.

A woman from Texas who belongs to a nondenominational Bible church writes that she loves *This Present Darkness* because "it is absolutely fascinating to get a glimpse of what the spiritual realm of our existence might be like!"[77] A woman from Canada, who read the book with her husband, son, and daughter, describes the story as both true and fiction. "Sure it's fiction but man," she writes, "this particular fiction has become my fact by deliberate choice because for me there is no down side in doing so. . . . If you're a christian, Frank Peretti pulls away the curtains and give [*sic*] a view of what 'might' be going on in the day-to-day goings on of angels in the upper and lower realms. So enjoyable, so entertaining, so satisfying in the end."[78] A stay-at-home mother in Oregon also thinks it was "a darned good story." She read the novel as a teenager and returned to reread it in her early forties. Peretti's fiction, she writes, "does the church a service by reminding us of the supernatural forces which actually *are* at work in our world and which many of us have done [our] best to forget in this 'modern' era. Do they function exactly as Peretti describes? No, I am certain they don't. This is clearly fiction."[79]

The many people who liked the novel liked the way it staged certain questions and gave them an imaginative space to try on an idea of what belief is like in contemporary American culture. They identified not with the literal claims but with the imaginative truth of spiritual struggle. It made them think of their own belief as a worldview in cultural conflict.

Of course, many readers didn't identify with it at all. As is always the case with mass culture, *This Present Darkness* has elicited mixed reactions. Some people who bought it and read it hated it. About 2 percent of the GoodReads ratings give *This Present Darkness* one star. Another 3 percent give it a begrudging two stars. These readers judge the book too didactic or too simplistic, or both. "Very Christian, very preachy," one woman writes. "Difficult to relate to any of the characters, only a handful seemed like they could be real people."[80] She notes she didn't actually finish the book. Another reader, similarly, says she "just couldn't get past Mr. Peretti's simplistic, black and white style."[81] A third woman, more harshly, writes, "I found this book on the train in Ft. Lauderdale and honestly considered throwing myself on the tracks."[82]

Evangelical historian Mark Noll's reaction wasn't that extreme, but he felt much the same way. Peretti's fiction, for him, is an example of the scandal of the evangelical mind.[83] Evangelicals in the 1980s weren't being influenced by the great tradition of conversionist Protestant theology. They weren't shaped by reading the eighteenth-century writings of Puritan preacher Jonathan Edwards or his heirs, Noll complained, but rather by the consumption of popular, Christian-themed merchandise.

By the end of the decade, the market for that merchandise had expanded to include two different ways of imagining evangelical belief. Romance novels presented belief as the possibility of fulfilled, abundant life. And Peretti's fiction offered a vision of cultural conflict. On the shelves of bookstores in every suburban community in America, Peretti's novels were soon joined by others that had the same idea.

3

The Rapture Dilemma

Tim LaHaye and Jerry Jenkins's *Left Behind*

Tim LaHaye was a Baptist pastor and a right-wing culture warrior, and he had an idea for a novel. It would be like a Frank Peretti novel, telling a story of spiritual struggle and how Christian belief compels cultural conflict. The story would start with a commercial airline pilot in his 747 cockpit, thinking about cheating on his wife. Then—*BOOM!*—the rapture would happen. All the real Christians would be gone in an instant, caught up into heaven, and the world would be in confusion and chaos and the antichrist would be plotting global dominion. That story would grab readers. The pilot would know this was the apocalypse foretold by the Bible. He'd realize God is real, the Bible is true, and the antichrist is bad, but he'd try to convince people, and they wouldn't believe him. The story could have an apologetics angle, showing people why they should believe and why they had to make a choice.

LaHaye thought this could be a blockbuster of an evangelical novel—and an "evangelical novel" both in the sense of a novel for evangelicals and a novel that evangelized. If it was a really good story, like the Peretti fiction being sold at B. Dalton's and Waldenbooks, non-Christians and nominal Christians would read it and be converted. Peretti's third book, after all, was about abortion, and it was selling at the mall! A story about the apocalypse, in which the action-hero protagonist realizes he has to use the Bible as his guide book? That could be a huge hit.

LaHaye knew just who should write it, too: Frank Peretti.[1]

Peretti declined. Sales of his new book were pretty good, and, combined, his first three novels had sold more than five million copies by the mid-1990s. He was in negotiations with a new publisher for a fourth book, *The Oath*. The publisher was talking about a massive promotional campaign.[2] Peretti didn't need a coauthor. He didn't want a coauthor. He passed on the offer.

So LaHaye went looking for someone else. His agent connected him with Jerry Jenkins.[3]

Jenkins was not too precious for collaboration. He was a working writer, and if the job paid, he would pound it out. He would tell you himself he didn't have lofty literary ambitions. "I make no apologies for writing to the masses," he said. "I am one of them."[4] He was an incredibly fast writer, too, producing forty to sixty pages of workmanlike prose per day.[5] He had started out at *Moody Monthly*, so he had his conservative Christian credentials, and by the 1990s, he had more than 120 books to his name, including authorized biographies of sports stars, singers, and celebrity preachers. He was happy to work with a coauthor, if he thought the book would sell.

The two men met at a hotel near the Chicago O'Hare airport. Jenkins lived in the area and LaHaye was traveling. LaHaye explained that he had the idea for the start of the novel, with the pilot on the plane, and he proposed to outline the prophetic timeline for the story, which he'd already basically done in *No Fear of the Storm*, a nonfiction book he'd published in 1992. Jenkins would then write a compelling story to fit the narrative frame. He would basically, as Jenkins later explained, put "fictitious characters in the way of these prophetic events," to help people really imagine the apocalypse.[6]

This wasn't a totally new idea. A number of apocalyptic Christian novels had been published in the early part of the twentieth century, popularizing the end-times theology set forth by the fundamentalist *Scofield Bible Commentary*. Their commercial success was limited, though. One early example was *Titan, Son of Saturn: The Coming World Emperor; A Story of the Other Christ*, written by an Ohio doctor named Joseph Birkbeck Burroughs. It sold ten thousand copies between 1905 and 1917.[7] Other apocalyptic Christian novels, like *Be Thou Prepared, for Jesus Is Coming* (1937), *They That Remain* (1941), and *Raptured* (1950), saw similar or smaller sales numbers. Inspired by Peretti's success and the current state of the Christian fiction market, LaHaye had bigger ambitions. He wanted a crossover hit.

Jenkins didn't mind being second choice, but he did have some reservations about the plan. He told LaHaye that a project like this required a clear idea of the target audience. Was this a book for believers, who already knew the theology and thus the basic plot? Or was it for people who'd never heard of the rapture, the tribulation, the antichrist, with a goal of persuading them?[8] Already in the composition of the story, Jenkins needed to know. How much did he need to explain? Jenkins quoted James 1:8: "A double minded man is unstable in all his ways." LaHaye was unmoved. He wanted to reach two different audiences, at once.[9]

The novel should do the same thing Peretti's did, LaHaye said, and awaken evangelicals to cultural conflict, showing them how their belief put them at odds with the world around them. LaHaye wanted to rally evangelicals to culture-war politics. But also, the novel should convert people to evangelical Christianity. The story of the rapture and the antichrist, imaginatively engaged through fiction, should help them see why belief mattered and compel them to feel like they had to make a choice to believe or not believe.

Jenkins wasn't entirely convinced, but he signed on anyway. He thought the novel could sell maybe 200,000 copies. He wrote up the first ten pages, with a hero named Rayford Steele, whose "fully loaded 747" is on autopilot as he's "thinking about a woman he'd never touched." Then, suddenly, the rapture happens, and about a third of the passengers disappear instantly out of their seats.[10] Jenkins sent the pages to the agent, and the agent shopped it around to evangelical publishers. Tyndale House, in Carol Stream, Illinois, bought the book with a $50,000 advance. Some within the company were skeptical of the novel's sales potential, but the publisher decided the book would sell. Tyndale House even had some ideas for how to distribute the book beyond evangelical bookstores.[11]

The Compelling Apocalypse

LaHaye believed an end-times novel could reach these two audiences in two different ways, because he believed end-times theology reached these two audiences in two different ways. Long before he came up with the idea of *Left Behind*, LaHaye was arguing that the doctrines of the rapture, the tribulation, and the antichrist should be a key emphasis of evangelical preaching. He was dismayed to see some conservative Protestants downplaying end-times theology. Both as a Baptist pastor and as a political activist, he thought end-times theology was not just right but also powerful. The idea of the rapture—imagining it, picturing it, and thinking how it could happen at any moment—really affected people. It moved them and mobilized them. LaHaye believed end-times theology motivated evangelicals to evangelize with real fervor. He thought it made them become more politically active. And he thought it was effective in converting people to evangelicalism.

Evangelicals believe in sharing the good news of Jesus's salvation with the world, starting with friends and neighbors. But they often don't. They become lackadaisical, maybe a little passive. But they can be motivated, LaHaye argued, by the idea that the rapture could happen at any moment. If they are waiting for Jesus to return, LaHaye said, and think he could return at any moment to snatch true believers from the earth before the beginning of the reign of the antichrist, that's a reason to share the good news now, today, before it's too late. Eschatology, far from being an arcane theological pursuit, "provides Christians with an at-any-moment expectancy," LaHaye wrote, which "produces an evangelistic church of soul-winning Christians."[12]

LaHaye pointed to the history of the doctrine. Plymouth Brethren minister John Nelson Darby articulated this eschatology in Great Britain in the nineteenth century. Since then, LaHaye said, "the gospel has spread to every continent of the globe."[13] The one thing followed the other.

The causal connection may have been fuzzy for some people, but for others it wasn't. Bill Bright, for example, was so moved by an end-times prophecy class at Fuller Theological Seminary that he quit school to evangelize American college students. "I'm not going to be sitting here studying Greek when Christ comes!" he said.[14] A few years later, he founded Campus Crusade for Christ.

According to LaHaye, first-century Christians were similarly motivated. He said early Christians were expecting the rapture at any minute, and because of that, they "turned the world upside down."[15] The doctrine was later lost in Catholic corruption, which LaHaye attributed to Origen and Augustine.[16] Christians then became passive. They stopped being missionaries. Evangelism didn't seem so urgent, the faithful lost their fire, and the church fell into apostasy.

The apocalyptic prophecies of the Bible—Matthew 24:30-31, 1 Corinthians 15:51-57, 1 Thessalonians 4:16-17, and the books of Daniel and Revelation—could seem obscure. They could lend themselves to endless debates about details, overelaborate maps, and embarrassing predictions. But a clear understanding of the basic belief in the rapture was the secret to a strong, vibrant church. Anywhere and everywhere Christians thought the rapture would happen and could happen at any moment, LaHaye argued, they became "soul-winning, missionary-minded, and spiritually productive" believers.[17]

The doctrine of the rapture doesn't just turn Christians into missionaries, either. According to LaHaye, it also motivates them to get involved in politics. This seems counterintuitive to a lot of people. If the world has no future, why would anyone work to make it better? As historian Paul S. Boyer argues, the logic of the theology would suggest that believers' energies "are better spent in winning souls for Christ than in trying to shape world events."[18] Evangelicals shouldn't try to make the world a better place if they believe the world is hopelessly doomed. As one rapture preacher put it, "God didn't send me to clean the fishbowl. He sent me to fish."[19]

For LaHaye, however, the compelling need to evangelize was also a compelling reason to get involved in politics. If time is short, the need to spread the gospel is urgent. And the liberty necessary to preach the gospel at home and abroad is a top priority. Evangelicals, informed by their eschatology, should be committed to the political work necessary to preserve liberty, whether that meant opposing increased taxes and increased regulation, decrying the growth of government, or supporting a strong, hawkish foreign policy.[20]

LaHaye, for his part, had been active in right-wing politics since the early 1960s, starting shortly after he became pastor of Scott Memorial Baptist Church in San Diego. He supported Republican Barry Goldwater for president in 1964, agreeing with the candidate that "extremism in defense of liberty is no vice." In 1965, LaHaye wrote the actor Ronald Reagan a two-page fan letter urging him to run for governor of California.[21]

LaHaye was also a member of the John Birch Society, a secretive, far-right group opposed to communism and what it held to be the conspiracy behind the conspiracy of communism. A few high-level Birchers were active in his church, and LaHaye became a close friend with the organization's second president, Georgia congressman Larry McDonald.[22] LaHaye called himself a student of conspiracy theories and said he believed the Illuminati manipulated world events from behind the scenes.[23] LaHaye spoke at John Birch training seminars and appeared in John Birch promotional films in the early '60s, explaining why conservative Christians had to get involved in politics. "If we don't stop the advance of communism," he said, "none of us will be free to preach the gospel."[24]

Birchers, like apocalypse-minded Christians, were pessimistic about the long-term prospects of humanity. They believed doom was all but certain and foresaw a future of global tyranny and dictatorship. Already, by the end of the 1950s, the Birchers believed the conspiracy was like an international octopus, "so large its tentacles now reach into all of the legislative halls, all of the union labor meetings, a majority of all religious gatherings, and most of the schools of the *whole world*." According to founder Robert Welch, "The human race has never before faced any such monster of power which was determined to enslave it. There is certainly no reason for underrating its size, its efficiency, its determination, its power, or its menace."[25] And yet, the point of the John Birch Society was not defeatism. They were committed to fighting. They were committed, if nothing else, to holding out for as long as possible. LaHaye took the same stance, politically and theologically. It made sense as a response to communism, and it made sense in response to the coming reign of the antichrist. Every day of delay meant more souls saved.

Still, some of LaHaye's political friends were skeptical. Could preaching the rapture really motivate Christians to get involved in politics? Wouldn't the expectation that true Christians would be snatched out of the world make people too "heavenly minded" and neutralize them, politically? After all, a lot of conservative

Protestants weren't involved in politics and were skeptical of political activity, thinking it was a distraction from the real, spiritual issues. "That has nothing to do with prophecy," LaHaye said. "It has everything to do with apathy."[26] When people really understood end-times Bible prophecy, they understood the need to fight for liberty for as long as possible.

The historical record says LaHaye is right, by and large. Apocalypse-minded Christians have been motivated by their expectations of rapture, the tribulation, and the antichrist to pay close attention to world events and take an active interest in American politics, both foreign and domestic. There is a myth that fundamentalists disengaged from cultural conflicts because of their theology. Historian Matthew Avery Sutton has shown, however, that they didn't. "They never retreated," Sutton writes. Rather, rapture-believers "have consistently insisted that God has called them to use their talents to occupy, reform, and transform their culture."[27] They took their marching orders from Jesus's words in Luke 19:13: "Occupy till I come."

For these Christians, political activism wasn't a choice. It was a divine mandate. They had to be involved. And since the end could come any day, it was urgent.

The theology, just like the fiction LaHaye was imagining, also had a second audience. The rapture, the tribulation, and the antichrist were compelling, LaHaye argued, to non-Christians. Getting people to imagine the apocalypse was an important tool for evangelism. Just provoking the imagination was a powerful first step. You could tell people about the Bible's prophecies for the future, and that would force them to make a decision, a preliminary choice that would prepare them for the ultimate choice about belief. First: Are these things believable? Yes or no? And then if someone decides to keep an open mind and say that the story about the coming end of human history is, sure, believable, and that it "could be true," then the evangelist could press further and ask, "Do you believe? Yes or no?" The theology could thus compel a choice.

LaHaye had some success with this evangelistic approach. Once on a flight from Salt Lake City to San Francisco, he wrote, he was "seated next to a salesman who claimed he had never read a Bible."[28] The man was, by his own account, almost completely unchurched. He preferred to golf on Sundays, if he did anything. LaHaye asked the man to read a passage from Revelation. "I handed him my Bible," LaHaye wrote, "with only a brief instruction: 'This is a prophecy about a future event.'"[29] The salesman was quickly converted. He moved from ambivalence to the suspension of disbelief, and from the suspension of disbelief to actual belief.

As Jenkins worked out the story, this idea came up over and over again. The fictitious characters in *Left Behind* have their lives interrupted by these prophetic events. They hear these things were foretold by the Bible, and they think, "Could it be true?" and then, "It has to be true." They run repeatedly into a dichotomous choice, to believe or not to believe. Yes or no? The novel returns repeatedly to the choice and reprises, again and again, the argument against middle ground.

The character Rayford Steele, for example, becomes convinced one cannot dodge this dichotomy. There is no space for ambivalence, no room to agree to disagree. He believes. He tries to convince people of the truth he so clearly sees in the aftermath of this act of God and is frustrated when people don't think they have to make a choice.

One woman, for example, says she doesn't know if Steele's apocalyptic theories are true, but she knows he "is sincere."[30] Steele scoffs.

"What good was that?" he thinks. "If he believed and she didn't, she had to assume he believed something bogus or she would have to admit she was ignoring the truth. What he told her carried no other option."[31]

Jenkins put off writing for a year while he worked with famed evangelist Billy Graham on Graham's memoir, *Just as I Am*.[32] When he came back to the novel, he realized the novel wasn't about the theology of the rapture or the timeline of the tribulation. It was about the characters making choices. "I put the characters on the page," Jenkins said, "and let the consequences play out in my mind as I record what happens."[33] With this story, the real story was about the characters and how they'd all had a supernatural experience with God intervening in their lives, and now they had to decide what they believed.

The readers, if you thought about it, would be in the same position. The novel would put them in the way of these prophetic events. And when they picked up the fiction, they'd be confronted with the choice of whether or not they thought this story was believable. That's just how fiction works. It addresses the reader with a request to suspend disbelief.[34] Readers have to decide whether or not they can entertain this staged presentation of reality. And if they answered yes they could, when they read *Left Behind* they would find themselves or versions of themselves in the story, and they'd identify with those characters as they were reading, and then they'd have to decide if they identified with the characters when the characters were converted. They would come to confront this choice, in the novel: Do you believe? Yes or no?

The emotional arc of the novel could be structured around conversion, as characters come to face this choice. The heart of the novel would be a depiction of belief as a choice, and a choice one has to make. People who already believed could be reassured they made the right choice; people who didn't believe could be challenged. And that way, the fiction could address two audiences.

Demanding a Verdict

In the evangelical bookstores of the 1990s, this idea of belief as a compelled choice was quite common. Alongside the idea of belief as the key to abundant life in the American suburbs, and the idea of unavoidable cultural conflict and worldview clashes, there was this other idea, about the necessity of choice.

Sociologist Peter Berger says this is the mark of secularity. Berger famously argued against what is called the "secularization thesis," which says that as societies progress and become more modern, there is a decline in religious belief. That's not true, according to Berger. What does happen is that societies become more pluralistic, and it becomes apparent to everyone that there are a bunch of different understandings of the ultimate nature of reality. Which means it's possible to believe a bunch of different things and it stops being possible to believe whatever you believe by default. "What previously was fate now becomes a set of choices," Berger writes. "The individual may choose his *Weltanschauung*," his view of the world and meaning and existence.[35] Berger goes further: you don't just get to choose; you have to choose. "The modern individual," he writes, "is faced not just with the opportunity but with the necessity to make choices as to his belief."[36] This means that even the most staunch believers live with a certain amount of doubt, and a certain amount of defensiveness, because whatever they believe, they can imagine choosing to believe something else. The philosopher Charles Taylor, expanding on this idea, says, "We live in a condition where we cannot help but be aware that there are a number of different construals, views which intelligent, reasonably undeluded people, of good will, can and do disagree on. We cannot help looking over our shoulder from time to time, looking sideways, living our faith also in a condition of doubt and anxiety."[37]

This condition of doubt and anxiety is visible in the apologetics section of the evangelical bookstore. There, a host of very popular texts address believers' anxieties and the problem of modern religious choice, arguing that the most important choice isn't really a choice, because there is only one answer. They make an argument urging readers to embrace the evangelical Christian construal of ultimate reality, explaining that reasonable people are compelled to choose it.

In *The Case for Christ*, for example, apologist Lee Strobel tells readers it is like they are on a jury. They should weight the evidence for and against Jesus. They should be open-minded. But they had to come to a decision. "Ultimately," writes Strobel, "it's the responsibility of a jury to reach a verdict."[38] The book sold half a million copies its first year. The apologist William Lane Craig, similarly, starts his popular 1994 book with an attack on relativism. There cannot, he writes, be multiple right answers to the question of whether or not Christianity is true. There can be no middle ground. Christianity is true or false. God exists or does not. If one person believes and another doesn't, it makes no sense for them to agree to disagree.[39] Even if not everyone will be persuaded by evidence and arguments, evangelicals should still force that confrontation. Force the choice.

Craig himself does this professionally. He has had at least ninety-eight public debates with atheists since 1982. As religion writer Nathan Schneider notes, such debates literally stage the dichotomy of belief versus unbelief. "In these debates, there can only be two sides, with nothing in between," Schneider writes. "One side must be right, and the other must be wrong."[40] Belief is presented as a forced either/or proposition.

The most popular apologetics book produced by an American evangelical was Josh McDowell's *Evidence That Demands a Verdict*. McDowell was on staff at Bill Bright's Campus Crusade in the 1960s. He helped train evangelists to go to college campuses and convert people. To do this, McDowell compiled what he called "documentation of historical evidences for faith in Christ."[41] This consisted mostly of long quotes pulled from various Christian scholars. As the title indicates, though, the evidence of the book was imagined to carry an explicit demand. It would force a choice. And, according to Bright, the choice wasn't really a choice. "The evidence proving the deity of the Lord Jesus Christ," Bright wrote in the foreword, "is overwhelmingly conclusive to any honest, objective seeker after truth." There would be some, of course, who wouldn't believe. Those people, Bright assured readers, were "simply *unwilling* to believe!"[42] There is no such thing as honest disagreement. There was no choice but to make a choice, and there was one right choice. Evangelicals could thus explain for themselves their own experience of secularity, with its mix of doubt and defensiveness, and be assured the other alternatives weren't legitimate options.

The book was wildly successful. It was first published in 1972, and by 1986, *Evidence That Demands a Verdict* was in its twenty-fifth printing, with more than a million copies sold. One editor of *Christianity Today* judged the book "doubtless the most popular apologetics handbook of our time."[43] The magazine ranked it thirteenth on a list of fifty books that shaped modern American evangelicalism.[44] It was ubiquitous in evangelical churches, homes, and of course, bookstores. No one could grow up evangelical in the 1990s without, at some point, seeing this book, with the picture of a judge's gavel on an open Bible on the cover, or McDowell's other really popular apologetics text, *More Than a Carpenter*, which evangelicals often bought in bulk to give away.

For American evangelicals, however, the gold standard of successful evangelical arguments was C. S. Lewis's *Mere Christianity*.[45] Lewis was BBC radio's "voice of faith" in Great Britain during World War II. The public broadcasting service wanted "a sensible, engaging, and authoritative voice that commanded confidence and elicited affection."[46] Lewis, a literature professor at Oxford and Cambridge, filled the role. He gave twenty-nine talks to an estimated average audience of 600,000 people.[47] The talks were collected into a single volume and published in 1952. The resulting text made a commonsense case for the reasonableness of Christian belief. Lewis's arguments were smart but not inaccessible. Lewis wasn't interested in a big philosophical project. He just wanted to show that Christianity comported with reality. It made sense, he argued, as a choice. In clear and friendly language, *Mere Christianity* asserted that belief was at least plausible and should be considered.

Lewis himself quickly turned away from apologetics. Even before *Mere Christianity* was published, he decided he wasn't enough of a philosopher to make the best case for the rational foundations of Christianity.[48] In 1948, he debated the subject of philosophical naturalism with Catholic philosopher Elizabeth Anscombe. The two were on the same side of the issue, but Anscombe thought Lewis's argument for their side was seriously flawed. Anscombe, well versed in Ludwig Wittgenstein's philosophy, showed Lewis he was making some basic mistakes. He failed to distinguish between "reasons" and "causes" and misunderstood the difference between "irrational" and "nonrational."[49] The encounter was embarrassing and "slightly bruising" for Lewis, according to biographer Alister McGrath.[50] Lewis, besides, felt more drawn to the imaginative work of fiction. He explained this in a letter to theologian Carl F. H. Henry a few years later. Henry, a proponent of smart and culturally engaged evangelicalism, wanted Lewis to do more of what he had done in *Mere Christianity*. Henry invited Lewis to write apologetics for his new evangelical magazine, *Christianity Today*. Lewis declined. He was done with "frontal attacks," he explained. He was turning his attention to "fiction and symbol."[51] It was a path LaHaye would later follow.

Mere Christianity was, regardless, hugely important to American evangelicals. Lewis became kind of the patron saint of evangelicalism, though he did not himself identify with the movement or adhere to its standards.[52] "Lewis's writing," according to historian Mark Noll, "constituted the single most important body of Christian thinking for American evangelicals in the twentieth century."[53]

By the 1970s, whenever there was a high-profile evangelical conversion, *Mere Christianity* seemed to be involved. The book was everywhere. When a dozen or more of the musicians in Bob Dylan's Rolling Thunder Revue had born-again experiences in 1976, there was a copy of *Mere Christianity* circulating behind the scenes of the tour.[54] When Chuck Colson, President Richard Nixon's "hatchet man," converted before being sent to prison for obstruction of justice in 1973, he was reading *Mere Christianity*.[55] When Campus Crusade decided it needed an apologetics textbook to help campus evangelists, the central argument was taken from *Mere Christianity*.

One reason *Mere Christianity* was so important was that it presented readers with this dichotomous choice and demanded readers choose. Lewis claimed there was no third way between belief and unbelief. Look at Jesus, he wrote. A lot of people don't want to believe in Jesus, but they don't want to disbelieve either. They want a middle option, where they reject the idea that Jesus is God but accept him as a great moral teacher. But that's illogical. "A man who was merely a man and said the sort of things Jesus said would not be a great moral teacher," Lewis argued. "He would either be a lunatic—on a level with a man who says he is a poached egg—or else he would be the Devil of Hell. You must make your choice. Either this man was and is the Son of God: or else a madman or something worse."[56]

Colson said it was this passage that pushed him to accept Jesus as his Lord and Savior. "Lewis puts it so bluntly," he recalled in his memoir, *Born Again*, "that you can't slough it off: for Christ to have talked as he talked, lived as he lived, died as he died, he was either God or a raving lunatic."[57] As Colson was reading, he could feel the middle ground disappearing. He knew he had only two options. "Either I would believe," he wrote, "or I would not—and believe it all or none of it."[58] Colson experienced his conversion as a choice, but also, importantly, as a choice he was compelled to make.

McDowell felt similarly compelled. When he first encountered that key passage in *Mere Christianity*, though, he wasn't particularly impressed. In 1958, nineteen-year-old McDowell left his native Michigan on a quest to disprove Christianity. God, as he saw it, was "a public relations myth."[59]

The quest led him to the British Library where, as he recounts it in his autobiography, he presumptuously examined the Codex Sinaiticus in its bulletproof display case. He could only see two pages of the manuscript, and he didn't read Greek, but the object nonetheless reassured him in his unbelief. This was, after all, "still a copy of a copy of a copy of a copy."[60] It couldn't be trusted. McDowell approached a librarian and demanded to know how much the text had been altered. The librarian sent him to Alan Cobb, a British barrister and amateur evangelical apologist. Cobb introduced McDowell to the works of C. S. Lewis. Cobb pointed McDowell to this specific passage of *Mere Christianity*, about how Jesus claimed to be God and so was either a liar, a lunatic, or correct. McDowell ignored it at the moment. But later it hit him. Sitting in an evangelical library near the Baker Street Tube station in London, McDowell suddenly knew that Cobb and Lewis were right. It seemed, in an instant, irrefutable and unavoidable.

"I felt like a train lurching into the station," McDowell later wrote, "letting off a last burst of steam while coming to a final stop. I was speechless. I didn't know where I was. I only knew I had arrived."[61]

He returned to Michigan and responded to an altar call on December 19, 1959, at 8:30 p.m.[62] It felt, to him, like he was submitting to an obvious truth. The dichotomy had forced him to surrender to Jesus.

McDowell returned to this passage in *Mere Christianity*. When he went to work for Campus Crusade, he made it the crux of the argument of his apologetics textbook. McDowell rendered the dichotomy in a chart that could be easily re-created by evangelists on any chalk board on any college campus.

The top line said, in all caps, "JESUS CLAIMS TO BE GOD."

Below that, McDowell wrote, "(TWO ALTERNATIVES)." An arrow pointing left indicates one option: "Claims were FALSE." Below that are two subsequent alternatives: "He KNEW His Claims Were FALSE" and "He DID NOT KNOW His Claims Were False."

If the former is true, according to the chart, Jesus was a liar who died because of his lie. If the latter is true, Jesus was sincerely deluded. That's one set of alternatives.

An arrow pointing to the right side of the page shows the other option: "Claims were TRUE." Below that, the conclusion, "He is LORD." This is followed by another two alternatives: "You can ACCEPT" or "You can REJECT."[63]

If the choice isn't clear, McDowell states it multiple times on the following page. "Jesus claimed to be God," he writes. "His claim to be God must be either true of false." Then he repeats himself: "Jesus' claim to be God must be either true or false," he says. "If Jesus' claims are true then He is the Lord and we must either accept or reject His Lordship."[64]

McDowell wanted to force people to make a choice. He was also very clear that, in another sense, the choice is not a choice. He personally experienced conversion as a realization. He thinks the dichotomy of *Mere Christianity* can force people to have that kind of moment of recognition, where they will be faced with a choice they can't not choose. "I cannot personally conclude that Jesus was a liar or a lunatic," McDowell writes. "The only other alternative is that he was the Christ, the Son of God, as he claimed."[65] If others are not so persuaded, McDowell, following Bright, thinks they probably aren't being honest with themselves.

Popular evangelical apologetics, in this way, imagined belief as something that arises out of a forced dichotomy. The experience of belief was the experience Berger described of feeling forced to choose. On the one had, you would know that your choice is a choice, but you also wouldn't have a choice about choosing. You would have to choose. Yes or no? In evangelical bookstores, belief was presented as a worldview, which forced you into conflict with your neighbors. It was presented, too, as an act of trust that God loves you and has a wonderful plan for your life, even the mundane daily parts. And as the market organized American evangelicalism and made this religious identity available through the consumption of Christian-themed merchandise, there was also this third idea of compelled choice.

Drama of Belief

Left Behind is, more than anything else, about this idea of belief. Academic critics, however, have tended to read *Left Behind* as primarily a political novel. Cultural studies professor Hugh B. Urban, for example, writes that *Left Behind* is "clearly a commentary on the processes of globalization and America's role in a transnational era."[66] He reads *Left Behind* side by side with neoconservatism's political program, and looks to the fiction for insight into the foreign policy of George W. Bush, who was elected president five years after the first novel was published. While Urban admits there is no "coded message woven subliminally into the *Left Behind* books," there is, he writes, a deep link between Bush's political vision and LaHaye and Jenkins's fictional narrative. He sees an "affinity" between "the Evangelical Ethic and the Spirit of Neo-Imperialism."[67]

Others have felt the same way. The fiction was popularly seen through this political lens, especially around the time the United States invaded Iraq. "We understand immediately," essayist Joan Didion wrote, on reading the novels in 2003, "this will be an end-times scenario with a political point."[68] Conservative political commentators notably did not see their ideas in *Left Behind*. A review in the neoconservative *Weekly Standard* described the novel (and Christian-themed merchandise generally) as a corruption of Christianity.[69] *National Review*, the flagship of American conservatism, reported that *Left Behind* was "bloated, stilted, and corny," and its politics, at best, goofy.[70]

But from the left, the novel could seem like it put a spotlight on everything that was so worrying about America's religious conservatives. Here were people who were not worried about the global conflagration that might result from an ill-conceived crusade in the Middle East—they were hoping for it! Here were people intoxicated on the hubris of a divine mandate. "The President's preferred constituency," Didion wrote, "feel secure about whatever destructive events played out in the Middle East because those events were foreordained, necessary to the completion of God's plan, laid out in prophecy, written in the books of Genesis and Jeremiah and Zechariah and Daniel and Ezekiel and Matthew and Revelation, dramatized in . . . the 'Left Behind' books."[71]

It is true the book and its sequels are political. As with *This Present Darkness*, *Left Behind* has some obvious political concerns. The novel expresses unqualified support for the state of Israel and extreme skepticism toward the United Nations. The novel also comments on the problems of abortion, the breakdown of the traditional family, feminism, and liberalism on college campuses. But this is mostly scene setting and background. For LaHaye and Jenkins, the fiction is actually about belief. As literary scholar Amy Hungerford rightly points out, *Left Behind* "highlights belief about as dramatically as any fictional scenario could." She explains further: "Believing in Christ is not only, for these writers, the defining characteristic of true religion, subject only to the free choice of the individual, but it defines the fate of every character in the novel."[72] The novel is structured around the narrative arc of conversion. The novel centers on questions about the cultural practice of belief and the experience of belief in contemporary, pluralistic society. The drama of *Left Behind* is the drama of belief.

There are two main characters in *Left Behind*. They are both heroes, whom the readers can root for and identify with as they respond to the apocalypse. Each starts in unbelief. And then changes. Faced with a choice, the protagonists realize they have to make a choice, and they choose to believe. They then see that the choice was the only honest choice, one they were compelled to make.

The first person to go through this process in *Left Behind* is Rayford Steele. Steele starts out as an unbeliever—specifically as someone who doesn't believe in the evangelical vision of the apocalyptic future. Before the rapture happens, he does not think it will happen. He can't even imagine it. His wife has been going to a new evangelical church, and she is learning a lot about Bible prophecy and the end times. She is especially excited about the rapture. "Can you imagine, Rafe," she asks him. "Jesus coming back to get us before we die?"[73]

He can't.

It seems so implausible.

Steele is faced, in this moment, with a choice, but he doesn't want to choose. He doesn't want to have to side against his wife. Steele wants to remain ambivalent, and he resents the way the question, "can you imagine?" actually makes that ambivalence impossible. He doesn't want to say no, he can't imagine the rapture. He wants to say, "That's nice for you, that you have this hobby of eschatology, but we don't have to talk about it. We can agree to disagree."

This tension in the Steele marriage started with church. Irene joined a new church that focused a lot on personal relationships with Jesus and the doctrines of the end times. The Steele family had been nominally religious before. Their placid Protestant church had "demanded little and offered a lot," mainly in mainline respectability and social connections (124). New Hope Village Church was different. People there wouldn't let Rayford Steele just be passive. They practically forced him to have a position on whether or not God is active in the world and in human history and, especially, in his life. Just as a way of making conversation, people regularly asked Steele "what God was doing in his life" (2). It was infuriating.

Steele responds by "checking out." He puts his energy into his career as a pilot with Pan-Continental Airlines. He spends his Sundays fixing things around the house or resting, maybe playing golf or watching a game on TV. He doesn't actively oppose his wife's religious activity but tries to avoid it. He doesn't want to be put in a position where he has to have a position, and either believe or disbelieve. He prefers the ambiguity of uncertainty. "I'm happy for you," he tells his wife, "that you can be so cocksure" (5).

So when the rapture does happen, Steele knows what it is. He's flying from Chicago to London when the flight attendant he's thinking about having sex with tells him people are missing. Dozens. At least. Their clothes are there in their seats, but the people have vanished. Steele doesn't then immediately confess belief. He doesn't become an evangelical. But he knows something. "The terrifying truth," Jenkins writes, "was that he knew all too well. Irene had been right. He, and most of his passengers, had been left behind" (19).

At the same time, Steele can also conceive of other possible explanations. He remains uncertain or convinces himself he can be uncertain because there are other theories. Another pilot, flying in the opposite direction, from Paris to Chicago, tells Steele his first thought was spontaneous human combustion. The disappearances are also reminiscent of "the old *Star Trek* shows" where people were dematerialized and rematerialized (26). It occurs to Steele that the event could be caused by a weapon, "some world power doing this with fancy rays" (27). That's only the start of the many explanations that are going around. When Steele tunes in to an all-news radio station, "every conceivable explanation was proffered" (29). Given that kind of confusion, he can't be sure. He knows, according to the novel, but doesn't believe as his wife believed. He isn't "cocksure."

Steele turns the plane around and returns to Chicago. The world is a mess of crashed cars and planes and panicked people trying to check on loved ones. Steele calls home but no one answers. "If you're there, pick up," he says to the answering machine. "I sure hope you're there" (49).

He doesn't think they are.

Steele meets other people convinced this event is an act of God, and it strengthens his feeling that the rapture is the most plausible explanation. On a TV in the airport, for example, he sees a story about how the event unfolded at a soccer game at a school for missionary kids in Indonesia. Most of the spectators disappeared. All but one of the players vanished midgame, leaving their jerseys and the soccer ball behind. The remaining student, suddenly alone on the field, killed himself. Steele thinks the student was driven to suicide because he knew the truth. "Of all people," Steele speculates, "that player, a student at a Christian school, would have known the truth immediately. The rapture had taken place. Jesus had returned for his people, and that boy was not one of them" (48). Seeing someone so absolutely convinced has the effect of making it more plausible.

When Steele gets home, the question of belief really becomes personal. His wife and young son are gone. They have vanished out of their beds. Waiting in the empty house for his college-age daughter, Chloe, who has also been left behind, Steele wonders "how they had missed everything Irene had been trying to tell them, why it had been so hard to accept and believe" (102). He commits himself to seriously considering the rapture. He "would be on a mission, a quest for truth" (103).

Once he has done this, he feels the rapture is the only possible explanation for what has happened. The other theories don't make sense. The rapture is true.

Steele turns to the Bible at this point, but it isn't helpful. He flips through. He can't find anything that specifically speaks to being "left behind." There's no index with a listing for the rapture. Nothing obvious jumps out. He reads several passages from Revelation where Jesus says, "I am coming quickly," but he doesn't know what that means since the Bible is very old (122). It doesn't really matter, though. At this point he knows. This is the rapture.

As it's presented in the novel, Steele reaches this conclusion without getting any new information. He thinks the rapture is plausible, feels he's forced to have a position on the question of whether it's true or not, decides he's going to be serious about it, and then reaches the conclusion that evangelical eschatology is not only true but is actually the only reasonable thing to believe. He is almost pushed to this conclusion by the inexorable logic of dichotomies.

The Only Logical Explanation

When Steele's daughter, Chloe, comes home, Rayford tells her her mother was right about the rapture. Chloe argues with him. She says there are lots of possible explanations, and it's just not clear what to believe. "In California," she says, "they're actually buying into the space invasion theory" (159). It might be easier to think your vanished loved ones are in heaven, but how could you know? How could you be sure? Rayford Steele is sure. To him it is now clear. He has moved past doubt. Chloe asks him, "You're saying the only logical explanation is God, that he took his own and left the rest of us?" Rayford agrees: "That's what I'm saying" (165).

This idea of how belief works—of how one comes to belief—is recounted again when the Steeles visit New Hope, Irene Steele's evangelical church. An assistant pastor there named Bruce Barnes has been left behind, because he didn't really believe. He believes now and presents belief to the Steeles as this sort of total certainty. Before, he says, when he didn't really believe, he wasn't totally committed the way he is now. "I thought I believed everything there was to believe in the Bible," Barnes says (195). But, before the rapture, he was worried about what other people thought and was always aware, in his thinking, of other people's views. When people asked him "if New Hope was one of those churches that said Jesus was the only way to God," he "did everything but deny it" (197). Barnes didn't want to have to take a strong position.

Barnes, more than anyone else, gives voice to the theology of the authors of *Left Behind*. However, he isn't interested in explicating the details of his (renewed) eschatological beliefs. He doesn't talk about the rapture itself, either what it is or how it fits into God's larger plan for the end of human history. His focus, instead, is on belief. Barnes explains how people are sinners in God's eyes, but "Jesus took our sins and paid the penalty for them" when he died on the cross (201). This is a "supernatural transaction." But the credit from Jesus's death can only be applied to the individual's life through belief. And you have to really believe. You have to "see the truth and act on it" (200). The apocalypse is important, as with Steele, it forces people to make a choice about what they believe, and whether they believe or not. It is important because it forces confrontation with a critical dichotomy. At the end of the world, everything comes down to a single either/or.

Chloe Steele argues with Barnes, just as she argued with her father, and as her father initially argued with himself. How can one be sure when there are other possible explanations? "There's every kind of theory you want on every TV show in the country," she tells the pastor. "And each is self-serving" (190). Barnes doesn't answer this directly. Instead, he makes a little speech about the suspension of disbelief. "I have asked for a few moments of your time," he says. "If I still have it, I want to try to make use of it. Then I'll leave you alone. You can do anything you want with what I tell you. Tell me I'm crazy, tell me I'm self-serving. Leave and never come back. That's up to you. But can I have the floor for a few minutes?" (190).

This is about one-third of the way into the novel, and can be read as being addressed to skeptical readers as well as the skeptical character. In his fiction-writing-advice guide, Jenkins says the suspension of disbelief is a critical component of the novel. "Readers are to temporarily choose not to disbelieve what might otherwise trip up their logical minds," he writes. "All I'm asking is what any novelist asks: a temporary, willing suspension of disbelief."[74] Jenkins knows readers have good reasons to not believe the story he's telling, so he only asks them to take the first step toward belief and imagine it could be true (even if it's not). He addresses them with an either/or choice: Is this story at least plausible? Barnes, likewise, asks that objections and alternative explanations be put aside, at least for the moment.

Barnes is here rephrasing Irene Steele's original question to her husband, "Can you imagine Jesus coming back to get us before we die?" The novel suggests that if people can imagine the rapture as possible, and if they feel forced to take a position on the question and take the question seriously, they will realize, as Rayford Steele did, that the rapture is the only possibility. There's a direct line from believing something is plausible to believing it with absolute certainty. Barnes strategically pushes his listeners (and the novel's readers) to take the first step. They must begin with the simple yes or no, accepting there is no third choice. The question makes ambivalence impossible. A choice must be made.

Steele is very impressed with this mode of argument and how it blocks off alternative explanations. It forces the listener's hand, in a sense. Presenting people with an initial dichotomous choice compels them to face the truth they know, deep down, is true, or to acknowledge their own active disbelief. Chloe Steele resists. She thinks there are a lot of possible explanations, and it's not clear how you could know which one was the right one. Rayford Steele, however, reflecting on his own thinking process, now believes bringing up the diversity of possible positions one could take is not honesty, but dissembling. Looking at his daughter, he thinks she is just finding ways to avoid being forced to reckon with the truth. "You'd have to be blind not to see the light now," Rayford thinks. "Had he been this pseudosophisticated at that age? Of course he had. He had run everything through that maddening intellectual grid—until recently, when the supernatural came crashing through his academic pretense" (237). Barnes's approach of asking for the suspension of disbelief disables the "maddening intellectual grid." It forces people, whether they are "pseudosophisticated" or not, to start by agreeing that the rapture is plausible or taking the position they won't even consider it. "Rayford thought Barnes was brilliant," Jenkins writes. "He had put Chloe in her place, leaving her no smart remark" (190).

Steele goes on to adopt this strategy himself. He presents evangelical eschatology as the only theory that can be considered. In one scene, he starts his explanation of the rapture by announcing that his theory is "more than a theory" (383). He pays a waiter so the discussion will not be disturbed (382). He then speaks for "a little over half an hour" without interruption (384). In another scene, he starts by setting out the terms of his proselytizing. "I'm not here to argue with you," he tells a woman he wants to convert, "or even have a conversation" (367). She must accept those terms. "I don't see how I have a choice," she says (368). Steele says he is giving her one choice, to listen to him or not. If she is going to agree to listen to his story, though, she has to agree to submit in the act of listening.

For himself, Steele responds positively to being forced to submit to belief. He is moved by Barnes's presentation on the need to see the truth and act on it, and to do his part in the "supernatural transaction" of salvation. Listening to Barnes, Steele "felt he had found exactly what he was looking for. It was what he had suspected" (201).

Steele leaves New Hope with a videotape of a sermon about the rapture. The pastor of the church recorded the message before the apocalypse and left it at the church for the eventual day it would be needed. Steele takes home a copy. He puts it in the VCR and settles in front of the TV. The now-raptured pastor, Vernon Billings, addresses the camera and says the rapture has happened. He says this with complete confidence. What is perhaps more remarkable is that Billings believes the person watching the video after the rapture will also have that confidence. "You know what I'm saying is true," Billings says (211). He explains that the Bible predicted everything that is happening but tells his future viewers, "You won't need this proof by now, because you will have experienced the most shocking event of history" (209).

Billings shows them a prooftext for the rapture, 1 Corinthians 15:51–57. "We shall not all sleep," the pastor reads, "but we shall all be changed—in a moment, in the twinkling of an eye, at the last trumpet" (210).[75] Steele doesn't know what this means. To him, the text is confusing. Some of it just sounds like gibberish. As he listens to the pastor, though, he understands that the Bible applies to his present situation and can be used to shed light on how God is at work in human history. Billings tells viewers they are going to face special challenges, because they've been left behind. Steele understands, too, that the point of the rapture and the subsequent time of tribulation is to force him to face this either/or choice. The rapture is compelling him to believe.

"It was time to move beyond being a critic," Steele thinks, "an analyst never satisfied with the evidence. The proof was before him: the empty chairs, the lonely bed, the hole in his heart. There was only one course of action" (214). Steele goes to his knees. He puts his palms down on his living room carpet, and his face to the floor in a gesture of supplication. In the video, the pastor says, "Pray after me," and Steele repeats the words he is told to say: "Dear God, I admit that I am a sinner. I am sorry for my sins. Please forgive me and save me. I ask this in the name of Jesus, who died for me" (216). As he sees it, he has no other choice.

Beyond Being a Critic

The other hero and convert of *Left Behind* is a reporter, Cameron "Buck" Williams. Williams's character follows the same narrative arc as Steele's. He too starts in a place of unbelief. As a journalist, he is professionally skeptical. As a journalist, however, he is also professionally open. He wants to get to the bottom of things and is attuned to the idea that things are not always as they appear. He doesn't just accept assertions. He does his own reporting. And he will follow a lead that might, at first, appear outlandish. He will accept, at least as a working premise, that the outlandish actually might be true. This is his job. And Williams is good at his job. He has won journalism's top prizes—including a Pulitzer before turning twenty-five—and is introduced to readers as the "youngest ever senior writer for the prestigious *Global Weekly*," jetting around the world and reporting on the most important stories (228, 6). And in his reporting, he's seen things.

A little more than a year before the rapture, for example, Williams reported on Russia's surprise attack on Israel. He was in Israel reporting on another story when it happened. The scene unfolds in a flashback early in *Left Behind*. "The assault became known as the Russian Pearl Harbor," Jenkins writes. "The Russians sent intercontinental ballistic missiles and nuclear-equipped MiG fighter-bombers into the region. The number of aircraft and warheads made it clear their mission was annihilation" (10). The Israeli military scrambled a response, but they were outnumbered and caught off guard, and "from what he heard and saw in the military bunker, Buck Williams knew the end was near" (11).

The destruction of Israel was miraculously averted at the last moment, however. An inexplicable firestorm, accompanied by a hailstorm, rain, and an earthquake, destroyed the airborne Russian forces. "The sky was afire," Jenkins writes. And the skeptical-but-open reporter "stood in stark terror and amazement as the great machines of war plummeted to earth all over the city, crashing and burning. But they fell between buildings and in deserted streets and fields. Anything atomic and explosive erupted high in the atmosphere, and Buck stood there in the heat, his face blistering and his body pouring sweat. What in the world was happening?" (13).

Williams thinks it could have been a miracle. Possibly it was God divinely intervening into human affairs to protect the Jewish state. He is impressed when Jewish scholars point out the apparent connection between the event and biblical prophecy. He was "stunned when he read Ezekiel 38 and 39," which describes an army attacking from the north "like a cloud" "in the later days," only to be thwarted by "flooding rain, great hailstones, fire, and brimstone" (13-14; see Ezek. 38:16, 22). Williams is not moved to belief but is moved to think it at least plausible that these events were divinely foretold in the Bible. There are other explanations, though. His editors at the newsweekly are not convinced the event was a miracle, and Williams admits he wouldn't buy this theory either, "had he not been there and seen it himself" (13). Thinking about the other possible explanations, he hesitates. He can't be certain. Christian friends push him to make a decision, but Williams "wasn't prepared to go that far."

But the event has changed him. It expanded what he could imagine. Now, to him, Jenkins writes, "nothing was beyond belief" (15).

Williams was raised a Christian. He is from Arizona, where his dad made a living as a trucker, transporting oil and gasoline. Wil-

liams went to church and Sunday school with his family but quit
religion as soon as he was allowed to decide for himself. His family's faith was too nominal. There was no "connection between the
family's church attendance and their daily lives" (109). Williams
had basically nothing to do with religion after leaving Arizona
for an Ivy League education and a high-powered career as an up-
and-coming journalist. "He had built his life around achievement,
excitement, and—he couldn't deny it—attention," Jenkins writes.
"He loved the status that came with having his byline, his writing,
his thinking in a national magazine" (357).

When the rapture happens, Williams is sleeping in first class
on Rayford Steele's Chicago-to-London flight. He's following a tip
that the world's bankers, a "secret group of international money
men," are secretly meeting and planning to establish a global currency (84). Williams is not convinced it is true, but just because it
is a conspiracy theory "doesn't mean it's not true" (85). He's awakened when another passenger, an old woman, cries out that her
husband is missing. Williams assures the woman that her husband
is probably just in the bathroom and will return momentarily. She
doesn't think that's right. Her husband's clothes are on his seat.
"The pant legs still hung over the edge and led to his shoes and
socks," Jenkins writes. The senior's glasses and hearing aid have
also been left behind and are sitting on top of the clothes. When
Williams goes to look for the man, he finds many people are missing on the plane. "All over the plane people were holding up clothes
and gasping or shrieking that someone was missing" (23).

Williams does not immediately know what this is. Unlike
Steele, he is not familiar with the idea of the rapture. He apparently doesn't even know the term. His first thought, trying to make
sense of things, is that it might be a new kind of kidnapping. "His
mind searched its memory banks," Jenkins writes, "for anything
he had ever read, seen, or heard of any technology that could re-
move people from their clothes and make them disappear from a

decidedly secure environment. Whoever did this, were they on the plane? Would they make demands?" (23).

When the plane lands in Chicago, Williams checks his email. His editor has asked the reporting staff to "begin thinking about the causes. Military? Cosmic? Scientific? Spiritual?" (55). They need to consider all the possibilities. Every explanation. The number of possible answers, however, seems to move the reporters to a place where they don't need to know the answer. "Whether we'll come to any conclusions," the editor says in a personal email to Williams, "I don't know, but at the very least we'll catalog the reasonable possibilities" (56). Just as the plethora of possible theories to choose from made Steele's quest for certainty more difficult, Williams is going to have to wade through a lot of explanations.

"Ideas are like egos," his editor says, mangling a familiar idiom, "everybody's got one" (56).

When Williams is introduced to the idea of the rapture, he's committed to the idea that anything's possible. "How could you rule out anything at this point?" he thinks (62). There's a doctor offering medical services in the Pan-Con Club, back at O'Hare. Williams has a minor cut, and the doctor treats it for free, calling it "a Rapture Special" (59). Williams doesn't know what that means, and the doctor doesn't have time to explain. He only says, "Is there any other explanation that makes sense?" (60).

Williams does not immediately investigate the rapture, though. He goes off on another investigation, following a rabbit trail of secret bankers and world currencies. This seems initially unrelated to the apocalypse, and it's not clear why the newsmagazine should give this investigation priority. But Williams's editor is convinced something suspicious is going on with the world's currencies while everyone is distracted by the mass disappearance, and he wants his best reporter to look into it. As the novel unfolds, the shadowy connections become visible. The "international monetarists setting the stage for one world currency" turn out to be connected to religious Jews interested in rebuilding the holy temple in Jerusalem. This, in turn, is connected with a group with representative leaders from the world's religions who are trying to establish a one-world religion (57). The religious, financial, and political powers are all coming together (141). They're aligning behind an obscure Romanian politician "who looked not unlike a young Robert Redford" (114). Williams is investigating the rise of the antichrist.

This shadowy global conspiracy is important to the authors. It helps the plot, for one thing. While the one protagonist is going to meet with a left-behind pastor and ask how he can be certain in his belief, the other barely escapes dying in a car bomb, fakes his own death, and goes on the run with a phony passport. This "keeps the storyline moving," as Jenkins explains in his how-to book on writing fiction.[76] But more importantly, the conspiracy is critical because it illuminates the novel's ideas about belief. As Williams pursues and is pursued by shadowy forces, the hero and the reader are presented with another choice about plausibility. Could there be a conspiracy, a "power behind the power," changing the world and concealing the truth (84)? Many people, of course, dismiss even the possibility of a global conspiracy, waving it away as crackpot thinking. "There are books about this stuff," Williams acknowledges. "People make a hobby of ascribing all manner of evil to the Tri-Lateral Commission, the Illuminati, even the Freemasons, for goodness sake" (175). But conspiracy theories can also be right, and Williams thinks you have to think they could be true. Presented with the possibility of a conspiracy, you have to make a choice about whether it could be true, and Williams thinks the more honest choice, the more open-minded choice, is to investigate.

The hero-journalist says the same thing about the rapture: you have to think it at least could be Bible-foretold prophecy. It's at least possible.

When Williams returns to investigate the rapture, respectable opinion is coming to a consensus. The opinion makers have made a decision about what happened to cause this mass disappearance. They think "it was natural, some kind of a phenomenon where all our high-tech stuff interacted with the forces of nature and we really did a number on ourselves" (355). There are still other options out there, but they seem less and less serious. "I've got an uncle who thinks it was Jesus," Williams's editor says, "but he also thinks Jesus forgot *him*. Ha!" (355). Williams won't dismiss the idea so cavalierly. He feels some social pressure to reject the evangelical eschatology. And yet, "something made him wonder if there wasn't something to this Rapture thing" (357). Presented with the choice of whether or not the rapture was really the rapture, he has to think the answer is yes.

He's more convinced when he meets Steele. Steele at this point is a believer and a full-time evangelist for the truth of the doctrines of the rapture, the tribulation, and the antichrist. "I have more than a theory," he tells Williams in an interview. "I believe I have found the truth and know exactly what happened" (383). Steele explains how the unfolding events were foretold by Bible prophecy. He cites chapter and verse. Williams is unfamiliar with the citations, and, as Steele reads from Revelation, Williams thinks the verses could be "mumbo jumbo." The confidence of Steele's reading, however, makes the end-times prophecy "appear clear" (385). For a moment, Williams gets a glimpse of the kind of certainty he wants, the kind of certainty he could have if he believed. Other, alternative explanations are blocked, pushed away. Steele's theory that the event is the rapture appears "profound and convincing" (386). It is, for Williams, "the only theory that tied the incidents so closely to any sort of explanation" (385).

Williams is not forced to make a choice, though, so he remains ambivalent. He can imagine the event is the rapture, but doesn't feel he has to make a decision about whether that's the truth or not. He is, after all, just collecting opinions for his magazine article. His job was to "round up all the theories, from the plausible to the bizarre" (386). He takes a professionally neutral stance.

Even in his neutrality, though, Williams can see the choice. Either this is true, or it's not. The evidence demands a verdict, and there's no way, honestly, to agree to disagree about these claims. Williams "knew instinctively," Jenkins writes, "that if any of it was true, all of it was true" (393). Eventually he would have to make a choice. It keeps him awake that night. "Could he be on the cusp," he wonders, "of becoming a born-again Christian?" (396). In one scene, Williams gets out of bed and paces, thinking over the pilot's arguments and the clarity of the choice. "Everyone in the world," he thinks, "at least those intellectually honest with themselves, had to admit there was a God" (394). He feels a growing sense of compulsion, like he can't not choose, and there's really only one right choice.

This rising action reaches its resolution when Williams goes to meet the antichrist. The obscure Romanian politician connected to the interlocking conspiracies of global currency and one-world religion has risen to power. Nicolae Carpathia is made head of the United Nations. He demonstrates an ability to "capture the imagination of the world" (358). He starts making bold, unexpected moves, proposing, for example, to relocate the UN headquarters from New York City to "New Babylon," in Iraq, and he calls for a resolution unifying the world's religions (353). As he does so, the "core group" of left-behind converts tries to figure out if Carpathia really is the antichrist or if it's someone else. They are pretty confident he is the antichrist. "I don't see," one reflects, "how I could come to any other conclusion" (427). The group warns Williams before he travels to the United Nations for a press conference announcing the new Carpathia regime. In his notebook, William scribbles, "*Carpathia. End times. Antichrist?*" (435). And then he realizes something. "He was no longer wondering or doubting,"

Jenkins writes (440). "This business of an Antichrist who deceives so many . . . well, in Buck's mind it was no long an issue of whether it was literal or true. He was long past that" (441). He knows. And he knows he knows. All of it is true.

Right before the press conference, Williams goes to the men's room in the UN building. He locks the door and prays, surrendering his life to Jesus. He makes the supernatural transaction, and it works: all doubt disappears. He chooses belief, and he couldn't not choose it. When Williams steps out of the restroom, he possesses total certainty.

The brand-new believer possesses a certainty so strong it can withstand even the antichrist. Carpathia controls perceptions of reality at the press conference. He exerts a "hypnotic power," deceiving people, controlling their minds. He commits a double murder in front of the whole room, then tells them that's not what they saw. It was a murder-suicide. He wasn't involved. They will remember only what he wants them to remember, and, more significantly, they will remember that he, Carpathia, is in power. "You will understand cognitively that I am in charge," the antichrist says to the hypnotized media, "that I fear no man, and that no one can oppose me" (457). Everyone there is deceived. Except the newly converted Williams. He and he alone knows the truth.

It is notable here that there are multiple perspectives on what happened in the room—but that doesn't trouble Williams. Different people literally see things in different ways, but that doesn't stir the slightest doubt in the journalist-hero's heart. He is now free from the condition of secularity. For him, there are not multiple ways of seeing things, multiple possible, plausible things to believe. There is instead a clean dichotomy: there are those who are deceived and those who know the truth (466).

Williams calls the believers in Chicago. "Let me tell you this: Carpathia is your man," he says. "No question" (468).

Williams flies back to Chicago at the end of the novel and reconnects with rapture believers: the pastor Bruce Barnes, the pilot Rayford Steele, and the pilot's daughter, Chloe. They are the ones who have chosen to believe, each feeling compelled to make this choice. They know the truth, know the rapture happened, the Bible really does predict the future, and the antichrist is bad. They form themselves into a "Tribulation Force," dedicated to opposing the new world government and world religion and all the deceptions of the antichrist. In the final scene, the four believers are walking through O'Hare airport, "striding four abreast, arms around each other's shoulders, knit with common purpose" (468).

Crossover Success

The book was not an immediate crossover success. Tyndale House published thirty-five thousand hardback copies in 1995. Hedging its bets, the company produced only twenty thousand dust jackets.[77] Twenty-thousand copies were sent to evangelical bookstores across America. They sold, and then the other fifteen thousand sold; there was a second printing, and Tyndale House agreed to turn *Left Behind* into a series. *Tribulation Force* came out in 1996. *Nicolae* was released in 1997. *Soul Harvest* came out in 1998.[78]

The series was a hit among evangelical Christians but little known outside the subculture of people who consumed Christian-themed merchandise. Cultural studies scholar Amy Johnson Frkyholm first heard about the books in 1997 and noticed that they seemed to exist in this world within a world, marking the boundaries of "in here" and "out there." "The books are passed along," she wrote, "from parent to child, brother to sister, within a church Bible study group or in other similar social settings. Readers become the books' evangelizers, passing them out to family and friends."[79] They didn't sell quite as well as Peretti's novels, but by

1998, *Left Behind* and its three sequels together sold about three million copies.[80]

Then, in 1999, the series made the leap to mainstream markets. *Apollyon*, the fifth novel in the series, was picked up and distributed by Walmart. The big-box retailer was looking for ways to connect with customers and adopted a strategy of identifying itself with white, middle American values.[81] One way to do this was by selling religious books. Walmart started stocking King James and New King James Bibles in the mid-1990s, when a Religious Right group called for a boycott of Walmart's big competitor, Kmart, over books. The American Family Association contacted 160,000 evangelical churches around the country, telling them Kmart was "one of the largest retailers of pornography in America," because Waldenbooks, then owned by Kmart, sold a line of pornographic novels featuring underage female characters. The group urged Christians to protest the degradation of family values and shop instead at "family-oriented stores." Walmart was eager to be a family-oriented store. The company struck distribution deals with a number of evangelical publishers, including Tyndale House. In 1999, the retailer started selling the *Left Behind* novels in about three hundred stores, in the process taking this Christian-themed merchandise to many, many people who had never shopped at an evangelical bookstore. The big chains of suburban super-bookstores, Barnes & Noble and Borders, decided they needed to sell these novels too, to stay competitive, and *Left Behind* became a true national phenomenon. Within a year of publication, *Apollyon* had sold 3.4 million copies, more than the previous four novels combined.[82]

Assassins was released six months later and sold almost one million copies in a week, breaking into the *New York Times* bestseller list. That was unheard of for evangelical fiction. Then Tyndale House decided to support the next installment in the series with a full-scale promotional push, and invested $1 million advertising *The Indwelling*. The book sold 1.9 million in two weeks. *The Mark*, published the month George W. Bush was elected president in 2000, had sold 2.5 million copies by early 2000. *Desecration*, published after the terrorist attacks of September 2001, sold 2.9 million copies.[83] *Armageddon*, published shortly after the United States invaded Iraq, was on the *New York Times* best-seller list for twenty weeks. And with every new installment, people were going back to the beginning of the series and buying as many as 270,000 copies of the original *Left Behind* per month, picking up the story about the pilot in the cockpit thinking about cheating on his wife when—*BOOM!*—the rapture happens, just like LaHaye had imagined it.[84] All told, the sixteen novels in the series sold more than 80 million copies.[85]

LaHaye was right: *Left Behind* could reach two audiences. The book transformed the market for evangelical fiction, taking it mainstream, making it public. That meant a lot of people read it, and they had a lot of different reactions.

Reader Responses to Left Behind

Some people read and were affirmed in their choice of belief. Others read and believed. The novels worked on them as LaHaye and Jenkins hoped they would, and they felt they had to choose and there was only one choice and they knew it, and they choose belief. There are no reliable numbers for how many were moved to belief by *Left Behind*, but the fiction's official website features hundreds of testimonies of conversion.

Some of the more riveting reader conversions were collected and published by Tyndale House. Norman B. Rohrer, an evangelical author of as-told-to autobiographies, wrote *These Will Not Be Left Behind* in 2003, a collection of thirty conversion narratives prominently featuring the *Left Behind* novels.[86] The first story in the book, for example, is about a Littleton, Colorado, woman named Darlene Snyder. Snyder had a very hard life. Her father, an evangelical minister, died of colon cancer when she was young. She grew into a rebellious 1960s teenager, talking back to authority, skipping out on her high school classes, and staying out late at night. When she was fifteen, her mother sent her to what Rohrer describes as "a Christian home for troubled kids," but things only got worse. She started having sex with "a rebel named Gary."[87] Then she was raped. At sixteen, Snyder ran away. She went to Florida and did a lot of drugs. "She used LSD, mescaline, and marijuana," Rohrer writes. "She took hallucinogenic mushrooms, barbiturates, quaaludes, methedrine, and cocaine—whatever gave her a buzz in her reckless pursuit of pleasure."[88] Snyder's life "stabled off" in the 1990s, but she still drank, used foul language, and avoided church. Her life changed, however, when she started listening to *Left Behind* on audiocassette. Driving between Littleton and Denver, Snyder "popped the first cassette into her player and turned up the volume."[89] The story soon overpowered her.

"Somewhere in the Rocky Mountains," according to Rohrer, "conviction shook her. She gripped the steering wheel with all her might, gasping with sobs as the narrator on the cassette tape continued. Two decades of rebellion were melting away like the snowpack in the spring."[90]

Snyder was transformed. In much the same way that characters in *Left Behind* are compelled to believe, she was compelled to believe. It was a choice, but also it didn't feel like that. As a sign of her belief, Snyder got baptized and bought the rest of the *Left Behind* audio books and wrote the publisher to tell them her story.

There's no way to know how many of the millions of people who read *Left Behind* were like Darlene Snyder. There is evidence, though, that there were some.

Many evangelical readers, however, seem to have read as a way to connect to their community, and for them the novels created

a playful space to think about and discuss different ideas. Frykholm, in her extensive study of the evangelical reception of *Left
Behind*, found readers engaged in extended negotiations with the
text. "Over and over again in interviews," Frykholm reports, "I ask
the question, 'Are these books accurate? Is this the way the world
is going to end?' Over and over again, I receive the same answer,
'Yes, but they are just somebody's interpretation. They are only
fiction.'"[91] The fiction didn't compel these readers to subscribe
to particular doctrines but allowed them to play with their beliefs.
One Baptist woman told Frykholm her reading led her to disagree
with her pastor about who could be saved, and when, and under
what conditions. Another evangelical woman told Frykholm how
the novel instigated conversations with her Catholic husband
about belief in Jesus versus belief in the rapture, and whether or
not end-times theology was important to salvation. "While *Left
Behind*'s immediate ideological context is structured by a particular message about individual salvation," Frykholm writes, "readers draw from broader social contexts to 'create the message' of
the text for themselves."[92]

As the book moved beyond the bounds of an evangelical market, more people read it, and they also mostly read it in this nego-
tiated way. They liked parts. They didn't like parts. On the social
cataloguing site GoodReads, for example, numerous readers gave
nuanced responses to the text. An Indianapolis woman enjoyed
Left Behind, but only because she "was able to get past the prea-
chiness" and "just read it as a mystery/thriller type novel."[93] A
St. Paul, Minnesota, man said he started reading only because he
worked in a chain bookstore in the first decade of the new century
and people repeatedly asked him if the series was good. "Turns
out, it wasn't too bad," he writes. "It's a fairly action-packed trip
across a post-apocalyptic Earth, following a rag-tag group of unlikely guerrilla fighters determined to fight the power. I enjoyed it
as such." The bookstore clerk gave up on the series after several

installments, when, as he puts it, "the praying started to get out of hand."[94] These readers could take the fiction and leave it too, as it suited them.

For other readers the message of the text was less malleable, or at least less fun to play with. They read the books as a definitive statement of evangelical identity—and they hated it.

One out of every five people who rated the book on Goodreads absolutely loathed it. "It was quite possibly the very worst book I've ever choked down," one New York man wrote. He read the book as a teenager because his parents made him. "Remembering these pages of absolute shit brings bile to my throat to this day."[95]

For some of these readers, *Left Behind* became a really important identity marker. Anthropologist James Bielo found that young, "emergent" evangelicals used the books as a way of distinguishing themselves from what they saw as "bad" evangelicals. "It was a readily identifiable source against which they formulated and articulated their own kingdom theology," Bielo writes. They "constantly used *Left Behind* and its eschatology as a foil."[96]

Perhaps the most intense oppositional reading comes from progressive evangelical blogger Fred Clark. Clark criticized the novels extensively on his popular blog, going line by line and plot point by plot point for more than a decade.[97] He spent five years just on the first book in the series, starting in October 2003 with an analysis of the pornographic resonance of the name Rayford Steele.[98] Clark concluded his review of the first book in September 2008, criticizing how unbelievable the story was. For him, the novel is about belief and compelled belief, but exactly the opposite of how the authors intended.

"This is the great and insurmountable failure of *Left Behind*," he wrote. "It set out to be a work of propaganda, a teaching tool mean to demonstrate—the authors would say to *prove*—that the events it describes could and indeed *will* really happen. Yet their attempt to present a narrative of such events instead demonstrates—I would say proves—that these events could not and indeed will not ever happen."[99]

As Clark reads *Left Behind*, it is not only implausible, it is so implausible as to compel disbelief. "Those events are not about to occur," he writes. "They will *never* occur. They *can* never occur. Don't believe me? Go read *Left Behind* and see for yourself."[100]

And sometimes, of course, readers read it one way one time and another way another time. One woman, for example, picked up *Left Behind* in November 2014. It was her second try at reading the novel. "Made it halfway last time," she wrote on Goodreads, "but it's been three years." She read sixty-eight pages the first day, and read another eighty-nine in the next three. She finished three days after that and rated the book three stars. She loved the setup for the plot and thought the villain was "awesome," but she struggled with other parts. "I wish I thought I would enjoy the rest of the books in this series," she wrote, "but I think because my own inner religious fight I would have a hard time feeling as though the religion push wasn't a personal thing." She said she might return to the series "if I figure out my religion."[101]

Left Behind reached a diverse range of readers, but it didn't quite compel them to belief in the way the authors had hoped. What the fiction did do was organize religious identity and give people ways to articulate their religious identity in their cultural context. In a culture where a lot of people believe a lot of things, and belief-by-default isn't an option, this best seller became a common cultural landmark, helping people position themselves and say what they believed and how they believed and what belief was like for them, personally, in contemporary American life.

4

Authenticity in Amish Bonnets

Beverly Lewis's *The Shunning*

everly Lewis wanted to write with an open heart to God. For
her, that was the point of being an evangelical author. She
started each morning in her Colorado Springs home with prayer,
devotional Bible reading, and breakfast for her husband, Dave,
and their three adopted children. Two of the children were twins
with special needs, and, after breakfast, Lewis homeschooled
them. Then the twins' professional caregivers took over, and
Lewis went to work at the music studio she owned with her husband. She had about forty music students each week. They took
her afternoons and some of each evening. Then, home again, she
fed her children, cleaned them, and tucked them into bed. The
house got quiet, and she would write.[1]

Lewis wrote for magazines, first. *Highlights for Children*. *Focus on the Family*. Then, in 1993, Zondervan Publishing decided
to launch a line of young-adult fiction, and Lewis got a contract
to write YA novels. That first year she wrote *Holly's First Love*,
then *Secret Summer Dreams*, *Sealed with a Kiss*, and *The Trouble
with Weddings*. These were all about Holly Meredith, a fictional,
evangelical thirteen-year-old with divorced parents and modern,
middle-school problems. The series continued with *California
Crazy*, *Second-Best Friend*, *Good-bye Dressel Hills*, and *Straight-A*

Teacher in 1994, then *No Guys Pact* and *Little White Lies* in 1995. Holly learned important lessons about trusting God and living an abundant life, and Lewis kept writing.[2]

She would write into the "wee hours" every night, sitting in her bedroom, with her fluffy dog, Cuddles, under her chair. Then Lewis would pray again. Then try to sleep.[3]

It was a good life, but strictly regulated, with little room to breathe or just exist. "All things are possible," Lewis said, "to those with a clock and a strict schedule."[4] Her life required discipline, discipline, discipline.

It made her think of her grandmother. Her mother's mother, Ada Ranck Buchwalter, had once thrown off all discipline to follow her heart and find her authentic self. Ada, according to family stories, had grown up in a strict, conservative Mennonite home. The Rancks were not quite Old Order Amish, but similar. "Very close cousins," Lewis would say. "Horse-and-buggy Mennonite."[5]

The religion was so strict that when Ada was a child, she loved music and liked to whistle as she worked, but her family thought it was frivolous and told her to stop.[6] She wasn't allowed any room to express herself or be an individual. She was supposed to follow a "plain path": work hard, submit to the rules, and marry a farmer. But the girl with music in her heart instead fell in love with a blue-eyed young man who loved Jesus and the Bible and wanted to be a preacher. Ada defied her father to marry Omar Buchwalter. She left her very structured life in the Mennonite community and, as Lewis told the story, "accepted Christ and married my grandfather, who became an Assemblies of God minister."[7] It took incredible courage. And she paid a price. According to the family story, Ada was shunned—completely cut off from her family and her church, in a strict practice of communal discipline. Lewis imagined the pain her grandmother, only eighteen, must have suffered and the moment of freedom she must have experienced when she was allowed finally to be herself. Lewis imagined Ada removing her plain head covering, the symbol of submission that conservative Mennonite and Amish women wear, and letting her hair free. How would it feel to finally, truly be herself?

Maybe it didn't happen exactly the way the family told the story. The Ranck family seems to have belonged to a conference of Mennonites, for example, that did not practice shunning.[8] But it was a family legend, and the facts mattered less to Lewis than the sense of it. The idea of it. It gave her a good feeling, lying in bed at night, trying to sleep, thinking about Ada following her heart.

Lewis decided to write this story: an adult novel, loosely based on her grandmother. She'd change it a bit. The heroine would be Amish, not Mennonite, since the Amish were more well known and more strict. Lewis thought of the Amish women from her childhood in Lancaster County, Pennsylvania, and how they'd all line up in their matching dresses, identical head coverings, all looking the same. One would always seem to stand out. "For every lineup of Amish women at a gathering of any kind, you'll always see one of them that has her hand kind of on her hip," Lewis said. "That's my character. She's the one that's pushing boundaries."[9] Of course, she'd add some drama, inventing a plot to pull readers in and push the story along. But it'd be a story, ultimately, about a woman finding herself, freeing herself from strict discipline, and expressing her true identity.

As she wrote, Lewis reimagined evangelical belief as an experience of authenticity. Belief, as she conceived it, was self-discovery and self-expression. Belief was being your true self before God.

Lewis had been a Christian since a conversion experience at six years old, when she, as she later recalled, "walked down the sinners' aisle" and opened her heart to Jesus at a revival meeting in Reading, Pennsylvania.[10] Her whole family was "pastors, pastors' wives, missionaries and evangelists," and she grew up in her father's Assemblies of God church. Her family always sat in the second pew.[11] Lewis agreed with Frank Peretti—who was also in the Assemblies of God—that true Christian belief was a world-view. It was irreconcilably opposed to all others, starting with a presupposition of the sovereignty of God and the clear, absolute distinction between right and wrong.[12] She also agreed with Janette Oke that belief was about trusting in God and that God wanted the best for you, in your daily life. That's what the *Holly's Heart* books were about. But as she wrote this new story—without maybe fully intending to—Lewis staged belief as a more individual kind of flourishing, more expressive, centering on the idea of an authentic imperative.

Lewis didn't have a whole plan, except to put her heart on the page and write as if she were praying. "Being 'real' for God is our goal as writers," she said, "isn't it?"[13]

Katie Lapp's True Identity

The Shunning opens with Katie Lapp, a twenty-two-year-old Amish woman, in the attic of her parents' home. She's going through boxes, preparing for her upcoming wedding, and finds a baby gown. It's satin. The sight of the fine fabric awakens something in Lapp. She holds it up. She can't help herself. She starts to imagine the world this dress must belong to.

"I was lost," Lapp says, "in a world of my vivid imagination—colorful silk, gleaming jewels, golden mirrors. Turning and swirling, I flew, light as a summer cloud, over the wooden floorboards. But with my dancing came the old struggles, my personal tug-of-war between plain and fancy. How I longed for beautiful things!"[14]

Lapp knows she's not supposed to feel these feelings. She is a plain woman, committed by baptism to the simple ways and strict disciplines of the Old Order Amish. She is supposed to be "an honest-to-goodness Amishwoman," like her mother (12–13). But her mother doesn't struggle, as she does, with fantasies of fancy things. Her mother flourishes living the Amish life. Rebecca Lapp—"Dear *Mam*"—thrives in her given role. At "a quilting frolic or a canning bee," "snapping peas or husking corn," the elder Lapp is inspired to tell stories that are, by turns, heartfelt and funny. She tells the stories of her life among the Amish, and the Amish women around her love them and hang on to them. Katie Lapp notices that the stories seem to come from deep within her mother. For as long as Lapp can remember, whenever her mother told a story, "her hazel eyes held all the light of heaven" (12).

Lapp's best friend, Mary Stoltzfus, seems to belong too. Even when the structure of Amish life seemed especially strict, Stoltzfus responded with delight. Lapp remembers when the girls had to stop going to school after the eighth grade. Stoltzfus was good at school. She "got the highest marks through all eight grades." But the church said she was done, and she was done and happy about it, ready to advance to the next stage of her life, preparing to take her place in an Amish home as a wife and mother, and live according to the strict, plain rules.

Lapp wasn't like that. "When it came right down to it," Lapp says, "Mary and I were as different as a potato and a sugar pea" (13). Lapp just never seemed to really feel Amish. It is something she puts on, in the morning, when she gets up at five to do the chores. She brushes her hair and twists it into a tight, smooth bun. She puts a "white mesh *kapp*," or head covering, on her head. She pulls on thick woolen long johns, a "solid brown choring dress," and a black apron. As she gets dressed she tells herself "maybe today would be different." Maybe today she could be the right kind of woman "in God's eyes" (45). But she doesn't identify with these clothes. She doesn't feel Amish in her heart.

Lapp's been Amish her whole life. Everything around her tells her this is who she is. Her friends are Amish, her family is Amish, and the food she makes is Amish. Her house is Amish, her horse is Amish, and she's been baptized Amish. She lives, in the fullest and most complete sense of the term, in Amish country. The first boy she loved was Amish, and she would have married him if he hadn't died in a boating accident. Now she's an Amish woman preparing for an Amish wedding, promised to the widowed bishop of her Old Order community, John Beiler. She has no reason to question any of this or doubt that this is who she is. Yet she does. She has this longing for something else, and it rises from within her, unbidden.

"Ever since I was little, being Plain has been burdensome to me," she says. "It's the music—all those songs in my head. I can't make them go away" (31).

Lapp, like Lewis's grandmother Ada, is always singing and making up songs. But in the fictional Hickory Hollow, the conservative religious community is very strict about music. Lapp's bishop—the one she's supposed to marry—calls the guitar an instrument of evil (125). He will only allow people to sing from the church-approved songbook. These songs are not from the heart, though. They are formal religion. Lapp's songs, on the other hand, are spontaneous and free. They come from within her, pure expressions of who she is.

As Lewis imagines the Amish, they are a people of rules. They practice their belief through adherence to the rules, the *Ordnung*. *The Shunning* doesn't give a lot of detail about the *Ordnung*, except to refer to it as "*die Alt Gebrauch*," the old custom or traditional way, the old order. It is unwritten. The Amish know the *Ordnung* because that's the way things are. If there's a question, the rules are interpreted and enforced by the bishop, Lapp's future husband. Sometimes people deviate from the order or violate the order, and then they're required to publicly confess and repent. If they refuse, they're shunned. That communal discipline is foundational to the Amish. Lewis writes that the Amish began in Switzerland in 1809, when four Mennonite bishops broke away to practice a more strict form of excommunication (131). Now the shunning—"*die Meind-*

ing"—hangs over the community with a feeling of dread. "The word itself," Lewis writes, "stirred powerful emotions among the People. Feelings of rejection, abandonment . . . fear" (132). That fear keeps everyone in line and preserves the Amish order.

Lapp knows that's not the only way to practice belief. Before he died, Lapp's first love, Daniel Fisher, had started to read the Bible. He'd met some evangelicals somewhere, and they'd given him "a paraphrased version of the New Testament." He'd started reading and was startled to read the apostle Paul critiquing "rule-keeping" (131). He read the verses to Lapp: "Christ has set us free to live a free life," the Bible said. "So take your stand! Never again let anyone put a harness of slavery on you. I am emphatic about this. The moment any one of you submits to circumcision or any other rule-keeping system, at that same moment Christ's hard-won gift of freedom is squandered." Fisher continued, "For in Christ, neither our most conscientious religion nor disregard of religion amounts to anything. What matters is something far more interior: faith expressed in love" (Gal. 5:1-2, 6 The Message). Belief could be a matter of the heart.

But that wasn't the Amish way. They believed in rules and through rules. "A good Plain woman," Lapp knows, "obeyed the Ordnung, was totally submissive" (204). Lapp had to obey the rules and take her place as the bishop's wife in Hickory Hollow.

"Yet why," *The Shunning* asks, "did she feel stifled? Trapped?" (131).

Pushed by her father and the bishop, Lapp confesses this music as sin and tries to conform to community rules. She stops singing the songs. She puts away the guitar. She even stops humming. This doesn't make her feel good, though. She thinks the religious rules ought to have the same effect on her that they have on her mother and her best friend, creating a context in which she can flourish and be fulfilled as an individual. But they're not having that effect. She confesses and conforms, but instead of feeling restored to the community, she feels estranged from herself. She feels trapped, "her heart imprisoned along with the forbidden songs" (131).

Lapp is confused by this. She feels her feelings are wrong. With an omniscient narrator, however, Lewis tells readers the truth: "The music had been a divine gift within Katie," *The Shunning* says. "God, the Creator of all things, had created her to make music. It wasn't Katie's doing at all" (78).

There are other signs, too, that Lapp's Amish identity isn't authentic. Like her hair. Katie Lapp has glorious red hair. Striking hair is standard for the romance genre. As Sarah Wendell and Candy Tan note in their study of romance novels, "Heroines—especially Old Skool heroines—are colorful, colorful creatures. Hair of titian, flax, honey, deepest auburn . . . no heroine ever has plain old brown hair."[15] Lewis's heroine, firmly in this tradition, insists on describing her hair as auburn. "Red," she insists, is "for worldly English barns and highway stop signs—not for the single most beautiful feature God had ever given a woman" (168). Lapp loves her hair and glories in it. But, like the music and the desire for fancy things, it sets her apart from her community.

The truth is readily apparent to anyone who notices. "Where was the broomstick hair and the hazel eyes—the family mark?" an aunt wonders. "Not even as far back as great-great-Grandmammi Yoder had there been a speck of red hair" (101). One of the widowed bishop's five children ask about Lapp's hair: Why is it so different? Why is she so different? The bishop dissembles. "Lots of folks have red hair," he says, but his observant son counters, "not around here" (99).

Then comes the revelation: The week before her wedding to the bishop, Lapp's father and mother sit her down for a talk. They need to tell her something. "You see," says her mother, "we never told you the truth, Katie—not all of it."

The young Amish woman feels a rising panic. Her heart beats hard and she's crying. Everything sounds like it's far away. Her ears are ringing. She is afraid of what she doesn't know and, more, of what she does.

"What . . . truth?" she asks.

"The truth," her mother says, "about who you are . . . really" (167).

Katie Lapp was adopted.

She is not Katie Lapp. There is no Katie Lapp.

"If I'm not Katie Lapp . . . then who am I?" she asks.

Rebecca Lapp answers, "You're Katherine Mayfield, Katie, that's who you really are" (167).

Lapp, it turns out, was born to a single mother who was, in the parlance of the novels, not Amish but "English." Her mother brought her to Amish country as a newborn and left her there, in her satin dress, to be taken in by the Lapps and raised as their own. The practice of adoption is unfamiliar to the Amish, but Lewis, herself an adoptive mother, wrote what she knew.[16] Or perhaps what she was afraid of. In the novel the adoptive Amish mother pleads with her daughter, telling her that she really does belong to the family and the community. The young woman is "English by birth and Plain by adoption" (167), Amish "in every way, 'cept blood" (204).

But the revelation confirms everything the protagonist of *The Shunning*—deprived even of her authentic name—has feared. She doesn't belong. This isn't her world.

The young woman tries, at first, to actively choose the life that has been chosen for her. She says, "I'm just Plain Katie, ain't?" and tries to go through with the wedding. Even as she dresses for the day, though, the unbidden desires rise again. She puts on her white wedding apron and her head covering, but she is, the novel notes, "thinking of the satin baby dress, resisting the thought of its splendid feel beneath her fingers" (186).

Lapp's parents think all this is just jitters, before the wedding. The girl will get married to John Beiler, and everything will settle down. The bishop, after all, is a good man. Several characters re-

peat this, throughout the story. He's a good man, a good Amish-
man, a God-fearing man. He's also imposing and stern in his
heavy black work coat, a felt hat, and a full beard. He's affectionate
toward his children but also strict, and when he reprimands one
child, the child seems to crumple. He's a strict bishop, too. Some
communities are gradually growing more lax, especially in their
prohibitions against music, allowing teenagers to own guitars, fid-
dles, and even CD players. But not Beiler. He resists change and
enforces the *Ordnung* (138).

Beiler is older than Lapp and has five children, and he's been
waiting—several people repeat this—a long time to marry her. "It's
such a long time," one character comments, "for the bishop to be
without a wife" (80). The emphasis on how long he's been waiting
may be tinged with something predatory. "The bishop's had his
eyes on you," one character tells Lapp, "for a gut [good] long time.
I've seen the way he watches you" (140). Lapp has seen a longing
in the look, and "the desire made her uncomfortable . . . aware
of her own innocence and her femininity" (72). When she thinks
about her married future, she thinks how she'll lie in the bishop's
bed where his first wife lay.

The real issue, though, is that Lapp just doesn't love him. It's
not about Beiler, it's about her heart. Lapp agrees he's good and
thinks he's kind. He's willing to marry her after her first love died.
But she doesn't particularly care for him. He doesn't make her feel
anything. When she dreams, she dreams of Dan Fisher. The one
man represents her heart; the other her duty, her discipline, and
what she's supposed to do.

There's a kind of inevitability to the wedding. "When it all boils
down, Katie," says Lapp's friend Stoltzfus, "you are supposed to be
marrying the bishop and don't ya ever forget it. He's a wonderful-
gut man" (180). The marriage feels like an obligation, "when her
heart," Lewis writes, "craved so much more" (191).

Lapp makes it to the wedding, taking her place on an Amish

bench. Her stomach is in a knot. She feels trapped, "trapped between two worlds—her place with the People, and her hunger for the modern world outside, forbidden as it was" (188).

The Amish sing a song from the church-approved songbook. They sing another, the prescribed second song for every service, *Das Lob Lied*:

> Put wisdom in our hearts while here
> On earth thy will be known,
> Thy word through grace to understand
> What thou would have us to do.
> To live in righteousness, O Lord,
> Submissive to thy word,
> That all our vows prove true.

Then someone reads from Matthew 19:1–12, where Jesus condemns divorce, and a preacher stands up and begins preaching about submission. The wife, he says, should submit to her husband in everything.

Another minister speaks: "If there is a brother or sister present today who can give cause why these two should not be joined in marriage, let him make it manifest at this time, for after this moment not one complaint shall be heard" (193).

Lapp stands up.

"I'm not fit to marry your brother in Christ, Bishop John Beiler," she says.

Then she turns and flees (194).

She runs from the ceremony, from her family, from the bishop, and from the Amish. She runs from her obligations and, most of all, from her own inauthentic identity. She follows her heart.

In a Romantic gesture, the protagonist declares her real identity literally to the heavens. "I'm Katherine now," she says to the sky. "My name is Katherine Mayfield" (203).

She faces real consequences for this. She is shunned. No one in her family can talk to her. Her friend can't talk to her. She is not even allowed, under the strict church discipline, to eat at the same table with other Amish people.

The protagonist spends the rest of *The Shunning* unraveling her Amish identity and discovering who she really is. "I was not meant be Amish," she says. "It's not working out for me to be Amish. I wish it hadn't taken so long for me to see it, but I know now what's the matter with me" (205). This is a process. She reclaims her birth name. "*I'm* supposed *to be Katherine Mayfield*," she thinks, "*whoever that is!*" (181). She renounces her baptism, saying it was illegitimate because she wasn't who she thought she was. "The kneeling baptism never happened to me," she says (218). "I wasn't who I thought I was back then" (223). The discipline of the *Ordnung*, she says, turned her into someone she wasn't. She takes her condemned guitar out of its hiding place and makes up a song (232–33). She gets rid of her Amish clothes and buys new dresses. "She loved the swishing song of the fabric," Lewis writes, "the silky feel of it against her skin. And, oh glory, the open neckline, free and unrestrictive" (209). She even gets rid of the head covering, "allowing the long auburn tresses to flow," just like Lewis imagined her grandmother did, all those years ago (203).

Katherine Mayfield decides finally to leave Amish country completely, to go find her birth mother. "I've been cut loose," she says on the final page, "to discover who I truly am . . . who I was meant to be" (282).

The Market for Authenticity

The Shunning was, in some ways, an odd evangelical novel. There are, for one thing, no conversions. The main character doesn't learn to trust God, or read the Bible, or even pray. The novel doesn't narrate an evangelical born-again experience but instead sets out a kind of horizon for salvation, inviting readers to imagine that—whatever salvation entails—it has to be authentic. The philosopher Charles Taylor calls this the "authentic imperative," which just means the command to "be yourself." There's an idea, according to Taylor, that human flourishing must be individualized. It's not enough that humanity as a whole flourishes (as nice as that might be). But it also has to happen at the individual level. Each person must flourish. And to flourish individually, you can't just surrender to expectations and demands placed on you by your culture. You have to discover your own desires, your heart's yearning, and realize the fullness of your unique humanity.[17]

This was, of course, the message of every Disney movie: follow your dream. It was also the message of the supermarket, after the consumer revolution following World War II. As the economy changed, American stores gave people more choices. The increase of variety had the effect of making even minor choices appear individually meaningful. You don't just buy blue jeans because you have to wear pants in public, you buy a specific brand of blue jeans because they say you are young, or sexy, or hardworking. You don't buy a car just to get somewhere. That matters to the car consumer, of course, but there's an additional meaning to the purchase, which is what that specific vehicle says about you. Each purchase became an expression of identity, a statement about the kind of person you were. "Rather than aim to sell commodities in as much volume as possible to the mass," writes historian Lizabeth Cohen, "the modern-day marketers, equipped with advanced psychographic tactics, identify clusters of customers with distinctive ways of life and then set out to sell them idealized lifestyles constructed around commodities."[18]

In this new, consumer-focused era of capitalism, however, marketers and manufacturers would sometimes find that consumers developed a deep resistance to these packaged identities.

They felt fake. But this only reinforced the "authentic impera-tive," making it seem like the most important criteria for making a decision. White evangelicals weren't exempt from this. In fact, white evangelicals were one of these clusters of consumers being sold an idealized lifestyle constructed around (Christian-themed) commodities. The evangelical bookstore was part of the market segmentation and fostered these urgent feelings about the need to be authentic.

Inside the bookstores in the mid-1990s, calls to authenticity were not as prominent as calls to culture war or promises that sub-mission to God was the key to human flourishing. But they were there. Several notable nonfiction titles from the period argued, in fact, that authenticity was key to a thriving evangelical church. In 1995, for example, a new book called *Rediscovering Church* ex-plained how authenticity had become a central concern for one megachurch about thirty miles northwest of Chicago.

Willow Creek was one of the most prominent evangelical churches at the time. In addition to attracting about fifteen thou-sand people to six weekend services in South Barrington, Illinois, the megachurch sold its model to other suburban churches across the country. Evangelical pastors flocked to South Barrington to learn the Willow Creek ways. There were about 1,400 congrega-tions officially using "Willow Creek principles" in the '90s. Un-officially, there were many more.[19]

When it started in the 1970s, the nondenominational church, like the evangelical bookstores of the period, focused on making Christianity relevant to daily, middle-class life. "If I ever preach an irrelevant sermon," said Bill Hybels, the church's founding pastor, "drag me out of the ministry!"[20]

This was a rejection, partly, of the style and approach of Hy-bels's childhood church, a Christian Reformed Church in Kala-mazoo, Michigan. In the 1950s, the denomination was, as Hybels later described it, "encrusted with the trappings of tradition." The church put a lot of emphasis on sixteenth-century creeds and Calvinist doctrine. When Hybels started teaching a youth group, he did too. His first lesson was on the theology of revelation, taken from the 1933 *Manual of Christian Doctrine*, written by Louis Berghof, a professor at Calvin Theological Seminary. Hybels started talking about "theophanies," and the youth group kids were lost. He quit, five minutes in, and promised the group that from then on he would "talk about something relevant to [their] lives."[21]

When it came time to start his own church in 1975, Hybels and cofounder Dave Holmbo began with a marketing survey. They went door to door, asking people why they didn't go to church. The number-one response they got was that people felt like the stuff at church just didn't matter. It had nothing to do with their anxieties or their aspirations. People worried about their marriages and their children, their jobs and their finances, and pastors, they said, "never even mentioned the struggles" that were "tearing them apart."[22] Hybels and Holmbo then designed a service that would appeal to these people, the "unchurched Harrys and Marys." They called it a "seeker service."

Willow Creek met in a theater and eschewed anything traditional. No cross. No stained glass. No organ music. No explanations of Calvinist creeds. The sermons weren't called "sermons" but "messages." A worship band played pop songs, mixing secular hits such as the Eagles' "Desperado" with original, evangelical music, done in contemporary styles. "We wanted to show lost people that we understood their challenges and longings and headaches and joy of their lives," wrote Lynne Hybels, Bill's wife.[23] The fledgling church put half of its weekly budget into multimedia presentations.[24] There were also skits and drama, and the whole thing was more like the *Tonight Show Starring Johnny Carson* than what baby boomers grew up thinking was "church."

At Willow Creek, they thought of themselves as "missionaries to the secular suburbs." A *New York Times* reporter observed that "what they offer for the spirit are 'relevant' sermons that blend Scripture with practical advice for a harried middle class."[25]

None of this was quite as novel as the legend of Willow Creek made it out to be. Hybels learned a lot of his approach, actually, from Robert H. Schuller, who started a drive-in theater church in Garden Grove, California, in the 1950s.[26] Regardless of how innovative these innovations actually were, though, they worked. People came, and they kept coming. Willow Creek grew, and kept growing. Attendance went from 125 to 1,500 in the first few years. It was ten times that by the 1990s.

By the 1990s, Willow Creek was widely hailed for its use of marketing and management theory. The *Los Angeles Times* marveled at this new thing, a church based on "a targeted 'customer' survey."[27] The *Chicago Tribune* called Hybels "a kind of spiritual CEO."[28] The *New York Times* reported that he was "reading the signs in Adam Smith's marketplace" and consulting with corporate leadership guru Peter Drucker.[29] Michael Lewis, a financial journalist, wrote that Willow Creek was a miracle of modern capitalism, repackaging Jesus just like marketing geniuses had bottled water to stimulate revived demand for a boring, banal product.[30]

"The fantastic success of Willow Creek," Lewis wrote, "means that across America evangelical pastors are brimming with the good news about things like market segmentation."[31]

Hybels increasingly worried about all this attention to marketing and management theory. It could make the church seem too packaged, too gimmicky and inauthentic. He started, in the mid-'90s, pushing back on the myth he'd created. "We don't think our success is about marketing," he told one reporter in 1994. "We're successful because when people experience that life change, their enthusiasm becomes contagious. We're just all about friends talking to friends talking to friends."[32] That might sound like viral marketing a lifestyle brand, but Hybels didn't want it to be thought of that way anymore. When he did that "customer survey," he didn't even know that was what that was.[33] "I don't do a sales job," he said.[34] When people didn't believe him, Hybels became more insistent: "It's not about the marketing."[35]

It was about this time that Willow Creek started especially emphasizing authenticity. In the early '90s, when a ministry magazine did a two-part profile on the church, the focus was on evaluation tools, reimagining evangelism as "networking," and making sure each church service had a "high user value."[36] In the late '90s, when the same magazine returned to Willow Creek, the church's leaders said authenticity was really the core of everything they did. "Relevance," really, was a question of authenticity. "We've got to answer the questions that searching people are asking," said pastor Lee Strobel. "We need to build authentic relationships with them so that we may share our faith in the context of an honest, no-strings-attached friendship."[37] When Bill and Lynne Hybels released their book on the history and vision of Willow Creek in 1995, authenticity was the central issue.[38]

The emphasis on authenticity was, partly, new language for what Willow Creek had always been doing. It was also a response to struggles and scandals that had been kept behind the scenes. First, in 1978, Hybels reorganized the structure of the church, placing himself in authority over everything.[39] This created a lot of tension among the leadership but was mostly kept secret from the congregation. Then there was a scandal. Dave Holmbo, Hybels's close friend and cofounder, was forced to resign in 1979. Officially, the church called it a "parting of the ways" prompted by "differing philosophies of ministry."[40] But that wasn't the whole truth. The church was covering up what Lynne Hybels, in *Rediscovering Church*, would call "a destructive, ongoing pattern of behavior."[41] This is typically evangelical code for some sort of sexual misconduct. Holmbo had become "enmeshed in sin."[42] When Holmbo was forced out, however, many people interpreted this as Hybels making a play for complete control of Willow Creek, and there was, as one elder recalled later, "wave after wave after wave of conflict."[43]

Then, in 1986, according to accusations that emerged in 2018, Hybels also became "enmeshed in sin." He allegedly groped and fondled his executive assistant. He did this repeatedly, she says, over a period of two years. On one occasion, he pressured her into performing oral sex. On another, he pressured her into watching porn with him in his home. Nine other women have also accused Hybels of sexual misconduct, ranging from subtle sexual propositions to oral sex.[44] Hybels denies the allegations. The former executive assistant told the *New York Times* that in 1989, Hybels told her to keep quiet. She did, because she was ashamed, and she wanted to keep her job, and she "really did not want to hurt the church," she said. The scandal did not become public.

At about that same time, Hybels had a kind of breakdown. A week before Christmas 1989, he put his head on his desk and starting crying. The sobs were uncontrollable, like something just broke.[45] He was exhausted. He was overwhelmed by feelings of anger and resentment. Then he pulled himself together, officiated a wedding, and preached at six Christmas Eve services. At one point an elder asked him if he still enjoyed leading the church, and Hybels snapped, "I can't afford to think about how I feel."[46] A year later, Lynne Hybels, in her own words, "broke." "For years I had battled depression," she wrote. "As 1990 came to a close I felt I was losing the battle."[47] Both Lynne and Bill Hybels started going to counseling.

A few years later, there was another scandal. Jim Dethmer, a teaching pastor hired to take some of the workload off Hybels, suddenly resigned in 1993. Rumors swirled. Was this a repeat of what happened with the Holmbo affair? To clear the air, Dethmer wrote the church a public letter, saying the pressure of performing had just become too much. There was so much focus on image, and he felt like he was a fraud. He was just pretending up there. "I am going to take steps," he wrote, "to protect myself from pretense, that most subtle of hypocrisies."[48]

It was in this context that the church started talking about the importance of authenticity. Hybels started saying leaders have to be honest and open about their struggles. Preachers can't be persuasive unless they're authentic. While Hybels's own openness appeared, even at the time, kind of vague, the ideal of authenticity was held up again and again. By the mid-1990s, "authenticity" was a key word at Willow Creek, and therefore at evangelical churches across the country.[49]

"The emphasis on emotional authenticity and healing made its way into the weekend and midweek services," Lynne Hybels wrote in *Rediscovering Church*. "It was probably most reflective of and in response to the needs of many staff and lay leaders during that era. It offered a necessary midcourse correction for a group of hardworking servants of God who had for too long lived in crisis mode."[50]

The same evolution toward an "authentic imperative" can be seen in the history of another prominent megachurch: Saddleback. Saddleback Church was founded in 1980, in Lake Forest, California. It wasn't associated with Willow Creek, but it was similar in a lot of ways. Both churches consulted with Robert Schuller and Peter Drucker.[51] Both were seeker-sensitive, preaching a practical application of the gospel to daily life in the suburbs. Both started with a marketing survey.

Rick Warren, a young Baptist minister, went door to door in Saddleback Valley, a suburban area about forty-five miles south of downtown Los Angeles. He used what he learned from the survey to develop a composite profile of the customer he wanted to target. Where Willow Creek had "unchurched Harry," Warren had "Saddleback Sam."

"Saddleback Sam" was imagined as an upper-middle-class white man in his late thirties or early forties. He was successful—even affluent—and self-satisfied, but also deep in debt, deeply unhappy, considering divorce, and afraid of age and death. He was skeptical of organized religion and tradition more generally, and really didn't think Christianity was relevant to his life.[52] The survey found the number-one reason Southern California suburbanites said they didn't go to church was "boring sermons."[53]

Warren then designed a church service to attract these people. He rejected everything that smacked of tradition. Nothing "churchy." No suit and tie for the pastor, no pews or stained glass for the building. Even though Warren was a Southern Baptist, he wouldn't brand the church with the name Baptist.[54] And most of all, at Saddleback the messages would be relevant. They would address the concerns of day-to-day life in the suburbs and suburban, middle-class struggles.

"Their big question," Warren wrote of his target audience, "is, 'So What?' They want to know what difference our message makes. I've found that the unchurched in America are very interested in Bible doctrine when it is applied in practical and relevant ways to their lives."[55]

Warren's early sermon series included "How to Survive under Stress," "How to Feel Good about Yourself," and "How to Keep On Keeping On."[56]

The seeker-sensitive strategy was successful, and the church grew. Attendance went from the hundreds, in the early 1980s, to the thousands a decade later. By the mid-'90s, regular attendance was around ten thousand people. With that success, Saddleback, like Willow Creek, was trumpeted as a marketing miracle. The *Los Angeles Times* reported that "Saddleback and other market-oriented churches have irrevocably transformed the business of church."[57] Halfway across the country, the *Des Moines Register* ran with the headline "Sales Tactics Fill Pews."[58] The *New York*

Times Magazine said, "Warren may be the most talented religious marketer in America."[59] *New Yorker* writer Malcom Gladwell compared Warren to business legends Ray Kroc of McDonalds and Sam Walton of Walmart.[60]

Warren, like Hybels, became uncomfortable with this emphasis on packaging and marketing, even as he continued to teach three-day, $155 church-growth seminars to thousands of evangelical pastors. "Salesmanship" made it all seem like a trick. Warren protested that when he did that initial marketing survey, he didn't even know what that was. "When I got here and started talking to people and asking them, what would you look for in a church, I didn't know that was a marketing study. I just thought, if I'm going to reach people, I've got to talk to them," Warren said.[61] Later he wrote he wasn't marketing, he was just being polite.[62]

There were also a lot of behind-the-scenes struggles at the church. Warren had panic attacks in the pulpit and seriously considered quitting the ministry. He hired a copastor named Steve Williams, and the two men had some conflicts and parted ways in 1984. Warren had multiple fights with his congregation over the vision of the church. In 1987, the church lost about $100,000 on a failed land deal. When Saddleback finally bought some land in 1990, county officials blocked construction. It took two years of fierce political conflict for the church to get approval to develop the property. Warren also got into a fight with the Internal Revenue Service over clergy housing exemptions, struggled to write a book about his model for a thriving church, and continued to have panic attacks—eventually diagnosed as the result of a rare brain disorder—that forced him to lie down in a dark room between services.[63]

"No church," Warren acknowledged, "becomes large without struggling."[64]

In this context, Warren started to write about authenticity. Authenticity became, for him, a kind of key. "The purpose of your life is far greater than your own personal fulfillment, your peace of mind, or even your happiness," he wrote, in what would become his 2002 best seller, *The Purpose-Driven Life.* "It's far greater than your family, your career, or even your wildest dreams and ambitions. If you want to know why you were placed on this planet, you must begin with God. You were born *by* his purpose and *for* his purpose."[65] The book begins where *The Shunning* ends, with a call to authenticity.

Neither Willow Creek nor Saddleback gave up on the idea of abundant life in the suburbs. Neither they nor the many churches across the country modeling themselves after them abandoned the practical, relevant sermons. But in the mid to late 1990s, they also started talking about authenticity. The idea of flourishing was individualized. Evangelical belief, these megachurch pastors said, wasn't about packaged conformity but about discovering your true self, becoming that self, and satisfying your deepest, most personal desires.

When Lewis's manuscript showed up at evangelical publishing houses in 1997, the theme resonated. The fiction was articulating something evangelicals were feeling. Even if it was an unusual evangelical novel at the time, it also seemed right to a lot of people.

Imagining the Amish

Lewis's novel was also unusual for another reason: it was about the Amish. Even though it was an evangelical novel, with evangelical themes and intended for an evangelical audience, the characters and the settings were Old Order Amish. Lewis was using the conservative religious tradition the same way that Regency romances used the period of British history when George IV ruled as prince regent. The Amish were a setting for her story, a screen for her projections. This was weird for evangelicals. Most evangelicals didn't have any connection with the Amish. They didn't have any firm ideas about what the Amish or even Mennonites were like. No one in the world of evangelical publishing had really written about them, before *The Shunning*.

The Shunning was, however, part of an American tradition of Amish fantasy. Since the beginning of the twentieth century, Americans have used the Amish to work out their ideas of authenticity. The Amish, as historian David Weaver-Zercher writes, are "remarkably useful symbols" for this purpose.[66]

This started in the early twentieth century, when Amish rejection of technology and resistance to progress started to really set them apart from their farmer neighbors. The Amish became symbols of "backward" thinking. This wasn't just about gasoline engines, though. Critics saw in the Amish a dangerous rejection of individualism, personal fulfillment, and self-expression.

A critic in 1907, for example, said the Old Order religionists were "lacking in courtesy, in suavity of manner, in politeness." They were rude, in every sense of the word. And this affected their aesthetic sensibilities as well. They lacked, the critic continued, "in delicacy of tastes, in appreciation of the beauties of nature and in love of art, painting, sculpture, music and literature."[67] It was thought, Weaver-Zercher writes, that "the asceticism of the Amish people had robbed them of their humanity."[68] With their strict disciplines and regulated conformity, the Amish couldn't flourish.

This is the argument of *Sabina: A Story of the Amish*, which is probably the first published novel to feature an Amish protagonist. It was written by Helen Reimensnyder Martin. Martin was a feminist, a Swarthmore and Radcliffe–educated author who wrote fiction about the oppression of women. For her, the ethnic Germans of her native Pennsylvania—especially the religious ones—offered the most egregious examples of oppressive patriarchy. It wasn't just that the Amish devalued women's labor. It wasn't just that the women were required to submit totally to their husbands. It wasn't just that they denied women an education. The Amish, Martin believed, even crushed a woman's desire for personal fulfillment. Amish patriarchy reduced women to "bovine dullness."[69]

In *Sabina: A Story of the Amish*, the main character falls in love with an outsider. She's not supposed to. Her father flatly states that the Amish keep their children close, their horizons narrow. The sons have to settle for farming; the daughters have to settle for marrying farmers. But Sabina is attracted to a non-Amish man who comes to Lancaster County to paint, and for a moment she imagines a larger life. It's not to be. She has a psychic vision of a face and falls into a fever and forgets she ever loved the Bohemian painter. The artist leaves for a period of study in Paris, and when he returns, he finds she has married and is now so dominated by the drudgery of caring for her Amish husband and two children that she doesn't even notice the man she once loved. At the end of the novel, Sabina doesn't even know whether or not she is happily married.[70] Sabina doesn't have the agency necessary to even feel unfulfilled. She cannot fathom the authentic imperative. The woman lacks not just the technology and gadgets of modern convenience but even her own subjective sense of self. She cannot be herself; she cannot know herself.[71]

Martin mainly wrote for upper-middle-class women. She was published in *McClure's* and *Cosmopolitan*. The Amish were useful, for her, though, for stories about "false consciousness." They were examples of the deep damage of inauthenticity.

Another way of imagining the Amish started to develop with the New Deal's Work Progress Administration (WPA), which funded efforts to find and document authentic American folkways. With the work of the WPA, David Weaver-Zercher writes, the Amish were "quickly and thoroughly recast as virtuous Americans" and "became increasingly robust representatives of America's past."[72] The artist Katherine Milhous, for example, did a series of WPA posters advertising Pennsylvania. A number of the posters just depicted Amish families or Amish children. Others presented the Amish as a living connection to American history. "Visit Pennsylvania," one said, with a picture of a woman in a black head covering, "where pre-revolutionary costumes still survive."[73] The Amish, who reject all violence, did not participate in the Revolution, but never mind.[74] Another Milhous poster advertised Amish-made ceramics. It said, "Colonial Pennsylvania exists to-day in many churches, costumes, crafts of the German Sectarians."[75] The market for "Amish country" tourism started at this time and became big business with the construction of the interstate system in the 1950s. By 1963, roughly 1.5 million tourists drove to Lancaster County every year, spending $45 million annually.[76] Though some people were still suspicious of the apparently authoritarian and dogmatic religion, increasing numbers of Americans looked at the bearded men, bonneted women, and quaint black buggies with feelings of nostalgia for an imagined past. They approached the Amish wistfully, with a sense of loss, even if they couldn't exactly articulate what they admired about that way of life. It seemed better, simpler, more fulfilling.

Some political conservatives, capitalizing on these feelings, started to use the Amish as examples of authentic American communities threatened by big government. This began as early as the 1940s but really became significant in the late '60s.[77]

The central principle of American conservatism, as articulated by conservative thinker Russell Kirk, was that "the best possible—or least baneful—form of government is one in accord with the traditions and prescriptive ways of its people."[78] In 1965, that principle was more palatable to the broad American public when those people were imagined as Amish, rather than, say, the white southerners of New Kent County, Virginia, who were fighting government-mandated integration of the public schools.[79] True conservatives, Kirk believed, opposed efforts to end "separate-but-equal" education. But not out of any racial animus. Rather, they acted from principled commitment to limited government and a belief that reform efforts in general were dangerous, ideological attacks on long-established traditions.[80] Conservatives had to defend even peculiar American folkways against ideologues. "The ideologues," Kirk warned, "who promise the perfection of man and society, have converted a great part of the twentieth-century world into a terrestrial hell."[81] This conservatism would seem like racism, though, if the threatened "American folkway" were Jim Crow segregation. So Kirk avoided writing about the Virginia segregationists, even as that case went to the Supreme Court. Instead, he held up the Amish as a prime example of what he was talking about.

In his syndicated column in the late '60s and early '70s, Kirk wrote repeatedly about government attacks on the schools of the "quiet and courageous" Amish. These were mostly obscure incidents involving local governments. Michigan, for example, required an Amish schoolteacher to get certified. Kirk interpreted this as an existential threat to the Amish. "Destroy the Amish schools, and in time you destroy the Amish sect," he wrote. "Only a totalitarian state refuses to tolerate the existence of such groups."[82] Kansas passed a law requiring all children to attend school until age sixteen. "The public-education zealots," Kirk wrote, "mean to integrate the Amish children into their secular paradise" even though it would "destroy that harmless and industrious sect."[83] Kirk wrote about similar incidents in Indiana, Iowa, and Wisconsin. Again and again, he argued that the Amish were good, peaceful, hardworking Christians, flourishing, except for the heavy hand of big government.

"Incidentally," Kirk wrote, "my columns on the Amish schools attract many letters from readers; this suggests that a good many Americans still are attached to the principles of private rights and religious freedom."[84]

When one of the Amish school cases that Kirk wrote about went all the way to the Supreme Court in 1972, there were, notably, no Amish involved. The Amish, because of their theology of *gelassenheit*, or nonresistance, decided not to fight the government regulation.[85] The National Committee for Amish Religious Freedom—which included no Amish people—pursued the case anyway.[86] For them, the Amish were less real people with particular theology than powerful symbols of a conservative idea.

The court ruled for the conservatives in *Wisconsin v. Yoder.* It was an important legal victory for private Christian schools.[87] At least one Christian school would later invoke the court's decision to argue for a religious right to racial discrimination.[88] Kirk, who stopped his column in 1975, found no occasion to comment on segregation academies or "the traditions and prescriptive ways" of segregated schools. The Amish were his preferred example.

By the end of the twentieth century, there was a variety of popular interpretations of the Amish. They were "publicly useful," as David Weaver-Zercher writes, "providing lessons for outsiders that, from these outsiders' points of view, had no essential connection to Amish ecclesiology."[89] Whether the Amish were imagined as ideal Americans or drudgery-bound dogmatists, though, the fantasy always involved an idea of authenticity. The Amish were examples of good old-fashioned values like hard work and community. Or they were examples of how claustrophobic conformity, and how oppressive arbitrary religious rules, could be.

Lewis, for her part, imagined the Amish both ways. She was of two minds.

When Lewis thought about her grandmother, she thought about how the strict Mennonites wouldn't let Ada Ranck whistle and how they shunned her for following her heart. Lewis believed it was the grace of God that saved her grandmother from life with the "horse-and-buggy" sect.[90] But also, there were things she admired about the Amish. Asked about them, she could wax rhapsodic. "Close-knit families," she said in one interview, "as well as the importance of community. . . . And, of course, cooking from scratch, sewing nearly everything one wears, growing vegetables, tending roadside stands, and walking along a deserted country road at twilight while the fireflies twinkle in the meadow—ah, the peace of it all!"[91] Lewis could sound like a travel agent, selling a tour of Amish country. She also frequently talked about how she valued her connection to the Amish. "Being born into the Anabaptist culture in Lancaster," she said, "and growing up close to the Amish, I absorbed the Plain tradition quite naturally."[92] The brief biography of her in *The Shunning* touted the authenticity of her "Plain family heritage."

This conflict made its way into the fiction, too. Long passages in *The Shunning* describe the glories of Amish country. In one scene, Lewis lingers on "the ribbon of road [that] dipped and curved past fertile fields on every hand . . . the nostalgic sight of horse-drawn carriages . . . the gentle creaking of a covered bridge, flanked by groves of willows—their long fronds stirring in a lazy breeze."[93] In another, she describes the rows and rows of canning jars in an Amish cellar, though they have nothing to do with the story, except to offer an idyllic setting.[94]

When Lewis recollected the Amish from her childhood in Lancaster County, the memories were also mixed. She remembered that the Amish would stand across the street from her father's church, like they wanted to come in but couldn't. She thought they looked "hungry for more of God or maybe just more of the scriptures." But then a moment later she would recall how their faith seemed intertwined with their whole lives. She remembered admiring the Amish women. They seemed "settled with themselves," she said. "They're grounded. They know their core."[95] At the same time, Lewis thought a lot of Amish probably struggled with depression, and some suffered spousal abuse. Many of them were repressed.[96]

Lewis holds both of these views in tension. *The Shunning* tells a story about a woman escaping the Amish, but it also imagines the Amish community as a place where a woman can thrive. The heroine's best friend, Mary Stoltzfus, wouldn't be herself if she left the Amish. When Katie Lapp puts on a nice dress, she feels like herself for maybe the first time. For Stoltzfus, it would be different. She recoils from fancy clothes, seeing that endless freedom of expression as a vortex of inauthentic choices. "Those worldly moderns," she says, "keep changing and changing their clothes and themselves 'til they don't know which end's up. They don't know who they are or whatnot all!"[97] For her the Amish conformity isn't stultifying. It's comforting and reassuring. The Amish life is good for her, because she belongs.

An older woman makes the same point, more explicitly. "I was born Amish, and I'll die the same," she says. "The Plain life is the only life I'll ever know." It's not resignation. It's more like peace. She's at home. She looks at Lapp, however, and sees she doesn't belong. "You seem out of place somehow," she says. "Always have."[98]

Lewis imagines that the Amish life feels different for different people. Each individual, as she presents it, "has his/her own way of realizing our humanity," and one has to find it for oneself. One has to learn to be oneself.

Lewis ultimately leaves the authenticity of the Amish life open to individual interpretation in *The Shunning*. It's a matter of personal choice. Readers can thrill to the setting of the story, enjoying the buggies and the bonnets and the odd Amish words. Or they can identify with the woman who wants to throw off all discipline and follow her heart. They can imagine what it would be like to keep their hair under a *kapp*, and what it would be like to take it off and shake their hair free for the first time. Readers are free to play with the fantasy, and however they do that, that's a kind of self-discovery. The evangelical novel invites them to experience that self-realization and imagine that, whatever belief is like, it has to be authentic.

Selling Amish Fiction

Lewis sent out the first chapters of her manuscript and a proposal in 1995. Three evangelical publishers made offers.[99] The best came from Bethany House Publishers, in Bloomington, Minnesota. Carol Johnson, the woman who had seen the potential in Jannette Oke's evangelical romance twenty years before, liked the idea of Amish fiction too.[100] There was a healthy appetite for Christian romances and more places than ever to sell them. The market was expanding and diversifying.

By the mid-'90s, there were more than 4,000 evangelical bookstores across the country, grossing about $3 billion annually. The stores sold music, gifts, and church supplies, but still did $200,000 of business in Bibles and about $1 million in other books. And sales were growing by about 10 percent per year.[101] There were still lots of independent shops, run by small, ministry-minded business owners, but the market was increasingly dominated by big, expanding evangelical chains: Family Christian Bookstores had 160 outlets, Joshua's Christian Stores had 72, and Baptist Book Stores (which would soon rebrand as LifeWay Christian Stores) had 66.[102] To compete, many of the independent stores joined marketing groups, which professionalized their branding, launched their "digital storefronts," and ran advertising campaigns. The Parable Group served about 300 evangelical bookstores. Munce Marketing served about 500.[103]

The real competition for both the independents and the chains, however, was the secular booksellers. It seemed like every bookseller was realizing that religious books would sell, even if the store itself wasn't religious. "Religion is hot," one industry insider observed, coming back from the American Booksellers Association in June 1995. It was a market trend, he said, that seemed "as if it broke like a wave from nowhere."[104] The white evangelical market had been growing since the '70s, and the mainstream booksellers saw no reason why they couldn't capture that segment of the market. Mall bookstores, big-box retailers like Walmart and Kmart, and the new suburban superstores like Borders and Barnes & Noble all started stocking Christian-themed merchandise.

The superstores, especially, had rapidly expanding shelf space they could stock with evangelical publishers' products. Borders boasted it could stock more than 100,000 titles in each of its 1,200 stores. At a Borders store, one journalist marveled, there were "books stacked to the ceiling. Books lined up in bookcases. Books spread out on tables, highlighted on platforms, displayed in twirling, 5-foot-high wire racks."[105] Barnes & Noble was the same. Each store had about 35,500 square feet of retail space and could stock as many 125,000 titles.[106] There was plenty of room for Christian fiction, and stores even dedicated whole shelves to "inspirational romance." So Bethany House knew it could sell an Amish novel, even if it was a bit different from other evangelical titles. Maybe it would even be a hot new thing.

When Lewis got the good news, the whole family celebrated. She put on one of her favorite recordings—a gospel choir performing a Fanny Crosby hymn popularized at Billy Graham crusades, "To God Be the Glory."

She turned it up:

> Praise the Lord, praise the Lord,
> Let the earth hear His voice!
> Praise the Lord, praise the Lord,
> Let the people rejoice!
> O come to the Father, through Jesus the Son,
> And give Him the glory, great things He hath done.

Lewis started dancing around the house, and her husband and three children danced too.[107]

Bethany House published *The Shunning* in 1997. The first year, 150,000 copies sold. The sequel, *The Confession*, came out the same year. The second novel follows the heroine, Katie Lapp/Katherine Mayfield, as she reunites with her biological mother, who, it turns out, is fabulously wealthy but dying, and desperately praying to be reunited with her daughter before she passes. The mother is an evangelical, with a personal relationship with God. But an imposter is pretending to be the woman's long-lost Amish daughter to steal the real Lapp/Mayfield's inheritance. Lapp/Mayfield has to prove that she is the woman's authentic daughter. The proof is her red hair. "Not many people," one character says of the mother-daughter connection, "have the privilege of wearing the rich colors of autumn all year long."[108] *The Confession* sold 75,000 copies in twelve months.

The third book in the series, *The Reckoning*, came out in 1998. That novel tells the story of how Mayfield learns that her first love, Daniel Fisher, actually didn't die in an accident but faked his death to run away from the Amish to become an evangelical. "Someday I hope you'll allow me to tell you the whole story," Fisher writes. "In the meantime, I have found a love I've never known . . . this I find in Jesus." Fisher explains that the Amish faith was really man-made rules and arbitrary tradition, passed down from generation to generation. Evangelicalism, in contrast, is a religion of the heart. It's an individualized faith. "Read the book of John in the New Testament," he tells Mayfield. "You'll find what your heart searches for."[109]

She does. Mayfield reads the Gospel of John in a leather-bound King James Bible and feels "something life-giving inside her."[110] It's a born-again experience. "She was captivated," Lewis writes, "by the message on the love of God . . . a *personal* heavenly Father who adored and cared for His children."[111] As she discovers this new divine love, she recovers the love of her childhood friend, too. They marry and live happily ever after. *The Reckoning* sold 100,000 copies in a year.

After their initial print runs, the books continued to sell. *The Shunning* sold about 100,000 copies per year, for ten years, crossing the 1 million mark in 2008. *The Confession* sold about 75,000 per year, *The Reckoning* about 55,000.[112]

The sales earned Lewis enough money that she could stop teaching music and commit herself to writing full time. She built a writing studio, at her home, and went to work on another trilogy: *Amish County Crossroads*. She published the first two parts in 1999, *The Postcard* and *The Crossroad*. She followed that with a stand-alone novel in 2000, *The Redemption of Sarah Cain*, about a woman who has to sacrifice a successful career to raise five Amish orphans. Each of these sold more than 500,000.

Lewis continued to write Amish novels at a pace of about two per year.

Others started to write them too. A decade after the release of *The Shunning*, Amish fiction had become its own distinct category of evangelical fiction. Fourteen new Amish novels were published in 2007, then a dozen more in 2008. There were twenty-six in 2009, forty-five in 2010, sixty-three in 2011. At that point, booksellers created an official designation: "Fiction / Amish & Mennonite." In 2012, a new Amish fiction title was published, on average, every four days.[113] Valerie Weaver-Zercher (married to David Weaver-Zercher) did a book-length study of the genre. She found that at least sixty different authors were writing Amish romances in the early twenty-first century, with authors like Wanda Brunstetter and Cindy Woodsmall competing with Lewis for sales.[114] The titles proliferated and the market segmented.

"You can read an Amish-themed romance set in Pennsylvania, Ohio, Indiana, Kentucky, Oregon, Colorado, Missouri, Kansas, Montana, Maine, Wisconsin, or Mexico," Valerie Weaver-

Zercher writes. "You can have your heroine young, youngish, or middle-aged, single or married or widowed. You can have her Amish, formerly Amish, soon-to-be Amish, soon-to-be-not Amish, born Amish but adopted by the English, born English but adopted by the Amish, neighbor to the Amish or snowbound with the Amish."[115]

These were, from one perspective, only minor variations on a major theme, but the variety encourages readers to express personal preferences. The choices present themselves as meaningful statements about consumers' identity. Each is a statement of self. In this way, the structure of the market reinforces the theme of Amish fiction, repeating the call to the customer to "be yourself." And in secular and evangelical bookstores across suburban America, a lot of people responded.

Reading The Shunning

Readers enjoy Amish fiction. On GoodReads, *The Shunning* has been rated more than twenty-two thousand times. A full 75 percent of the people who rated *The Shunning* say they either liked it or loved it. One woman from upstate New York reported that she read it straight through. "WOW," she wrote. "I couldn't put it down. I almost felt like I was Katie Lapp."[116] Best sellers are by definition popular, but Lewis's fiction is especially beloved by its fans. For comparison, three of the best-selling novels of 1997 were John Grisham's *The Partner*, Danielle Steele's *Special Delivery*, and Michael Crichton's *Airframe*. Sixty-seven percent of GoodReads raters liked or loved Grisham's novel, 58 percent liked or loved Steele's, and 57 percent liked or loved Crichton's. Lewis is really popular, even for a popular writer. Some of her later works, such as 2002's *The Covenant* and 2005's *The Preacher's Daughter*, rate even higher on GoodReads. Her readers read her work for pleasure.

Part of what the readers enjoy is the way the novel invites them to reflect on who they are, and how that shapes their religious beliefs. Again and again, in their GoodReads reviews, *The Shunning*'s readers try to articulate what they like about the Amish in the novel, what they don't like, and what that says about them. They ask themselves, could I be Amish?

"What is up with my obsession with the Amish?" one woman wrote in the spring of 2012. "Would I really be happy living amongst the Plain? I would die without my iPhone and car . . . yet anything that mentions the Amish lifestyle finds itself on my bookshelf."[117]

"I've always thought I might want to be Amish," a Texas woman reflected. "[*The Shunning*] made me not want to be Amish anymore. Too much cooking."[118]

Another woman had the opposite reaction: "Not a book that kept you captivated from page to page," she said. "However, I did have a yearning to churn butter."[119]

Other readers felt both ways at once. One woman wrote that there are "so many values and traits that I admire in the lives of the Amish . . . but also certain practices"—shunning, in particular—"I wouldn't agree with. I have a hard time accepting that following the Lord would mean never speaking to or of a member of your family again."[120]

Valerie Weaver-Zercher says readers use the Amish fiction genre to imagine being Amish and having an Amish (or "Amish-ish") experience.[121] It's a bit of escapism. A little vacation. "They physically exit hypermodernity," she writes, "and slip on the heroine's habits for a few hours of vicarious canning, egg-gathering, and hand-holding in the buggy."[122] As with many vacations, though, they leave in order to come back. Readers "escape" their lives in order to think about their lives. The novels create the space and time for reflection and self-assessment. Readers imagine an Amish life, and what that would be like, and then think about themselves, and whether they would feel fulfilled in an Amish life or burdened by the mundane chores. They use the differences between their own lives and the imagined "plain" alternative to think about who they are.

Not all of *The Shunning*'s readers like *The Shunning*, of course. On GoodReads, about 1 percent of raters give the novel the lowest possible rating. Their objections are mostly aesthetic. "The writing was mediocre," wrote a woman in her fifties. "The characters weren't likable. The story was melodramatic. And I didn't buy the whole premise."[123] Multiple readers found the plot predictable or obvious. Some were frustrated at the ending, which defers resolution to the sequels. A woman from Missouri said she only read *The Shunning* because her mom is a big fan of Beverly Lewis, but she couldn't finish. "Just not my style," she wrote.[124]

For most of the readers, though, the style serves as an invitation to self-reflection and, maybe, realization. At a Christian fiction book club in Plano, Texas, Valerie Weaver-Zercher found that Amish-fiction readers used the books to talk about themselves. The group's conversation swerved, she writes, "between the content and characters of the book itself and the stuff of their own lives, especially faith."[125] This is, of course, a hallmark of popular religious reading in America. Middle-class religious readers—whether they're evangelicals, liberal Protestants, or Jews—read therapeutically, looking for the life application.[126] "Popular religious reading involves aggressive personal appropriations of religious texts," writes American studies scholar Erin A. Smith, "to make them 'useful' in our daily lives."[127] Texts are "useful" if they manage anxieties, articulate aspirations, and make readers feel like their lives matter. Lewis's debut novel, with its main character searching "to discover who I truly am . . . who I was meant to be," is really useful to many white, middle-class, evangelical women.[128]

The Shunning's readers are invited to reflect on who they really are and connect that to their experience of belief. Frequently, in their GoodReads reviews, readers bring together their reactions to the Amish, their ideas about their authentic selves, and affirmations of evangelical "heart religion." As they read, they find themselves affirming a vision of authentic Christianity, a religion not of rules but of hearts open to God.

"I found myself," one woman wrote, "agreeing with some of the characters who bring out the difference between God's rules and the rules of men."[129]

"I had no idea," another noted, "Amish culture was in so many ways contrary to the Bible—not much mercy or grace, just rules . . . but anytime people write new rules and laws for walking with God, there will be issues."[130]

The novel encourages them to open their hearts and follow their hearts. One woman wrote that the fiction made her feel good about her life choices. "I know what's best for me," she wrote, "no matter if others want me to do things the 'right' way."[131] Another, finishing the series, summarized what she felt like she'd learned: "In a nutshell," she wrote, "we each must find our place in the world, or at least in our own corner of the world, be happy in ourselves, and not live for others."[132]

These women could imagine themselves to be Katie Lapp, or Ada Ranck, taking off that head covering, shaking their hair free, and being who God meant them to be. They could imagine themselves free of rules and disciplines, the strictures of expectations, just following their hearts. They imagined themselves free. They could imagine themselves authentic.

Thousands and thousands of these women send Lewis letters. She reads them on her sofa in the writing studio she built at her Colorado Springs home with money from *The Shunning*. Her readers ask her, sometimes, about becoming Amish. They ask her too about writing. How do you get published? But mostly, Lewis says, the women just open their hearts. They tell her how their own lives are hectic and fragmented, governed by strict schedules and discipline, discipline, discipline. They talk about trying to write with small children, and how they feel like they're supposed to write but feel guilty they're not being good mothers. They tell her about their own mothers. They tell her about their daughters. Or they tell her they can't have children. Is adoption right? Should they adopt? If you don't adopt and God doesn't give you kids, do you just live forever with this longing? Do you learn to live with the yearning? "I've counseled a number of women on this," Lewis says, and she tells them to look in their hearts, and they'll know if they should adopt.[133] Lewis's readers tell her how they've struggled with God and struggle to connect with God. They tell her how they've prayed. They tell her how they've struggled with family members, been rejected by churches, and are alienated from other Christians. "I've been shunned and I'm not Amish!" they write.[134] They tell her they love her books, which is really the reason for writing. They can read her heart, open on every page, and that is the point of being evangelical, isn't it?[135]

Amid Emerging Ambiguities

William Paul Young's *The Shack*

William Paul Young didn't want to be authentic. He really didn't care about culture wars or worldviews in conflict, and he wasn't flourishing. He wasn't even thinking about flourishing. He was thinking about killing himself.

Young had a plan, partially formed, to fly to Mexico. He didn't want his kids to find his body. They could never know. No one could know. He would go down into his secrets and shame, and no one would know, and he would be gone in that blackness, submerged in the awfulness of his self, and the shame would finally swallow him whole, and it would be over. It would all be over. It would be silent.

On the other end of the phone, his wife was furious. She said, "I know." But Kim didn't really know. She knew the part about him having an affair with her best friend, but she didn't know who he was. What he'd done. His secrets.

"When you begin to know who I am," he thought, "it will be game over for me."[1]

He would kill himself. Or he'd have to face Kim. That was the only other option.

"If we're going to do this," he told her, "I have to tell you everything."[2]

Young was born in 1955 in Grand Prairie, Alberta, Canada, the eldest child of two future missionaries, William Henry and

Bernice Young. The Youngs were in their twenties, part of a small denomination called the Christian and Missionary Alliance.[3] The church, like Janette Oke's Missionary Church, believed in submitting totally to God to experience God's wonderful plan for your life. For the Youngs, that wonderful plan involved an adventure of service, spreading the good news of Jesus to the Dani people in the highlands of Netherlands New Guinea.

The colonial Dutch government had only opened the remote highlands to missionaries in 1954.[4] There, in the Baliem Valley, the Dani tribe seemed untouched by the outside world. Dani women cultivated sweet potatoes with stone tools. Dani men engaged in perpetual ritual warfare to placate malevolent spirits. The people wore few clothes and practiced rites of cannibalism, believing they could absorb the powers of their enemies by eating their flesh.[5] In 1956, the Youngs moved to the valley with a stock of penicillin, the message of Jesus, and their ten-month-old son.

The Dani people first saw the missionaries as ancestral ghosts. They debated whether or not to kill the ghosts, and whether or not they could.[6] They decided not to, but they were still scared. The child didn't scare them, though. He was a child. His parents let him spend his days with their children, playing and hunting and being a Dani. Young thought he was a Dani. "I am around the tribal people from morning to night," he later recalled. "They teach me how to do everything. They teach me how to hunt. How to shoot arrows. How to play with the clay."[7]

They also abused him. The sexual molestation began around the time he was four. Young's first memories of it are when he was four and a half, "and by then," he said, "it was in full swing."[8]

Within a few years, Young was himself a sexual predator. "By the time I'm six years old, I've already been reconfigured," Young said.[9] According to Young, people have a hard time understanding this, but the abuse made him an abuser. He learned, in his own victimization, how to victimize others. He recalls trying to trap young girls, his age or a little younger, to force himself on them.

His parents were, Young believes, completely unaware of what was happening. Perhaps they were preoccupied with serving God and the Dani people. Perhaps they just didn't see. Perhaps they didn't know what they were seeing.

When Paul was six, his parents sent him away from the Baliem Valley and the Dani people. Following Christian and Missionary Alliance rules, they sent him to a boarding school for missionary kids. But it wasn't an escape from sexual violence. The abuse continued.

"I got to boarding school, and the first night the biggest boys came and molested us first graders," Young said. "My life was full of nightmares. The worst nightmares you can imagine."[10]

Abuse was a widespread problem at Christian and Missionary Alliance boarding schools.[11] The children were beaten violently and randomly for infractions large and small. Sometimes they were slapped and punched. There were instances when the missionary kids were forced to eat their own vomit, and instances where they were forced to sit in their own feces. One child was beaten for breaking his arm. The caretakers, called "aunt" and "uncle" by the missionary kids, regularly humiliated the children and then manipulated them into taking responsibility for the distress they were causing the adults. The children were told that if they complained, it would ruin their parents' ministries. They were told that if they ruined their parents' ministries, they were responsible for sending people to hell. Both "aunts" and "uncles" touched children in inappropriate ways and forced the children to expose themselves. Some of the men forced the children to masturbate them. Some forced the children to perform oral sex.[12]

Another missionary kid, sent to one of the schools at six, like Young, wrote that "the people who read us Bible stories . . . prowled the dorm halls at night, preying on the defenseless. Older boys, victims themselves, learned to mimic their elders in that depraved environment to serve their own lustful desires, and they used blackmail and physical pain to silence us."[13]

Young survived all the abuse. He adapted to it. He internalized the shame of his abuse and made it a secret. He theologized it, too. He decided he deserved what he got because he was so bad, sinful, and dirty. But he could be better. He could earn love, and he could work to become the person who didn't deserve these things that happened to him. He would embrace the Bible rules for being a good person, and then he could have a good life.

"I became a religious performer," Young said. "I was working hard to create a religious persona that people would admire and approve and have affection for."[14]

Young grew up and became a kind of picture-perfect evangelical. He loved the rules and embraced the rules. He relished their certainty. He flourished in the suburbs, just like everyone said he was supposed to. He graduated from a small Christian college in Portland, Oregon, with a degree in religion. Then he became a college campus minister. He met his wife, and they got married and had six kids. They joined a Foursquare Church. They lived in Gresham, Oregon, about fifteen miles east of Portland. He left ministry and worked in an office in the city and came home and read his kids stories before bed at night.[15] He took the family camping in the Columbia River Gorge in the summers. On Sundays they all went to church. And all of it felt like a lie.[16]

"Shame and lies are what holds this whole thing together," Young said, "and then bad doctrine keeps it all locked up on the inside."[17]

The facade of his flourishing finally cracked in 1994, when his wife caught him having an affair. She called him at his office and said, "I know." Young, in retrospect, wondered if he wasn't trying to get caught. That wasn't his first thought, but after a lot of therapy, it occurred to him that he was trying, on some level, to prove he was unlovable. Kim couldn't love him. She could only love the lie. He seemed like a good person who did the right things and followed the rules, but that's just because the shame was submerged, the bad stuff pushed down in the dark of his soul, and the truth of his twisted, sexual self was secret. If she really knew who he was and how broken he was, she could never stand him.

That's how he thought about God, too.

Young realized he'd never had an honest relationship with God. He'd never accepted God's love. He'd never learned to trust and live in the open-ended ambiguity of a loving relationship. For him, belief had been about doing the things you're supposed to do to be good, knowing deep down that you're not. For him, it had been this idea that if you perform well enough (and keep your secrets secret enough), then you could earn that abundant life. But it didn't work, because he was still himself. And after eleven years of therapy, he realized just how wrong he'd been about what belief should be.

He sat down in 2005 to try to explain that. He wrote a parable, as he thought of it, to help his kids imagine belief in a kind of different way: Imagine that a man went to a shack and met God. What would that be like? He would be confounded, but then he would learn that's okay. The story wasn't about being your true self. It wasn't culture wars or worldview conflicts. It wasn't about the rules for a good life. "Faith," Young wrote, "does not grow in the house of certainty."[18] It grows, instead, in uncertainty, ambiguity, doubt, and tension. Imagine belief, Young argued, as an honest relationship. Imagine that God is a God who loves you even when you don't know what to make of God.

Living with Ambiguity

The novel starts by directly addressing readers and their doubts about the story. "Who wouldn't be skeptical," the opening line asks, "when a man claims to have spent an entire weekend with God, in a shack no less?" (xi). There are good reasons to be dubious about this supernatural story of a religious experience in the woods. The narrator says, "It is a little, well . . . no, it is a lot on the fantastic side" (xvii).

The narrator has doubts himself. He tells readers that's okay. Reading doesn't mean abandoning all your critical capacities, just like being in a relationship doesn't mean never asking questions. If a relationship is honest and open, you can be open about your questions and honest about what you don't know.

The narrator says that's how it is with him and the protagonist of the novel readers are about to read. The protagonist is the narrator's neighbor, Mackenzie Allen Phillips. The narrator has known Phillips for "a bit more than twenty years" (xi). The two men are close. They go to the same church. They help each other out. They get coffee and talk. But even though the narrator can vouch for his friend's good character, he cannot just assume Phillips's story of his experience with God is true; he cannot naïvely take it for granted.

"Most days," he tells readers, "I am right there with him, but on others—when the visible world of concrete and computers seems to be the *real* world—I lose touch and have my doubts" (xviii).

The narrator models a certain sort of belief, which is not firm or adamant but may, for its flexibility, be stronger. It exists between certainty and uncertainty. It's an act of trust, which means not always, immediately knowing the truth of things, and being okay with that.

The narrator says the best approach to reading the story is to not try to resolve the uncertainty. Instead, readers should embrace a broader, more generous sense of how something can be true (xviii).

This sort of belief, of course, is familiar to fiction readers. The claim is basic to fiction: that something that is untrue in one way can be importantly true in another. A fictional story that doesn't correspond to real events in real life is not simply a lie. It isn't just false, but rather, it's false for the sake of showing something true. In made-up characters and made-up situations, readers seek out moments of recognition, where they can nod and say, "that's right." They agree to pretend something is true, and act like it is true even though they know they are pretending, because the untruth communicates a truth. The untruth and its truth might be rationally incommensurable, but this poses no real problem for fiction readers. They can believe a story while also freely admitting they don't believe it.

The literary critic James Wood has argued that this is exactly why literary belief is different from religious belief. Fiction readers engage in not-quite-belief. They suspend disbelief. Which is to say they believe, but they also reserve other options. They know they can always "close the book, go outside, and kick a stone."[19] Religious belief, Wood says, requires people to give up any reservations. They have to embrace their religion's idea that the world is the way the world is and reject the possibility of other ideas, other options. *The Shack*, though, invites readers to imagine that religious belief is the same as literary belief. It's about being in that kind-of in-between space and getting comfortable with that ambiguity. Believers don't have to understand everything. They can just be along for the ride. The novel is inviting readers to "try on" belief like that.

The narrator, for example, still directly addressing readers, says there is going to be some confusion about the authorship of *The Shack*. The story is Phillips's story, but Phillips didn't write it. The narrator did. But he wrote it as Phillips. The narrator is also in the story, as Phillips's neighbor, and he describes himself in those passages as Phillips would, in the third person. To add to that confusion, the narrator signs the foreword "Willie." That might seem like a reference to the author, William Paul Young, but Young never goes by William. He goes by Paul. On the cover of the book, it doesn't even say "William," but "Wm.," because Young goes by his middle name. The protagonist also goes by his middle name, Allen. That might make readers identify Phillips with the author, but Willie's point is that he isn't Phillips, even though it really is Phillips's story—so also he is (xvii). The author is Phillips, who isn't the author but Willie, who isn't the author but Young, who is Phillips, who isn't the author, but Willie, and so on. The instability is intentional, and the book calls the reader's attention to it, to create this feeling of uncertainty.

There's a tradition of experimental literary writers playing with author-characters, who are and aren't the author. David Foster Wallace, for example, once wrote a novel where the main character, David Wallace, was confused for another character with the same name, and the main character also tells the reader he is the real person, the author, and not just a character. To prove it, he gives readers his social security number, which, it turns out, is not a real social security number but a number the author made up.[20] In experimental literature, though, this is generally meant to be confusing, and to push readers to think theoretically about texts, and authorship, and the constructed nature of realities they take for granted.[21] In *The Shack*, the narrator is making the opposite point: readers can let go of the question of who the author is. It's not that important. They can just accept the ambiguity. It might even be good for them. That's what belief is like.

Perhaps to underscore the point that knowing and certainty aren't important to the novel, the novel also changes genres three times in twenty pages. Readers, if they're going to enjoy this book, can't be sticklers for those kinds of rules. They can't cling to certainty.

The Shack is a crime story. Mackenzie Allen Phillips takes his kids camping in Oregon, and his young daughter Missy is kidnapped. The police are called. The FBI comes. They say they suspect the girl is the fifth victim of a serial killer they have been trying to catch for five years across nine states. The serial killer likes young girls, under the age of ten. He hunts in camping grounds around state parks, disappearing each time into the wilderness and reappearing in a state farther west to snatch another girl.

"We have good reason," an agent says to Phillips, "to believe that none of the girls have survived" (47).

Then the FBI finds a secondary crime scene. The car seen leaving the kidnapping is found abandoned off a narrow mountain road in the forest. Farther in, they find a shack. The shack. It's "a run-down little shack" in a hidden valley near a lake.

"A century or so earlier," Young writes, "it had probably been a settler's home. It had two good-sized rooms, enough to house a small family. Since that time, it had most likely served as an occasional hunter's or poacher's cabin" (58). And then as the scene of a murder.

Phillips, following the FBI into the woods, hoping against hope that his daughter is alive, only gets a glimpse of the inside. He sees an old table, a sofa, and, on the floor by the fireplace, his daughter's ripped and bloody dress. She is dead.

Then investigation disappears into the background, and *The Shack* becomes a different kind of story. The novel unburdens itself of its genre and becomes something else. For a while, it's a novel about coping with tragedy. Or struggling to cope. The story focuses on how Phillips feels: "numb, adrift in a suddenly meaningless world that felt as if it would be forever gray" (49). He is overcome by depression, which he calls "The Great Sadness." He cannot be comforted. Religion especially seems useless in the face of his suffering. "Sunday prayers and hymns weren't cutting it anymore, if they ever really had." Phillips "was sick of God and God's religion, sick of all the little religious social clubs that didn't seem to make any real difference or effect any real change" (63).

Even before his daughter's death, Phillips was conflicted about God. His first religious experience was abusive. As a child, he was "beaten with a belt and Bible verses" (xii). His father was a violent alcoholic and a strict church elder. If that wasn't enough to turn the child against God, at age thirteen he reported the abuse to a church elder while confessing his sins at a youth revival, only to have the elder inform his father of the betrayal. The punishment was swift and brutal. His father tied him to a tree for two days and beat him badly.

This makes it hard for Phillips to relate to God as a father (92, 94). The concept of a loving paternal figure is difficult.

When he thinks about God, he suspects God is "brooding, distant, and aloof" (xv). When he thinks of God, he sees his father's face. But also, he knows that's wrong. He also imagines God as an idealized grandfather, though he knows that's problematic for different reasons. He has a more abstract conception of God too, the conception expressed in the ontological formula familiar to evangelical worship songs, almighty and all-loving. Phillips doesn't wholly buy any of these pictures. "I don't know," Phillips says. "Maybe he's a really bright light, or a burning bush. I've always sort of pictured him as a really big grandpa with a long white flowing beard, sort of like Gandalf in Tolkien's *Lord of the Rings*" (71). For Phillips, each image is tinged with the thought that it's wrong. That conflicted feeling may be the strongest feeling Phillips associates with God.

When he thinks about it theologically, the problem isn't the existence of God. The real problem for Phillips is the problem of evil. How can he believe in God, whether God is thought of as a father or as an almighty and all-loving being, when bad things happen? How can he tolerate the ambiguities and uncertainties of a violent, evil world? He is too angry at God not to believe God exists. But then he thinks, what is the difference between God and the serial killer God created? Isn't the all-powerful, almighty, mighty-to-save God responsible, ultimately, for his daughter's horrific death (63)?

Phillips struggles with the idea that God is good. He thinks God betrayed him. He thinks, at the very least, God isn't trustworthy

(132). He thinks that while God may be good in some abstract or official sense, God doesn't care for and love him personally, perhaps because he doesn't deserve it (151). At the same time, Phillips longs to be wrong about this.

Phillips is not entirely alienated from belief. He has some seminary education and spends some time thinking about theology. He prays at night with his children and talks to them about Bible stories. He still attends church. He belongs to a pew-and-pulpit Bible church, as it's described in the novel: a nondenominational institution that could be called "the Fifty-fifth Independent Assembly of Saint John the Baptist" (xv). Phillips is uncomfortable at church. He feels more spiritual "surrounded by nature and under the stars" (20). But he goes to church. He takes his kids to church. On the outside, he's the picture of a good evangelical husband and father, even if inside he's always anxious and uncomfortable.

His wife is more religious than he is. Phillips envies his wife's faith (63). Nannette Samuelson Phillips had a good relationship with her father and has such a personal, intimate relationship with God that she calls God "Papa." She is a chaplain who specializes in working with terminal oncology patients and "thinks about God differently than most folks" (29–30).

Most folks, Phillips thinks, are just pretending, as he is. It's all a performance, a cover-up for their feelings of shame and inadequacy. "Nobody wanted God in a box," Phillips thinks sarcastically, "just in a book. Especially an expensive one bound in leather with gilt edges, or was that guilt edges?" (63).

Then Phillips gets an invitation. It's a note in the mail, on a slippery, icy day. It's typewritten. And seems to come from God. "It's been a while," it says. "I've missed you" (16). The note says Phillips should go to the shack that weekend. Phillips thinks at first that it's a sick prank, or perhaps he's being taunted by the serial killer, but then he decides he has to go. Just to see what happens.

Here *The Shack* changes a third time, shedding one genre and taking on another. The novel becomes a magical narrative about a supernatural, spiritual retreat. Phillips follows the instructions on the note. As he approaches the building in the woods, reality seems to waver. "The shack itself looked dead and empty," Young writes, "but as he stared it seemed for a moment to transform into an evil face, twisted into some demonic grimace" (76).

Then the evil of the place is so overwhelming that Phillips feels like he should kill himself. He feels "the emptiness of the place invading his soul" (78). He goes inside and sits down. This is where his daughter was killed.

He sees a bloodstain. He sees what she must have seen, in her horrible last moments. Phillips dozes off, for probably only a few minutes, and then gets up to leave. He walks away—and as he does, he sees everything change.

Winter becomes spring.

Snow becomes flowers and birds are singing.

The rundown shack becomes something sturdy and beautiful, a well-constructed, well-maintained cabin by a lake in a flower-filled glade.

He thinks he must be going crazy.

"It was all so impossible," Phillips thinks, "but here he was, or was he really here at all?" (87).

Coming to Terms with God

Before Phillips opens the shack door, God answers. Phillips is wondering what he's even supposed to call God: "Mr. God"? "Father"? Then she rushes out and hugs him. She greets him "with the ardor of someone seeing a long-lost and deeply loved relative" (82). God is a large black woman. She shouts his full name, Mackenzie Allen Phillips, and then calls him the short version familiar to friends and family: Mack. "Mack, look at you!" she says. "My, my, my, how I do love you" (82). This is God the Father.

Phillips is confused. He stands there "with his mouth indeed open and an expression of bewilderment on his face." He says, "Am I going crazy? Am I supposed to believe that God is a big black woman?" (89).

God doesn't present herself or himself to Phillips as an imperative, however. Phillips isn't "supposed" to do anything. God, as Phillips is told by God, isn't interested in obligating him to do anything and doesn't value anything done out of obligation. She doesn't care about those kinds of rules. She isn't interested in his religious performance. He should respond to God however he wants to respond to God. He is free to believe or disbelieve, to be open or closed, to accept what he sees or not.

Phillips says, "You're asking me to believe you're God, and I just don't see . . ." He doesn't complete the sentence. God disagrees: "I'm not asking you to believe anything, but I will tell you that you're going to find this day a lot easier if you simply accept what is, instead of trying to fit it into your preconceived notions" (124).

According to God, Phillips's expectations and preconceptions about God, his "religious stereotypes," are wrong (94). God presents herself in a way that reveals this.

God, first of all, is not white. Phillips is surprised by this but is also surprised he is surprised. He never consciously attributed a racial identification to God the Father. Nonetheless, he had assumed God the Father would be white (87). Seeing God appear as black calls attention to his false assumption and helps him realize that God does not rightly fit into his categories, racial or otherwise.

He had assumed other things, too, without actually articulating them. He had assumed, for example, that God the Father would be "churchy." Without really thinking about it, he had imagined that God, for example, would prefer the music of George Beverly Shea, the musical mainstay of Billy Graham's evangelistic crusades. Instead, Phillips finds God the Father listening to music he's never heard before—or even heard of. When he goes into the shack, God is listening to some "West Coast Juice." According to God, it's "like Eurasian funk and blues with a message, and a great beat," from a group called Diatribe, made up of boys who haven't been born yet. Phillips finds the whole thing disorienting.

Even more disorienting than the unexpected music or skin color is God the Father's gender. Phillips finds it disturbing that God is wearing a dress (93). He didn't expect God the Father to be gender-queer. He didn't expect to find her referred to as "her" and "she." He finds it upsetting that even though she presents as female and identifies as female, she is still God the Father. He tells God it is "a bit of a stretch" to call her Papa when she appears as a woman.

She asks him why.

Phillips says "in his head, at least," he didn't believe God was male. And yet, he did believe that. He didn't believe it in the sense of making a mental assent to the proposition "God is male," but that's how he imagined God. "All his visuals for God," in fact, "were very white and very male" (94).

According to God, this thinking is wrong—not just the content of it, but the structure. If God had been merely misidentified, correcting Phillips's understanding would be a simple matter of replacing one identity ("our Father in heaven") with another ("our Mother in the shack"). The novel suggests, though, that God is beyond human categories. In God, there is a tolerance of incommensurables. God lives in the in-betweenness. God is real in ambiguities. To know God and have a relationship with God, you have to give up on the fixed boundaries for everything.

"I'm not trying to make this harder for either of us," she says to Phillips. "For me to appear to you as a woman and suggest that you call me 'Papa' is simply to mix metaphors, to help you keep from falling so easily back into your religious conditioning" (94).

God appears to Phillips in such a way to disturb his too-human images of divinity, but God also intends to upset the more abstract definitions. "Many folks," God tells Phillips, "try to grasp some sense of who I am by taking the best version of themselves, projecting that to the nth degree, factoring in all the goodness they can perceive, which often isn't much, and then calling that God." But that is not God. "I am far more than that," God says, "above and beyond all that you can ask or think. . . . By nature I am completely unlimited, without bounds" (100). Even the ontological formulations of a God who is absolute and great in every way are critically wrong. They are too limited and limiting.

The other two persons of the Trinity are not as confounding, for Phillips, as God the Father, but they also unsettle the categories he has used to understand the world. Jesus unsettles the opposition between God and man, between sacred and profane. He's God in human form, but also, Phillips tells him, he's not as handsome as you'd think.

Jesus is first seen in jeans and a plaid shirt with the sleeves rolled up. He's wearing a tool belt and carries work gloves (84). He looks Arabic, but he tells Phillips he is "a stepbrother of that great family," a "Hebrew," "from the house of Judah" (87). He jokes about his Jewish nose (115). He goes by the name Jesus, but also Yeshua, Joshua, and Jesse.

Phillips feels more immediately comfortable with Jesus than he did with Papa. Jesus attributes this to their shared humanity. There are moments, though, when Phillips focuses on the fact that this human is also God and is struck by the strangeness of that. Lying on the dock in the lake by the shack, watching the stars with Jesus, Phillips wonders how Jesus can be inspired to awe by the sight and also, at the same time, be the stars' creator. Jesus explains that when he created the stars he was the preincarnate Word, but now he sees them as the incarnate Word, as God who is fully human (112). He is God and man.

Jesus uses the incarnation, how God became man, to talk to Phillips about how his own spirituality is limited when he accepts the false division between natural and supernatural realities, not recognizing the sacred in the profane and the spiritual in his own carnality. Jesus heals humans by unsettling this opposition.

"The human," Jesus says, "formed out of the physical material of creation, can once more be fully indwelt by spiritual life, my life" (116).

Phillips pronounces this almost unbelievable. Almost, but not quite. He is then "struck anew by the absurdity" of the claim. "Here I am," he says, "lying next to God Almighty, and you really sound so . . ." Jesus finishes his sentence, "human," and then jokes, "but ugly." The two share a good laugh (117). Even at his most unsettling, Jesus is comforting and friendly.

The Holy Spirt also messes up Phillips's categories. She appears as "a small, distinctively Asian woman" (83). Her name is Sarayu, though Jesus suggests she has other names as well (113). The word is a masculine Sanskrit word stem meaning "wind," and it is the name of a tributary to the Ganges. Though the word is masculine, Sarayu is female. The text does not call attention to her indeterminate gender, however, but instead highlights her indeterminate appearance. Phillips thinks she looks Chinese, "or Nepalese or even Mongolian," but she shimmers like a mirage (84–85). She is there and not there at the same time, present and absent, liminal to sight.

"Her nature was rather ethereal," Phillips thinks. "She obviously is not a being who is predictable" (134).

Sarayu takes Phillips to a garden. Phillips would have thought God's garden would be "perfectly manicured," but instead he sees "blatant disregard for certainty" (135). Everything seems to be everywhere. There's no order, no reason. Except there is. He just can't see it. Phillips is surprised to learn that the garden is laid out in a fractal pattern, a never-ending series of patterns repeating within patterns that looks, from a distance, simple and perfectly, intricately designed. It doesn't look like that up close. It looks beautiful but appears without order. "Looks like a mess to me," Phillips says, and Sarayu is thrilled by the comment (135).

For her, the order is not contradicted by the chaos, nor the chaos by the order, since the two are interrelated. Both things are true. This is the moral of the garden. "This garden is your soul," the Holy Spirit explains. "And it is wild and beautiful and perfectly in process. To you it seems like a mess, but I see a perfect pattern emerging and growing and alive—a living fractal" (146). God is working in the liminal space between order and chaos. Phillips's life is both/and, where he had assumed it had to be either/or. His categories for understanding his own life, like his categories for understanding God, were falsely fixed and certain. In truth, everything is caught up in the "verdant wildness" that keeps Phillips just a little off balance (136).

God tells Phillips that disorientation is part of the point of the weekend at the shack. God wants to show Phillips that his images of God were wrong. More than that, though, God wants him to let go of the conflicted feeling he associated with God. God wants Phillips to believe in a new way: embracing ambiguity and living in the tensions. Phillips doesn't need to comprehend God or correctly categorize God. God just wants to get the "head issues" out of the way.

"I realize," Phillips says toward the end of the weekend, "how few answers I have . . . to anything" (216).

Papa agrees but says answers aren't actually that important. What's important is a relationship with God. "All I want from you," Jesus says, "is to trust me with what little you can and grow in loving people around you with the same love" (196).

This alternative way of relating to God is modeled by God. The Trinity, as imagined in *The Shack*, is a mutually affirming relationship between the three persons, characterized by love and open-ended trust. Phillips at first wonders which one of the three persons is "really God." The three answer in unison: I am (87). God exists in between singular and plural.

God, however, is less interested in explaining Trinitarian theology than in revealing the picture of the relationship of the persons of the Trinity, the interrelationship of God with God. "What's important is this," God the Father says. "If I were simply one God and only one person, then you would find yourself in this creation without something wonderful, without something essential even." Humans would be without true, honest relationships. "All love and relationship is possible for you only because it already exists within me, within God myself," Papa says (103).

Phillips accepts three are one and one is three but still assumes there must be a hierarchy in the Godhead.

"Isn't one of you more the boss than the other two?" he asks (126).

No. There is no hierarchy in God.

"Once you have hierarchy," Jesus explains, "you need rules to protect and administer it, and then you need law and the enforcement of the rules, and you end up with some kind of chain of command or a system of order that destroys relationship rather than promotes it" (128).

The key characteristic of the Trinity, as imagined in *The Shack*, is that God the Father, the Son, and the Holy Spirit relate to each other differently, without needing a chain of command or a final authority. The relationship is not structured by power. They are in a "circle of relationship." They regard each others' interest as important as their own, and trust that the others each regard their interests in the same way, and avoid the conflicts that create the need for control. They trust each other. They don't try to contain each other, either in definitions or with other forms of control. They are thus truly free because they are totally vulnerable. This image of God is so critical, God believes, because it liberates people. It can free them from the need for control.

"You were made in our image," Jesus says, "unencumbered by structure and free to simply 'be' in relationship with me and with one another" (129).

When Phillips leaves the cabin in the woods, the cabin goes through the same radical and sudden transformation it did at the start of the weekend, when he approached it and reality seemed to waver and buckle. Now, however, he accepts it. At the beginning, the sudden change in perspective made him feel like he was being "swept away into the center of madness" (80). Now he can accept both realities, unperturbed. The cabin is, in some sense, dead and empty. It is, in some sense, like an evil face, a demonic grimace. This is where his daughter died. There's a bloodstain by the fireplace. But also it is the place where he met God. Both of these things are true. The shack exists in incommensurable terms, pluralistically, contestably, always in-between, and the protagonist of *The Shack* grows and changes so he can accept this, and even embrace it.

Phillips leaves the shack a man who believes. And belief, as it's imagined here, means dwelling in the indeterminacies. That's the novel's resolution.

The Shack ends by reminding readers of their reasons for doubt, their reasons to be skeptical about this story, but then inviting them to accept that doubt and live with the uncertainty. Maybe it doesn't matter so much what's true. Maybe belief isn't an act of knowing, but just a posture of openness. In the last fourteen pages, the novel reverses and rereverses its claims about what's true, in the world of the novel, and what's not, asking readers to give up their need for a final, certain answer to the question.

First, Phillips wakes up. He has, he realizes, fallen asleep without meaning to, as he prepares to leave the shack. Now awake, not knowing how much time has passed, he sees that the shack is once again a decrepit, decaying building with a bloodstain on the floor.

"He was back in the real world," the narrator says. "Then he smiled to himself. It was more likely he was back in the unreal world" (261).

Phillips then drives away but gets in an accident. He has a car wreck. He wakes up a second time, now in the hospital. For a second time, he doesn't know how much time has passed. He has only vague memories of what happened. Everything about the past weekend is uncertain. "He wasn't sure," readers are told, "if they were real or hallucinations conjured up by collisions between some damaged or otherwise wayward neurons and the drugs coursing through his veins" (265). Then he does remember, and the reality of the experience seems settled. The weekend with God really happened.

Then it's unsettled again. Phillips is told he has been in the hospital since Friday. The car wreck happened on the way to the shack, not on the way back, and he was never there.

Phillips makes a decision, at this point, to believe what he believes anyway. He did have the weekend with God. Even if he didn't. Perhaps the facts do not all fit and some of the things he believes don't mesh, exactly, with other things he believes. He can live in that tension.

At the end, the narrator Willie returns to directly address the reader again, saying Phillips doesn't have it all figured out, but that's okay. And maybe readers can relate. It's a spiritual journey. "He's a human being who continues through a process of change," Willie says, "like the rest of us" (273). It's a spiritual journey, and everything's kind of open-ended.

Evangelicals Embrace Ambiguity

Young's way of imagining belief was different from that of the most popular evangelical novels. *The Shack* wasn't like *The Shun-*

ning, Left Behind, This Present Darkness, or *Love Comes Softly.* But Young wasn't the only one thinking differently in the first decade of the new century. There was a group of evangelicals talking about the need for "a new kind of Christian." Evangelicalism, they said, needed to take a "postmodern turn" and reimagine belief.

This started in a think tank for megachurches. The Leadership Network was founded by Bob Buford, the evangelical CEO of a Texas cable-TV provider. The Network brought together megachurch pastors, including Bill Hybels and Rick Warren, and business management experts, notably Peter Drucker, to talk strategies, models, and methods. The organization funded the promotion of its programs to smaller churches and start-up churches across the country.[22]

In the late 1990s, the Leadership Network identified a demographic problem. Megachurches weren't reaching people in their twenties. The big suburban churches successfully appealed to children, teenagers, young families, older families, and senior citizens. But the eighteen-to-thirty-five demographic—college students, recent graduates, and young professionals—was missing. They termed this the "dropout hole."[23] The Leadership Network convened a study of the problem in 1996 with a special research group of younger evangelical ministers who had demonstrated some success reaching out to people in their twenties.[24]

The group was headed by Doug Pagitt, the thirty-year-old youth pastor of a Minneapolis megachurch. He was supported by Chris Seay, twenty-five, a third-generation pastor who had started a church for the disaffected evangelical students of Baylor University in Waco, Texas, and Mark Driscoll, twenty-six, who had founded a self-consciously "hip" church in Seattle.[25] There were about twenty men, total. They were supposed to be the next celebrity pastors. Like Hybels and Warren before them, they could learn from management experts and come up with new ministry models to reach a new generation. Their church-growth methods and worship-service styles could then be replicated across the country.

In 1997, however, when the group met at a Christian conference center in Colorado Springs, they became convinced it was necessary for evangelicalism to take "a postmodern turn." Brad Cecil, a youth pastor from Fort Worth, Texas, had read some contemporary philosophy and argued that the real problem with the "dropout hole" was philosophical. This was more than a generational disconnect, he said. They couldn't just market Christianity to Gen Xers the way Warren and Hybels had to baby boomers. It wasn't a marketing problem.[26] Cecil said the real issue was "primarily a shift in epistemology—the way people process information and view the world."[27]

Driscoll had also been reading some philosophy. He knew a little of the work of the philosopher John Caputo, a prominent proponent of a French school of thought called "deconstruction."[28] Driscoll declared himself "glad to see the end of modernity." He later encouraged the group to think of themselves as missionaries to "emerging and postmodern cultures."[29]

It wasn't completely clear to the men what "postmodern" meant. It doesn't seem like they all had the same sense of the term. But that, actually, was part of what it meant to them. They wanted to embrace the multiplicities and indeterminacies, the realities of their own lived experience of pluralism, and accept the resulting tensions. Cecil said it had something to do with "the Web" and the way hypertext on the Internet had changed communication, and with it, people's processes of thinking. "Postmodern" wasn't just a stage that young people were going through. It was something larger. It was, as the philosopher Jean-François Lyotard had said, "the condition of knowledge in the most highly developed societies."

That condition, according to Lyotard, was characterized by "incredulity toward metanarratives."[30] This is notably not the same as simple disenchantment. It is not a claim that people have given up on metanarratives. It is saying, rather, that people live with a sense of in-betweenness or liminality. People in the post-modern condition are perpetually between multiple big stories that they can use to explain their lives and the world. They live in the intersections. They occupy an intermediate, interstructural, interstitial situation, which, according to Lyotard, "refines our sense of differences and reinforces our ability to tolerate the incommensurable."[31] In the postmodern condition, then, one shouldn't expect to find broad disenchantment or secularization, but rather to see people with an acute sense of the multiplicity of options and, perhaps, an easy acceptance of them. They might not experience their in-betweenness as a problem, and might not try to solve it, but instead they find a way to live with the tensions. Evangelicals could also do that. They could embrace the tension. They could become postmodern.

One megachurch intern at the meeting recalled that it was the first he had heard the word "postmodern." It immediately made sense to him. "I heard people describing out loud an expression of the Christian faith," Tim Keel later wrote, "in a language that was native to me, that named the tensions I was holding within myself related to the church, our culture, and the gospel."[32]

The Leadership Network was not interested in funding the description of a new philosophical epoch, however. The men were charged with developing programs and coming up with methods to reach people in their twenties. Cecil suggested they become "missional." "We must think like missionaries again!" he told the gathered men. "Learning a new language. A new culture."[33] The key, he said, would be to think about truth as experiential, rather than propositional, and to reimagine belief as a relationship.

For others, though, becoming "postmodern" was more about being culturally savvy. Driscoll's Seattle church, Mars Hill, adopted and adapted youth culture: the clothes, the hair, the music.

It was post-grunge, alternative, and indie. "This is where we live," said one twenty-seven-year-old woman at Mars Hill in 1999. "This is our culture. These are the people that we're around all day long. This is the music we listen to."[34] The church was in touch and relevant. In his sermons, Driscoll would drop references to Radiohead, Marilyn Manson, and *South Park*, and he'd talk about how the Bible approved of oral sex within marriage.[35]

This wasn't that different from previous generations of evangelical outreach, except maybe more brash. Driscoll got a bit of a reputation for his swearing and was tagged "the cussing pastor."[36] His language was offensive to some older evangelicals—one pastor called his cursing "inappropriate, unbecoming, and dishonoring to Christ"[37]—and even some of Driscoll's peers grew critical. When he was invited to be a guest preacher at a church in Texas, he was warned that foul language would not be culturally appropriate. Driscoll said "fuck" in the first sentence of his sermon.[38]

Driscoll also felt that "postmodern ministry" called for a more aggressive masculinity. Megachurches, Driscoll felt, were too gentle, too soft and feminine. "They tend to be very effeminate," he said. "Manly men are repelled by this, and many of the men who find it appealing are the types to sing prom songs to Jesus and learn about their feelings while sitting in a seafoam green chair drinking herbal tea."[39] Megachurches made it seem like evangelicalism was just for "chicks and some chickified dudes with limp wrists."[40]

Driscoll and the other men in the Leadership Network's research group clashed about this. The other men weren't about to rush out and put women in their pulpits, but they didn't think the hypermacho approach was right, either. They were worried about becoming known as the "young assholes of evangelicalism."[41]

The megachurch think tank also reminded the young men it wanted to invest in things that were "positive and pragmatic." The goal was to "move toward more creation and less critique."[42] There was a bit of a breakup in 2000. Driscoll and some others separated, going their own way.[43] The next year, Brad Smith, president of the Leadership Network, announced that the think tank had identified a "groundbreaking group of innovators." They were, he said, "a new breed, with a new calling, new tone and new priorities."[44] The group launched a website called Emergent Village, to foster an ongoing conversation, and came out with a book, *A New Kind of Christian*, by Brian McLaren, the pastor of a non-denominational church in the suburbs of Washington, DC. The "postmodern" evangelicals would now be called "Emergent."

McLaren's book argued that a lot of evangelicals could be open and should be open to a new kind of ambiguity. Belief could be reimagined as something open-ended and comfortable with in-between spaces.

A New Kind of Christian stages a dialogue between two characters talking through a crisis of belief. Daniel Poole is an evangelical minister, considering leaving the ministry. He is, he says, "running out of gas" after fourteen years. "I feel like I'm losing my faith," Poole says. "Well, not exactly that, but I feel that I'm losing the whole framework for my faith."[45] The other character is a former minister who now teaches high school science. Neil Edward Oliver, "Neo," explains how this isn't a crisis of belief, or doesn't have to be. It can be an evolution, a transition to a new paradigm, an open-ended adventure. "You're suffering from an immigration problem," he says. "You have a modern faith, a faith you developed in your homeland of modernity. But you're immigrating to a new land, a postmodern world. You feel like you don't fit in either world. You can't decide whether to settle in a little ghetto or to move out into the new land."[46] Poole should greet the demise of his old framework gladly and welcome the new era, open to what it might bring.

In the introduction, McLaren connects this to his own biography. He writes that in 1994, at the age of thirty-eight, he was sick of being an evangelical pastor and was going through a personal crisis. He felt disillusioned. He felt "disembedded" from contemporary evangelicalism. He went into the mountains of Pennsylvania and, from a cabin overlooking a valley, acknowledged the thought he had been avoiding: he was going to leave the ministry. He compares the thought to thoughts of suicide. He couldn't live with the internal conflict anymore and wanted to end it.[47] As he had that thought, though, another broke through. "What if God is actually behind these disillusionments and disembeddings?" McLaren asked. "What if the experience of frustration that feels so bad and destructive is actually a good thing, a needed thing, a constructive thing in God's unfolding adventure with us?"[48] He had been trying to avoid the feeling of internal conflict. He had been afraid of the risk of ambiguity. Now he wanted to embrace those things. In the book, he invited others to imagine their crisis of faith as, actually, an experience of what belief is like in contemporary American culture.

The book, notably, was not put out by an evangelical publisher. *A New Kind of Christian* was published by Jossey-Bass, a secular San Francisco press that specialized in books on leadership, including Peter Drucker's books. The book would be sold at Leadership Network conferences, but it was outside the normal distribution channels for an evangelical book. It wasn't clear that Christian bookstores would stock it, and suburban superstores like Borders and Barnes & Noble might put it in the business-leadership section instead of "religion" or "spirituality." However, the book caught the attention of Phyllis Tickle, the influential religion editor at *Publishers Weekly*. Tickle started talking about *A New Kind of Christian*. She told people it was an exciting new thing, the next big thing in religious publishing. When mainstream journalists sought her out at the Christian Booksellers Association conference in 2001, asking her what might make a good story, the next *Purpose-Driven Life*, Tickle directed them to McLaren's book.[49]

A New Kind of Christian sold more than 100,000 copies in a year—enough to encourage other publishers to come out with books on "emergent," "emerging," and "emergence" Christianity. Zondervan developed a special imprint, EmergentYS.[50] Baker came out with a line of books called the Emergent Village Resources for Communities of Faith.[51] Other books weren't branded with the word "emergent" but spoke to the same themes. In *Blue Like Jazz*, published by Thomas Nelson in 2003, Donald Miller wrote, "I used to not like God because God"—like jazz—"didn't resolve."[52] It sold more than a million copies. In *Velvet Elvis*, published by Zondervan in 2005, Rob Bell wrote, "the Christian faith is only alive when it is listening, morphing, innovating, letting go of whatever has gotten in the way of Jesus."[53] In twelve months, it sold 116,000 hardback copies.[54] Like the evangelical novels of the same period, these books were sold in evangelical bookstores, but also at big-box retailers and suburban superstores and, increasingly, online.

The "platform innovators," meanwhile, published a slew of books on strategies and methods for reaching young people in a "postmodern" age. These were aimed at smaller audiences but helped establish this new religious identity, a new kind of evangelicalism.

Often, however, the books got tangled up in criticism of megachurches and spent more time on "deconstruction" than on the creation of new, replicable models for "emergent" ministry. A Leadership Network–sponsored book, *Postmodern Youth Ministry*, for example, opened with a critique of the idea of a single, effective approach. "This book will *not* give you a model for your youth ministry," it said. "Instead of promoting a new paradigm, we must deconstruct the old paradigms and then propose a series of reflections on culture, the church, and the state of youth ministry."[55] The book then devoted forty pages to exploring the "postmodern shift," starting with the question "What is true?" and the philosophy of Plato and René Descartes, and then moving to the problem of "foundationalism," with a sidebar praising the film *The Matrix* ("a postmodern gospel drama").[56] All of this was laid out as a pastiche of quotes and intersecting commentaries. In the end, the book argues that youth ministries should "help our students extricate their faith from their epistemology. That way, although their modernism is deconstructed, their faith won't be."[57]

Another book, cowritten by McLaren, Leonard Sweet, and Jerry Haselmayer, promised to provide a "primer on ministry in the emerging culture."[58] The emphasis was on practicality. This would be a user-friendly intro, the ABCs of the postmodern turn. The authors could organize it like a dictionary, an alphabetical intro to the "new language" of the new Christianity. But they quickly found that goal conflicted with the idea of postmodernity they were trying to promote. Could a guide to postmodernism really be linear? Shouldn't it resist or at least problematize the idea of a step-by-step, how-to guide? They seriously considered organizing it by use-frequency: not ABCDEFG ... but ETAIONSHRDLUCM-FGYPWBVKXJQZ.[59] They didn't, finally, try to deconstruct the alphabet, but they found other ways to subvert their own practicality. Offering a model for postmodern sermons, for example, they argued for the importance of surprise and unpredictability. An emergent sermon would reject logical progressions and instead create an experience. "Make your sermons pointless!" the authors wrote.[60] As a program for megachurches to solve the problem of the "dropout hole," it was decidedly antiprogrammatic. To mitigate this, at least a little, the publisher brought in a leadership consultant to create experiential team activities for the book. They called them "EPICtivities."

The tension at the core of the emergent project is perhaps best seen in a pair of dueling forewords to a third book, *The Emerging Church*, by Dan Kimball, which Zondervan published in 2003. The first is by Rick Warren. Warren writes that the emerging church is just a new iteration of the megachurch movement, an update to his own "seeker-sensitive" model. "While my book *The Purpose-Driven Church* explained what the church is called to do," Warren writes, "Dan's book explains how to do it with the cultural creatives who think and feel in postmodern terms."[61] The second foreword is by McLaren. McLaren's endorsement of the book opens with an attack on megachurches and their emphasis on marketable models. "Too often in recent years, church leaders have acted as if being sensitive to seekers means sliding into a one-size-fits-all, franchise, clone, mimic-the-model mentality," McLaren writes. These churches have been "gimmick-prone and thoughtlessly (sometimes desperately) pragmatic."[62] Emergent Christianity was, from one perspective, the rejection of the megachurches. From another, it was the megachurch methodology for a new generation.

True to Lyotard's idea of the acceptance of in-betweenness, Kimball's book does not attempt to resolve that tension. Instead, he has it both ways. "You can't box-in the emerging church," Kimball writes. "Instead of one emerging-church model, there are hundreds and thousands of models of emerging churches. Modernity may have taught us to look for a clean model to imitate. But in today's postmodern context, it's not that simple."[63]

There were some churches that identified with the term "emergent." It was always vague what it meant, but that was part of the point. "It appears," sociologists Gerardo Marti and Gladys Ganiel wrote in their study of several of these churches, "that ambiguity is a necessary and strategic aspect of Emerging Christians' religious orientation." Emergent Christians wanted to embody "a willingness to live with tension, ambiguity, and gray areas."[64]

The "emergent church" was mostly associated with books and publishing, however. The books created an identifiable, if amorphous, religious identity. "Emergent" meant, at least partly, an internal critique of evangelicalism. People used it as a way to say they were inside of and outside of evangelicalism, at the same time. They were part of the subculture but also felt some tension with the subculture. The anthropologist James Bielo interviewed ninety people who called themselves "emergent" or "emerging," and when he asked them to talk about what that meant, they returned to this idea, again and again. "Invariably," Bielo writes, "when asked to tell their Christian story Emerging Evangelicals posit a distance between their sense of self and the conservative Evangelical subculture. They explain various elements of Evangelicalism that they no longer accept, how their distastes became realized, and how the details of their current life respond to those perceived shortcomings."[65] They discovered their in-betweenness and explained it, frequently, by talking about Christian-themed merchandise. They thought some of it misrepresented their faith and their sense of their belief, like WWJD bracelets and punning Christian T-shirts.[66] They frequently talked about *Left Behind* and how they disagreed with it.[67] But other Christian-themed merchandise was really important to them, like *A New Kind of Christian* or *Blue Like Jazz*. These were people who shopped at Christian bookstores but didn't completely feel like they belonged there.

Publishing The Shack

No one thought *The Shack* belonged in Christian bookstores. Least of all Paul Young.

He didn't even plan to have it published, at first. Young didn't think of himself as an author writing a "book." It was a gift for his kids. It was something his wife, Kim, asked him to do. After years and years of therapy had healed their marriage and helped him think about belief in a new way, she wanted him to share what he'd learned. So in May 2005, Young started scribbling down snatches of ideas on a yellow legal pad while riding the train on the forty-minute commute between Gresham and Portland.

It wasn't a story, at that point. Just thoughts. Then Young thought he should try to make it like a parable, because "a story has a way of getting past our defenses," so he started adding some narrative elements.[68]

There were moments when the story just flowed, and it felt almost like the Holy Spirit was speaking through him. Young described it as like getting carried down a river. One Saturday, for example, he sat down at his computer, with all the pads and scraps of scribbled writing, to type them up, and he didn't move for more than eight hours, and when he was done he had four chapters.[69]

He finished *The Shack* in August. But it still wasn't a book. Young had fifteen copies made at an Office Depot—one for each of his six kids, for Christmas presents, plus a few for other relatives and some friends. Then, perhaps feeling proud of what he'd done, he emailed a copy of *The Shack* to the host of a podcast he listened to, Wayne Jacobsen.

This happened to Jacobsen all the time. Jacobsen was a former Foursquare Church minister who, after twenty years working in ministry, decided he didn't believe in organized religion. He didn't believe in religion. "Religion," he said, "is what human effort does to accomplish God's work. I don't think Jesus came to start a religion. He came to invite us into a relationship with him."[70] Jacobsen started writing books encouraging Christians to stop going to church. True Christian spirituality, he said, couldn't be institutionalized.

In 2005, he also started a podcast, *The God Journey*, with another ex-minister, Brad Cummings. Podcasts were new at the time, but an increase in iPods and other MP3 players, along with simplified tech for uploading and downloading audio files, made them an exciting new way to connect with people and share ideas. *USA Today* described podcasts as "programming by the people, for the people. No big overhead. No censors. No pesky professional standards to live up to."[71] The most popular show had about nine thousand downloads, and new shows were starting every day. One was Jacobsen's, with the tagline, "thinking life with God outside the box of organized religion," and it was attracting listeners like Paul Young.

Jacobsen got Young's email on a Friday night and replied right away. He told Young he got a lot of unsolicited manuscripts and he couldn't promise a full response. He would read the first twenty-five pages, he said, but unless they really grabbed him, he wouldn't promise more than that. "I was actually looking for an excuse not to read it," he later said. He printed out twenty-five pages, went downstairs to read, and as he read he started weeping. He spent twenty minutes crying.

When he tried to explain this later, Jacobsen just said the book "kinda ushers you into an encounter with God."[72]

The book was also a mess, and Jacobsen thought it needed to be reworked and rewritten to reach a broader audience. He wrote Young and told him he loved the book, but it needed to be revised before it could be sent to a publisher. Young didn't feel he could do that, so he asked Jacobsen to take the job and "make it more marketable."[73] Jacobsen, Cummings, and Young then spent eleven months revising the book. They rewrote it, by Jacobsen's calculation, four times. They added dialogue and rearranged plot. They reworked scenes and added new insights.

By 2007, the book was ready for a publisher. But no publisher was interested. Jacobsen shopped it around but only got rejections. It's not clear why, even with the boom in emergent and emergent-style titles, publishers weren't interested. It's possible the book was still too disorganized and uneven. Possibly the portrayal of God the Father as a woman was seen as too controversial. The racial identities of the persons of the Trinity would raise eyebrows, at least, and any depiction of the Trinity was sure to elicit criticism. The gatekeepers of the evangelical market decided the book didn't belong.

But maybe, Jacobsen, Cummings, and Young thought, that didn't matter anymore. The channels of distribution had changed. Diversified. Apocalyptic fiction and Amish romances were selling at Walmart and Barnes & Noble and now online, at Amazon.com. Besides, there was the podcast. Hadn't the Internet changed everything? It was the great disrupter—couldn't it also disrupt evangelical publishing? Just like Jacobsen didn't need a church to form a community of like-minded Christians, who all explored spirituality together, *The Shack* didn't need an evangelical publisher. The publishers and their distribution networks had brought people together, as evangelical consumers, since the 1950s, but there were a lot of people who didn't feel quite at home there, didn't quite fit there, and they would buy books too. What if Jacobsen, Cummings, and Young built an alternative, just for *The Shack*?

They established Windblown Media—the name a reference to the idea that the Holy Spirit is not contained by institutions but "blows where ever it pleases"[74]—with a pooled investment of $15,000. Jacobsen and Cummings advertised the book on their podcast and got about 1,000 preorders. They printed a first run of 10,000 copies in May 2007.[75] They sold out in four months. A second print run of 22,000 sold in two months, and a third-run of 33,000 sold in a month.[76]

By the end of the year, Windblown had sold 88,000 copies. The novel had still not made it past the gatekeepers of American evangelicalism, but there were, indeed, other ways to distribute books. *The Shack* took these alternative routes to readers. Most early copies were sold through the Windblown website. Amazon also started selling *The Shack*, purchasing the book by the thousands and listing it on the website as a mystery/thriller. Barnes & Noble—with one eye on their online competition—started selling *The Shack* in their suburban stores in November. They stocked the book cautiously at first, but it sold and they ordered more. The books were packaged and shipped out of Cummings's garage in Thousand Oaks, California, about forty miles north of Los Angeles. Orders came in so fast that Cummings struggled to keep up.[77] The book was a genuine hit, a self-publishing phenomenon. By May 2008, sales were nearing 1 million.[78]

Then Windblown Media made a deal with Hachette.[79] If evangelical publishers weren't interested in a story of a spiritual retreat with the three persons of the Trinity, the multinational conglomerate had no such compunctions. Based in France, Hachette had recently acquired Time Warner Book Group and its imprints, and was doing major business in US book sales. Hachette had the highest rate of titles-to-hits of any publisher at the time, according to *Forbes* magazine.[80] It did a robust business in religious titles. One of the conglomerate's US locations was in Nashville, Tennessee, and focused on books for the evangelical market. While the New York and Boston offices handled literary stars such as Sherman Alexie, David Foster Wallace, and J. D. Salinger, the Nashville office sold Joyce Meyer and Joel Osteen. The Nashville office took on Young. They began moving large volumes of *The Shack*, landing it on the *New York Times* best-seller list. *The Shack* held the top spot there for 50 weeks and was on the list for 177 weeks.[81] Then Walmart agreed to carry *The Shack* in all its stores.[82] Hachette sold 6 million copies in six months.[83]

The Shack was a phenomenon. It was popular enough in 2008 that comedian Jay Leno could use it in a joke about subprime mortgages on his late-night talk show, trusting that enough of his middle America audience would be familiar with the book for the joke to work.[84] Oprah Winfrey mentioned the title on her show the same year while talking to Jeff Bezos, the founder of Amazon, about the company's new E-reader, the Kindle. Winfrey hadn't read *The Shack*, but she knew it was a top-selling Kindle title that fall. Some audience members cheered just at the mention of the name of the book.[85]

Christian bookstores started stocking it too. It was, chairman of the Evangelical Christian Publishers Association (ECPA) Dwight Baker said, a moment of realization when that happened. The gatekeepers weren't keeping the gates anymore. For Baker, it seemed like a rebuke from God. "For all the analytics, all the tools we have, you still get humiliated on such a regular basis," he said. "God's saying, 'There's a guy with a message and he has a big job to do and you publishers can't catch on, so I'll get that message to readers in my own way.'"[86] *The Shack* made the ECPA's best-seller list and stayed there for nearly two years. In 2009, the ECPA gave *The Shack* the diamond award for 10 million copies sold. It stayed on the best-seller list into 2011.[87]

It didn't happen all at once, but with *The Shack*, the evangelical market was changed. Evangelical publishers had worked for years to get books to cross over into the general market. *This Present Darkness* showed it was possible. *Left Behind* crossed over and became a giant success, reaching two audiences. With *The Shunning*, it became normal to sell evangelical books outside of evangelical bookstores. But then with *The Shack* it became clear that books could "cross over" in both directions and, in fact, that "Christian-themed merchandise" didn't need evangelical publishers or evangelical distribution networks. The market had been absorbed into the general market, and in the process the distinct identity of evangelical book buyers was becoming very blurry. Amish fiction could be labeled "inspirational" instead of evangelical, and *The Shack* might be marked "spiritual" or even "spiritual but not religious." If evangelical bookstores only carried evangelical books to compete with Walmart, Barnes & Noble, and Amazon, then what was an "evangelical" book? The bookstores had long brought together different imaginative ideas about belief, from *Left Behind*'s culture war to *Love Comes Softly*'s abundant life. But the success of *The Shack* showed that there wasn't a single market anymore, to clearly mark the boundaries of "in here" and "out there." The

evangelical market had always been incommensurable with itself, but now, with the postmodern turn celebrating belief in the
interstitial space of metanarratives, the market fragmented and
broke apart.

Reading The Shack

A number of notable evangelical leaders reacted to *The Shack* with
hostility. They condemned the book, saying it misrepresented
evangelical faith. The first was Chuck Colson, a prominent figure
of the Religious Right. He reviewed it on his radio show, which
aired on more than one thousand Christian stations. The book
wasn't all bad, Colson said, but "sadly, the author fails to show
that the relationship with God must be built on the truth of who He
really is, not on our reaction to a sunset or a painting." *The Shack*
veered into universalism, teaching that there are "many equally
valid ways in which God reveals Himself." Discerning Christians,
Colson advised, should "stay out of *The Shack*."[88]

Tim Challies, a popular evangelical blogger, wrote nearly five
thousand words criticizing the book. He had noticed, he said, that
the novel was very popular with evangelical students and with
"those who are part of the Emergent Church." That didn't concern
him, exactly, but it did pique his interest. He ordered the book off
Amazon to write a review for his blog.

"On the whole," he wrote in 2008, "the book is readable and
enjoyable." More, "much of what Young writes is good and even
helpful." But he also had concerns. The most significant problem,
he said, was that Young misrepresented the Trinity. In *The Shack*,
there is no hierarchy in the Godhead. But, according to Challies,
that's not what the Bible teaches. God the Son and God the Holy
Spirit submit to God the Father, but God the Father never submits
to the Spirit or the Son. Hierarchy isn't bad, Challies explained.

"While the Bible does teach that we are to submit to one another, it also teaches that God has ordained some kinds of hierarchy," including husbands over wives, parents over children, and duly appointed authorities over their subjects. Young's rendering is, therefore, "unbiblical."

Challies was also concerned that the book seemed to slip into universalism. It didn't outright make an argument that everyone will be saved, regardless of whether or not they accept Jesus Christ as their Lord and Savior. Maybe, he wrote, Young is just unclear, but that's an issue. Further, the novel seems to downplay the importance of the Bible. God, in *The Shack*, suggests that people will learn to listen to God, intuiting the leading of the Holy Spirit and receiving personal revelations from the world around them. "Such teaching is dangerous," Challies wrote. "What authority is there if not the Bible?"

Challies's biggest concern, though, was just how readable the novel was. "The book," he wrote, "has a quietly subversive quality to it. Young seems set on undermining orthodox Christianity." He encouraged Christians not to read it.[89]

Other critics also focused on the book's depiction of the Trinity. Albert Mohler, president of Southern Baptist Theological Seminary, said *The Shack* was a referendum on evangelicalism's commitment to true Christian doctrine. "The Christian church has struggled for centuries," Mohler said, "to come to a faithful understanding of the Trinity in order to avoid just this kind of confusion."[90] Mark Driscoll, speaking at an evening service at Mars Hill, made the same point in more forceful terms. He called *The Shack* heresy four times in eight minutes.

Driscoll was especially offended at the depiction of God as a woman. "It's Goddess worship," he said. "If God the Father is really God our mother, that changes everything. That means when Jesus prayed 'Our Father in heaven,' he should have prayed 'Our Mother in the shack.'"[91]

It wasn't just church leaders who were concerned about Young's heresies. His mother, Bernice Young, was deeply disturbed by the book. When she got to the part of *The Shack* where God the Father comes through the door to greet the protagonist, and he is a woman, she was shocked. "Your brother," she said to one of Young's sisters, "is a heretic!"[92]

Most readers didn't seem to care, though. The after-the-fact attempt at gatekeeping didn't concern them. On the social cataloguing site GoodReads, more than half of readers gave *The Shack* five out of five stars. More than eight years after the book was released, people were still raving about it. "Wow Wow WOW!" wrote one woman from New York. "I loved this book!"[93]

Another woman from Arizona posted that "this was about the 4th or 5th time" she'd read the book. "It always brings me closer to God in a 'real' way," she explained. "There are lessons that I need to learn over and over again, and they are knit into the fabric of this beautiful and fantastical story."[94]

Not everyone loved it, but their criticisms were mostly not the criticisms of evangelical leaders worried about heresy. In one representative week in 2016, three people gave *The Shack* a bad review on GoodReads. One called the book racist for its use of an African American stereotype, another complained about the writing, and a third wrote simply, "Ugh."[95]

That was the minority opinion, though. The same week, more than twenty readers praised the book. A typical example was one Minneapolis woman who found herself incredibly moved while reading. "This book make me bawl my eyes out," she wrote. "I highly recommend this book if you're into soul searching."[96]

A lot of people were into soul-searching at the start of the twenty-first century. If that put them into tension with evangelicalism, well, that wasn't a bad thing. That's where faith could thrive—in the uncertainty, ambiguity, and in-between spaces of American religion.

William Paul Young's *The Shack*

The Fracture of Evangelicalism

Young stopped thinking of himself as an evangelical in the years after the publication of *The Shack*. He didn't completely disconnect from evangelicalism. He would never be completely disconnected. "Those are my people," he said. "I mean, I'm entrenched in that history."[97] But he felt the growing distance, the intensified estrangement.

Partly it was the criticisms. Called a heretic again and again, Young started to accept it. There were rules, and he'd violated them. There were boundaries, and he'd trespassed. But he found he didn't really care. If the gatekeepers said he was outside, he didn't feel the need to fight them. He was fine outside.

"A lot of this is about power and control," Young said in 2008. "Doctrine and the interpretation of doctrine has become like property. We don't live in a feudal system, where you build a wall around your castle. We've turned intellectual property—whether it's your idea of the Trinity or whatever else—into the ground that we wall off and defend."[98]

Young just rejected the idea that institutions and labels were important to his or anyone's relationship with God. He'd been a religious performer. He'd followed the rules. That's how he'd kept his shame hidden, for so many years, until it threatened to drown him in his own secrets and he had no choice but to tell the truth or end it all. Now he rejected all that, and that's what *The Shack* was about.

"The soul is not found in a religion; it's found in a relationship," Young said. "Jesus took the rules out of religion and put love in its place."[99]

By 2012, he stopped calling himself an "evangelical" at all. When *Publishers Weekly* asked him how he'd describe himself religiously, Young said he was fine with "spiritual but not religious."[100]

Young didn't feel alone in this, either. A lot of evangelicals didn't feel like they were evangelicals anymore. The success of *The Shack* seemed to testify, as one journalist wrote, "to an evangelical America in flux." Things were changing. Things were coming apart. "To a secular outsider," wrote Zach Dundas for *Portland Monthly*, "evangelicalism may look like a pious monolith. In fact, it is a broad and fractured mosaic."[101] Once, the evangelical book market had held all the pieces together and constructed a single religious identity. Evangelicalism was a world within a world. There was a clear line separating "in here" from "out there" and a yawning chasm between them. Now the line wasn't so clear. Now there were lots of lines, lots of separations, and lots of people who felt like they were living in those in-between spaces. They found they were fine, in between incommensurable metanarratives. Maybe it was even better. Maybe that's what real belief was like.

The book market fragmented and fractured at the start of the twenty-first century. And with it, evangelicalism. Christian bookstores had organized evangelicalism for white, middle-class Americans. Now they disorganized it again. Christian fiction had helped people articulate what belief was like, in cultural practice, and how it could be imagined. Now, with another novel, it was reimagined and rearticulated as something else. For Young, and for a lot of American evangelicals, that was fine.

Conclusion

The Question That Remains

When Donald Trump came and won the imagination of vast numbers of American evangelicals, the best-selling fiction authors who had shaped and formed and fostered that imagination with their novels said almost nothing.

What was there to say? Didn't the art speak for itself? They had written about faith and life and inspired millions to imagine the way their beliefs might play out in the world. They had asked readers to dream about their lives and their families and the way the world was going, and they had directed readers' attention to certain hopes and other fears. Trump spoke to those hopes and fears. The best-selling fiction imagined a past where things were better and simpler, and Trump promised to Make America Great Again. The books imagined conspiracies destroying small-town America, aided by deceptive neighbors and invisible, invading forces. Trump promised to Drain the Swamp, Lock Her Up, and Build the Wall. The books said authenticity was good and institutions bad, and Trump embodied both sentiments.

The evangelical fiction mostly wasn't political, but it prepared readers to imagine the world in certain ways and to embrace certain values. It prepared people to accept Trump as their political champion. Largely, they did.

A few authors seemed uncomfortable with this. William Paul Young told audiences that he wasn't a Republican but a Canadian.[1] When the election neared, he wrote on his blog that he didn't think Christians should be invested in the fates of nations or concern themselves with elections. Frank Peretti wrote a little about politics on his Facebook page in 2015. He tried to think out loud about how the government could protect the religious liberty of people who opposed homosexuality as he did, even as gay rights advocates won big victories in the courts. "Accommodation is the key word here. Compromise. Meeting in the middle," Peretti wrote. "What does it take to love, and not destroy, one's neighbor?"[2] The angry and chaotic comments that followed weren't conducive to any kind of conversation, though, and Peretti withdrew. He didn't say anything more about hot-button issues and was silent about the 2016 election, except to note that he wasn't checking his messages anymore.

The one author who really relished political conflicts and would likely have come out in support of Trump died before that could happen. Tim LaHaye backed conservative Republicans from Barry Goldwater to Mike Huckabee. He loved the scrum of election season and would likely have thrilled to see white evangelicals emerge as such a powerful bloc of voters—81 percent! But the ninety-year-old didn't have the strength to engage one last time, and he died in July 2016.[3]

The others avoided politics and any potential controversy. Jerry Jenkins, LaHaye's coauthor, promoted his writing workshops and writing advice seminars. Janette Oke, in Canada, had never made many public statements. She lived her life and focused on her family, just as the characters in her novels did. If she had wanted to do a press event, the Hallmark Channel might have asked her to talk about the inspiration for the pioneer-day fantasies it was repackaging as a sweet TV drama, *When Calls the Heart*, then in its third season and averaging about 2 million viewers every week. But Oke avoided public events. Beverly Lewis had a very active presence on social media—posting on her Facebook page several times a week and frequently engaging commenters in conversation—but she focused on promoting her books and talking generally about faith and family.

But whether the authors spoke or didn't speak, whether they thrilled to Trump's rhetoric or felt uncomfortable with elections altogether, it was not hard to see that their fiction encouraged a particular kind of politics. The novels promoted individualism, first of all. In Oke's romance novel, the heroine flourished when she realized God's love for her. She received abundant life. But it was just for her and her family. There was no vision of common flourishing or care for the general welfare—abundant life was atomized, parceled out like suburban lots. When a woman read the novel in bed at night—one light on the side table while her husband and children slept—she was invited to imagine that God wanted her to have the best life, and imagine how that would change her relationship with her spouse, her kids, and her daily tasks in her suburban home. That woman was never asked to imagine how her abundance related to her neighbor's needs, or how her fullness and flourishing were bound up with that of other people. She was never asked to think of what it would be like to be part of a new community where her debts were forgiven as she forgave the debts of others.

The same individualism can be seen in Young's novel. Social obligations are death to the spirit in *The Shack*. Institutions are boxes trying to trap souls. Freedom comes only in personal connection to God, which is realized completely alone. That individualized imagination lends itself to a politics of self-interest, a focus on personal freedom, and a disinterest in—or even suspicion of—the common good.

The best-selling fiction, second, encouraged readers to oppose pluralism. Pluralism is imagined as the cause of cultural upheaval, and readers are asked again and again to imagine how upsetting difference is. In *Left Behind*, it is pluralism that prompts crisis. The characters respond to supernatural events in different ways, because they believe different things and come from different perspectives, but these are not presented as reasonable disagreements. Instead, the realization that other people perceive something differently causes doubt. And the doubt causes chaos. How do you know you're right about what you see if others see the same thing and think something else? This question might spur you to humility and encourage you to listen to other people with different experiences and perspectives, recognizing that you don't know everything and other people know some things it would help you to know. But it's also, of course, upsetting to discover that you are wrong, and it is threatening to think you could be wrong. The novel asks readers to focus on this anxiety. It asks them to imagine feeling attacked and imagine defending themselves. Every encounter with difference is presented as a site of struggle.

Peretti's novel, similarly, conceives normal civic life as "spiritual warfare." A local election, a new edition of the town's newspaper, a real estate deal, and the start of the school year are all imbued with irreconcilable conflict. Every neighbor is an enemy, if not an ally. New neighbors are a special threat. Perhaps most upsetting, Peretti's novel invites readers to imagine that criminal accusations of sexual assault are only made for ideological reasons. They are literal lies of the devil in *This Present Darkness*, and the good Christians will dismiss them immediately. Facts are not neutral, after all. So facts that don't fit the agenda must be rejected. This was not primarily about politics, but it shaped political imagination. It prepared people to reject information that would be bad for their side. This helped Trump more than once in 2016 and in the following four years, when he was president.

Christian fiction was not the only reason white evangelicals supported Trump, but for many his approach resonated. When the candidate stood up at a Christian college in Sioux Center, Iowa, warned of the dangers of immigrants, talked about how Christianity was under siege, and said, "I could stand in the middle of Fifth Avenue and shoot somebody and I wouldn't lose any voters," it resonated.[4] His white evangelical hearers could imagine that refugees were really terrorists and evidence of a shocking crime was just "fake news." In fact, they already had. This was the story of the fiction they bought at the Christian bookstore, including the store in Sioux Center, less than a mile from where Trump spoke.

The next spring, I walked into the Christian bookstore in Mishawaka, Indiana, and asked myself, "What is evangelicalism?" I felt like I knew. Or at least had a sense. And then it felt like I didn't, the idea melting into air.

Part of the problem was that I'd been away for a while. I lived in Tübingen, Germany, for eight years, only returning to the United States a few months before Trump was elected. I was in Germany because my wife ran a campus ministry in the old university town. The ministry was very evangelical in some ways but also unlike anything I'd ever seen before, as she and a team built an eclectic community of college students and proclaimed that God was already at work in their lives through the love of Jesus, regardless of where they were at with faith or belief. I went back to school, earning a masters at the University of Tübingen, and I started studying with Jan Stievermann, a brilliant scholar of the history of American Christianity. When he got a job at Heidelberg University, two hours north, Jan took me with him. I became his assistant and worked on my doctorate. I read widely, trying to understand this history from the inside and the outside at once. I read Cotton Mather, and his sprawling and weird Bible commentary—the first written in the British colonies. I read the autobiography of Lorenzo Dow, an itinerant preacher and abolitionist who never combed his hair, never owned more than one pair of clothes, and shouted, screamed, cried, begged, joked, and story-told his sermons across the American frontier. I read the newspapers of early Pentecostals explaining how the Spirit moved in what they believed to be the last days. I read the private letters that organized the founding of *Christianity Today*. And I read lots of evangelical novels, laboring away on a dissertation about fiction and bookstores and imagination. As I would ride the train from Heidelberg back to Tübingen after a long day of work—reading a Christian romance, or a Christian zombie novel, a detective novel, an apocalyptic spy thriller, or any of the many, many fictions of belief—sometimes it would all hold together in my mind: evangelicalism. Then at other times it wouldn't and didn't seem like it could all hold together. When I returned to the United States a few years later, I wasn't sure if I knew what I knew.

Some scholars of American evangelicalism have a strong sense of what evangelicalism really is because of their childhood experience in the faith. That is their anchor for normal evangelicalism—good or ill—and all the other varieties radiate out from there. I never had that. My parents were Jesus people, self-consciously radical. When I was nine, they left their church in the suburbs of San Francisco and moved to Texas, where we joined an apocalyptic back-to-the-land commune. We farmed with horses, prayed to the point of collapse, and waited for the antichrist to come and kill us. I remember cowering one Sunday as our burly, bearded preacher shouted about how he was ashamed of us, and God was ashamed of us. He grew more and more angry until he picked up his large leather Bible and smacked it on the edge of the solid oak pulpit. Then he hoisted the pulpit up in his arms and slammed it into the ground. Later that day we drove by a Baptist church with a giant inflatable bouncy house in the yard. Twenty or thirty young people, boys and girls together, were laughing and talking and jumping as high as they could. At the height of each jump, some would wrap their arms around their knees like a cannon ball and some would spread their arms wide to fly. None of them seemed scared. It wasn't clear to me if we were part of the same thing, "evangelicalism."

Identifying three or four of five "key emphases" of theology or belief doesn't solve the problem of a definition. Many scholars studying the history of evangelicalism are happy with that approach, adopting David Bebbington's "quadrilateral" of emphases or characteristic marks: biblicism, crucicentrism, conversionism, and activism. It doesn't seem like it works, to me. It allows for too much gerrymandering, letting scholars redraw the line where it suits them, while not accounting at all for evangelicals' own gerrymandering and the way they draw, redraw, and reredraw the lines of who is and isn't a part of it at different moments of time. I want a definition that accounts for differences and deals with change, deals with history.

I have the same problem with political definitions, though. It doesn't seem inevitable to me that the majority of white evangelicals supported Trump. Things happened. Contingencies came into play. Events could have gone differently, and many times almost did—in 2020, 2016, 1990, 1980, 1950, 1850, and back through time. People are complicated and life is weird. History is weird. Evangelicals are a multiplicity, always going in a lot of different directions at once as people try to grapple with the world and God at the same time. In retrospect, perhaps you can see that dinosaurs evolved into backyard chickens, or the religious equivalent of that, but it's just not plausible to pretend you knew that was going to happen all along. The straight lines are misleading. It's wrong to think of this religious identity, "evangelical," as so singular that it can all be explained as one thing, beginning to end.

Evangelicalism is better conceived as an imagined community, a rolling conversation organized by real structures and institutions in the world that make that conversation possible. Like the evangelical book market and the Christian bookstores.

As I walked around that Mishawaka bookstore, I looked at the "Closing. Everything 10–40% Off!" sign and other indications the store would soon shut its doors. This was happening across the country, I knew. The structure that had carried and sustained the fiction that inspired and shaped evangelical imagination was now crumbling. Evangelical books had once only been available in evangelical bookstores, making evangelicalism a distinct consumer culture and subculture. Then the big bookstores started carrying the books too. Then everything was sold online. Buying one book was disassociated from the market of books and the larger consumer and religious identity. And the small stores that made evangelicalism available for purchase in the suburbs were disappearing.

It happened slowly and then all at once. There were always some new stores that opened and some that closed, but one year there was a subtle shift, and more closed than opened. In 2005, there was a net of about 100 more new stores. In 2006, the same story. Then, the next year, there were about 90 new stores in the country, but 160 went out of business.[5] The year after that the financial crisis happened.

Christine Wiedenfeld felt the crisis hit in her store in Crystal Lake, Illinois. The store had been operating in the Chicago suburbs since 1973, but in 2008, her customers just stopped spending money. "When the housing market fell, we fell," she said. "When the stock market sunk, we sunk."[6]

The stock market recovered after a few years, but it didn't matter. Evangelical bookstores kept going out of business. Attendance at the Christian Booksellers Association's annual conference dropped from fifteen thousand in 1999 to about five thousand in 2010.[7] In 2011, 63 more stores closed.

Stan and Anna Myrl Long went out of business that year. They had come to California in 1964, driving together across the country to follow a call and reinvent themselves. Not quite forty, they felt like they had a mission. A way to serve something bigger and achieve the American dream. They sold music, Bibles, gifts, and especially books. They didn't make a lot of money, but they felt like they were doing something worth doing. It was a ministry. They did that for twenty-six years. Then they went out of business.

The Longs had been thinking of retiring, but they didn't want to go like this. As they stood in their Rancho Cucamonga store in February 2012, even the bookshelves had those little tags on them. Everything most go.

"Tears have been shed, I must admit," Stan said.[8]

For Family Christian—"the world's largest retailer of Christian-themed merchandise"—it took about ten years for the change in the market to bring down the company. But it happened. Family Christian had its last profitable year in 2007. When the financial crisis hit, the chain saw sales drop by about $70 million. In 2012, Rick Jackson, an entrepreneur and evangelical from Atlanta, took over the company to try to save it. Jackson's plan was to convert Family Christian to a nonprofit, lowering operating costs. The plan didn't work. By 2015, Family Christian had more than $100 million in debts and sales were down almost 30 percent from 2008, with no signs of turning around. Jackson proposed a rapid-fire bankruptcy sale, selling Family Christian to another corporation he owned and sloughing off some debts in the process. Creditors objected, and a federal judge nixed the plan.[9] Suppliers forgave millions to try to help Family Christian keep going. It didn't work. Sales kept falling, and when I walked into the Mishawaka store in 2017, all the outlets were shutting down.[10]

The bookstores held evangelicalism together as more or less one thing. What replaces them when they're gone? Politics, maybe. Or the identity will fracture, and there will be two, three, seven evangelicalisms, each held together by its own network. A variety of things could serve this function: famous preachers, Christian musicians, magazines, seminaries, speaking circuits, parachurch missions, political groups, and any other network that brings people into imagined community. But the book market was an important one in the second half of the twentieth century and the start of the twenty-first, particularly because it brought so many different ideas together. The shelves in these small suburban stores united a variety of discordant dreams, divergent discussions, shifting emphases and concerns, and all these invitations—again and again—to imagine.

The imagination was too small, I think. Too narrow. From my perspective, American evangelicals ended up too focused on their own private domains, too fearful of strangers, too fearful of change, too invested in the arrogance of always knowing the right answer. Imagining the chaos of modern life, the confusion, the hardship, and day-to-day struggle, the best-selling fiction gave the wrong answers. But I want more and more varied imagination, not less, so I will mourn the vanishing book market anyway.

And even though the answers were too often wrong, I still find the question compelling. I want to be a part of that conversation, not because I agree with what's being said, but because I think the discussion is important. Wherever the conversation that is evangelicalism has strayed, and whatever happens to the structure holding that conversation together, the question still grabs me: God became a human, died, and rose again, so what should you do with your random Tuesday?

That's what Janette Oke asked when her baby died. That's what Frank Peretti asked when he woke up in a trailer home and prepared for work at a ski-equipment factory. That's what Tim LaHaye asked when no one read his apocalyptic theology and he went looking for a fiction writer, and what Jerry Jenkins asked when he churned out page after page of prose. It's what Beverly Lewis asked when the house was quiet after piano lessons, and what Paul Young asked when he could no longer live with his shame. Their answers resonated with others who suffered, too— the millions of readers who felt a connection with them, and told their friends, and went to Christian bookstores looking for more of those answers.

The question is compelling, even if the answers are not. And if the answers fall short, that doesn't make me want to abandon the question but ask it again with more urgency. God became human. He did some stuff and got killed. Then he resurrected from the dead. What difference does that make to my life? What does it mean in yours? What does it say to my suffering, or my neighbors'? What does that singular event in history, when God ripped open the fabric of time and existence to enter everyday life and change it forever, change for a man or a woman who is about to buy a novel in Mishawaka, at a store that's going out of business?

The story of Jesus Christ is at the heart of the Christian imagination. It's an amazing story: of powerful forces at work, of life-changing love, of a coming kingdom unlike any other, and of subverted expectations about God. Evangelicals are right to believe that if that story is true, it changes every other story we tell about ourselves and the world. They are right to see that the gospel is an invitation to imagine that everything is different, everything is being transformed, everything made right and made new.

The way people imagine this working out will change and the politics of their imagination will shift over time. Such is the nature of history. The networks that sustain the communities doing the imagining will also change, rising and falling, growing and shrinking, appearing and disappearing as time passes. This book is about one of those networks and how it shaped a culture and a faith for a period of our recent past. But the question that calls for our imaginative engagement will, I think, continue. One person will turn to another and ask a question not so different from the question the first disciples asked each other as they tried to reckon with the resurrection. Jesus defeated sin and death, they will say. So how do you imagine your life tomorrow?

Notes

Introduction

1. Zach Williams, "Old Church Choir," recorded December 2016, Provident Label Group, track 2 on *Chain Breaker*, 2016.

2. James E. Ruark, *The House of Zondervan* (Grand Rapids: Zondervan, 1981), 142.

3. Colleen McDannell, *Material Christianity: Religion and Popular Culture in America* (New Haven: Yale University Press, 1995), 222.

4. "Hot Christian Songs," *Billboard*, March 11, 2017.

5. Kate Shellnutt, "Lecrae Brings Reformed Rap to Jimmy Fallon's Tonight Show, Again," *Christianity Today*, January 10, 2015, http://www.christianitytoday.com/news/2014/september/lecrae-brings-reformed-rap-jimmy-fallon-tonight-show.html.

6. Nerisha Penrose, "Lecrae on New Album 'All Things Work Together': 'I'm Finally Comfortable in My Skin,'" *Billboard*, September 22, 2017, https://www.billboard.com/articles/columns/hip-hop/7973688/lecrae-interview-new-album-all-things-work-together.

7. "The Chronicles of Narnia: The Voyage of the Dawn Treader," Box Office Mojo, [April 7, 2010], https://www.boxofficemojo.com/release/rl2657388033/.

8. C. S. Lewis, *The Great Divorce* (New York: HarperCollins, 1946), 1.

9. A review of Nielsen BookScan data shows US bookstores sell

223

about eight thousand copies of *Mere Christianity* during slow months. Sales go up to about twelve thousand around Christmas and in August, when people send their children off to college.

10. "Translation Philosophy," ESV.org, n.d., https://www.esv.org /translation/philosophy/.

11. Frances FitzGerald, *The Evangelicals: The Struggle to Shape America* (New York: Simon & Schuster, 2017). Steve Donoghue, "'The Evangelicals' Examines the Collision of Politics and Faith," *Christian Science Monitor*, April 19, 2017, https://www.csmonitor.com /Books/Book-Reviews/2017/0419/The-Evangelicals-examines-the -collision-of-politics-and-faith; Douglas Brinkley, "Path of Evangelicals in America Leads to Era of Trump," *Boston Globe*, March 31, 2017, https://www.bostonglobe.com/arts/2017/03/30/path-evangelicals -america-leads-era-trump/gWQVwWtZhi1VfmNTKLRRAM/story .html.

12. FitzGerald, *The Evangelicals*, 2.

13. Thomas Kidd, *What Is an Evangelical? The History of a Movement in Crisis* (New Haven: Yale University Press, 2019), 3.

14. "The Digital Pulpit: A Nationwide Analysis of Online Sermons," December 16, 2019, Pew Research Center, https://www.pew forum.org/2019/12/16/the-digital-pulpit-a-nationwide-analysis-of -online-sermons/.

15. See Robert Darnton, "What Is the History of Books?" in *The Book History Reader*, ed. David Finkelstein and Alistair McCleery (London: Routledge, 2002), 9–26.

16. See, for example, Ien Ang, *Watching "Dallas"* (London: Routledge, 1982).

17. Beth Moore, "Q & A with Beth Moore, Author of 'The Undoing of Saint Silvanus,'" Books-a-Million, September 20, 2016.

Chapter 1

1. Laurel Oke Logan, *Janette Oke: A Heart for the Prairie* (Minneapolis: Bethany House, 1993), 207–10.

2. Denise Marie Siino, *In Her Steps: Women of Courage and Valor* (Nashville: B&H, 2005), 135.

3. Logan, *Janette Oke*, 207.

4. Janice Radway, *Reading the Romance: Women, Patriarchy and Popular Literature* (Chapel Hill: University of North Carolina Press, 1984), 31–34; Alice K. Turner, "The Tempestuous, Tumultuous, Turbulent, Torrid, and Terribly Profitable World of Paperback Passion," *New York Magazine*, February 13, 1978, 46–49.

5. Logan, *Janette Oke*, 209.

6. Michael Winship, "The Rise of the National Book Trade System in the United States," in *A History of the Book in America*, ed. Carl F. Kaestle and Janice A. Radway (Chapel Hill: University of North Carolina Press, 2009), 56–77, here 56.

7. Winship, "The Rise of the National Book Trade System," 64.

8. Winship, "The Rise of the National Book Trade System," 61.

9. William Vance Trollinger Jr., "An Outpouring of 'Faithful' Words: Protestant Publishing in the United States," in Kaestle and Radway, *A History of the Book in America*, 359–75, here 360–61.

10. Trollinger, "An Outpouring of 'Faithful' Words," 360.

11. Trollinger, "An Outpouring of 'Faithful' Words," 365.

12. Candy Gunther Brown, *The World in the World: Evangelical Writing, Publishing, and Reading in America, 1789–1880* (Chapel Hill: University of North Carolina Press, 2004), 55.

13. Trollinger, "An Outpouring of 'Faithful' Words," 365.

14. See David Paul Nord, *Faith in Reading: Religious Publishing and the Birth of Mass Media in America* (Oxford: Oxford University Press, 2004); John Fea, *The Bible Cause: A History of the American Bible Society* (New York: Oxford University Press, 2016).

15. Brown, *The World in the World*, 39.

16. A. P. Fitt, "Wanted!," in *Moody's Latest Sermons* (Chicago: Bible Institute Colportage Association, 1900), n.p.

17. Timothy E. W. Gloege, *Guaranteed Pure: The Moody Bible Institute, Business, and the Making of Modern Evangelicalism* (Chapel Hill: University of North Carolina Press, 2015), 9.

18. Gloege, *Guaranteed Pure*, 181.

19. See also William Vance Trollinger Jr., "Report from the Front Lines of Fundamentalism: William Bell Riley's the *Pilot* and Its Correspondents, 1920–47," in *Religion and the Culture of Print in Modern America*, ed. Charles L. Cohen and Paul S. Boyer (Madison: University of Wisconsin Press, 2008), 199–214.

20. Larry ten Harmsel, with Reinder Van Til, *An Eerdmans Century, 1911–2011* (Grand Rapids: Eerdmans, 2011), 14, 23.

21. For a history of Dutch Calvinist immigrants, see James D. Bratt, *Dutch Calvinism in Modern America: A History of a Conservative Subculture* (Grand Rapids: Eerdmans, 1984).

22. Ten Harmsel, *An Eerdmans Century*, 44.

23. James E. Ruark, *The House of Zondervan* (Grand Rapids: Zondervan, 1981), 18.

24. Cf. D. G. Hart, *Defending the Faith: J. Gresham Machen and the Crisis of Conservative Protestantism in Modern America* (Phillipsurg, NJ: P&R, 1994), 89.

25. Erin A. Smith, *What Would Jesus Read? Popular Religious Books and Everyday Life in Twentieth-Century America* (Chapel Hill: University of North Carolina Press, 2015), 87–88, 103.

26. Ruark, *The House of Zondervan*, 18.

27. Ruark, *The House of Zondervan*, 20.

28. See Mark Sidwell, "The History of the Winona Lake Bible Conference" (PhD diss., Bob Jones University, 1988).

29. Ruark, *The House of Zondervan*, 38–39. For a fuller story of Eerdmans and Zondervan's market expansion, see Daniel Vaca, *Evangelicals Incorporated: Books and the Business of Religion in America* (Cambridge, MA: Harvard University Press, 2019).

30. Ruark, *The House of Zondervan*, 43.

31. Bruce Bickel and Stan Jantz, *His Time, His Way: The CBA Story; 1950–1999* (Colorado Springs: CBA, 1999), 31.

32. Bickel and Jantz, *His Time, His Way*, 31.

33. Colleen McDannell, *Material Christianity: Religion and Popular Culture in America* (New Haven: Yale University Press, 1995), 246.

34. Michael Hirsley, "Christian Book Market Booms," *Chicago Tribune*, July 22, 1990, http://articles.chicagotribune.com/1990-07-22/news/9003010903_1_christian-fiction-crossway-books-publishers-weekly.

35. Randall Balmer, *Mine Eyes Have Seen the Glory: A Journey into the Evangelical Subculture in America* (Oxford: Oxford University Press, 1989), 199.

36. Kenneth N. Taylor, *My Life: A Guided Tour* (Wheaton, IL: Tyndale House, 1991), 304–5, 313.

37. Ruark, *The House of Zondervan*, 142–43.

38. McDannell, *Material Christianity*, 246.

39. Jan Blodgett, *Protestant Evangelical Literary Culture and Contemporary Society* (Westport, CT: Greenwood, 1997), 42.

40. Ruark, *The House of Zondervan*, 144.

41. "Paper Back Talk," *New York Times*, October 31, 1976.

42. See Kevin M. Kruse, *White Flight: Atlanta and the Making of Modern Conservatism* (Princeton: Princeton University Press, 2005); Darren Dochuk, *From the Bible Belt to Sun Belt: Plain-Folk Religion, Grassroots Politics, and the Rise of Evangelical Conservatism* (New York: Norton, 2011); Mark T. Mulder, *Shades of White Flight: Evangelical Congregations and Urban Departure* (New Brunswick, NJ: Rutgers University Press, 2015); Richard Rothstein, *The Color of Law: A Forgotten History of How Our Government Segregated America* (New York: Norton, 2017).

43. See Lizabeth Cohen, *A Consumers' Republic: The Politics of Mass Consumption in Postwar America* (New York: Random House, 2003);

44. Marabel Morgan, *The Total Woman* (Old Tappan, NJ: Revell, 1973), 61.

45. Morgan, *The Total Woman*, 120–21.

46. See Amy DeRogatis, *Saving Sex: Sexuality and Salvation in American Evangelicalism* (New York: Oxford University Press, 2014).

47. Charles Taylor, *A Secular Age* (Cambridge, MA: Belknap Press of Harvard University Press, 2007), 18.

48. For a range of criticisms of Taylor's *Secular Age*, see Michael Warner, Jonathan Van Antwerpen, and Craig Calhoun, eds., *Varieties*

of Secularism in a Secular Age (Cambridge, MA: Harvard University Press, 2013).

49. Janette Oke, *Love Comes Softly* (Minneapolis: Bethany House, 1979), 13. Hereafter, page references from this work will be given in parentheses in the text. All italics and irregular spellings are original.

50. Pamela Regis, *A Natural History of the Romance Novel* (Philadelphia: University of Pennsylvania Press, 2003), 112–14.

51. Sarah Wendell and Candy Tan, *Beyond Heaving Bosoms: The Smart Bitches' Guide to Romance Novels* (New York: Simon & Schuster, 2009), 16.

52. See Dennis D. Engbrecht, "Merging and Diverging Streams: The Colorful and Complex History of the Missionary Church," History of the Missionary Church, mcusa.org, and Melvin E. Dieter, *The Holiness Movement of the Nineteenth Century* (Metuchen, NJ: Scarecrow, 1980).

53. See John C. Pollock, *The Keswick Story* (London: Hodder & Stoughton, 1964).

54. Siino, *In Her Steps*, 135.

55. Logan, *Janette Oke*, 94.

56. "God's Way," written by Lida Shrivers Leech in 1911. See Ernest K. Emurian, *Living Stories of Famous Hymns* (Grand Rapids: Baker Books, 1955). For Oke's love of the hymn, see Logan, *Janette Oke*, 156.

57. Logan, *Janette Oke*, 156.

58. Logan, *Janette Oke*, 155.

59. Logan, *Janette Oke*, 157.

60. See also Silliman, "The Bible in the Evangelical Imagination," in *The Bible in American Life*, ed. Philip Goff, Arthur E. Farnsley II, and Peter J. Thuesen (New York: Oxford University Press, 2017), 305–15.

61. Logan, *Janette Oke*, 158.

62. Logan, *Janette Oke*, 209.

63. Logan, *Janette Oke*, 212.

64. Marcia Z. Nelson, "InProfile: Carol Johnson; Christian Fiction Comes Softly," *Publishers Weekly*, September 29, 2010, http://www.pub

lishersweekly.com/pw/by-topic/industry-news/religion/article/44627 -inprofile-carol-johnson-christian-fiction-comes-softly.html.

65. Logan, *Janette Oke*, 213.

66. "Gold / Platinum / Diamond Book Awards," Christian Book Expo, n.d., http://christianbookexpo.com/salesawards/gpd-past -winners.php.

67. "Brooke's Reviews: Love Comes Softly," GoodReads, January 30, 2008, https://www.goodreads.com/review/show/14092321?book _show_action=false&from_review_page=2.

68. "Tiffany's Reviews: Love Comes Softly," GoodReads, February 29, 2008, https://www.goodreads.com/review/show/16726790.

69. "Emily's Reviews: Love Comes Softly," GoodReads, March 10, 2008, https://www.goodreads.com/review/show/17459407.

70. Lynn S. Neal, *Romancing God: Evangelical Woman and Inspirational Fiction* (Chapel Hill: University of North Carolina Press, 2006), 106.

71. Neal, *Romancing God*, 117.

72. LaDonna Whitmer, "LaDonna's Reviews: Love Comes Softly," GoodReads, October 17, 2007, https://www.goodreads.com/review /show/7844130.

73. Crystal Rae Nelson, "A Warning against Christian Romance," *Young Women Stepping Heavenward*, n.d.

74. "Bekah's Reviews: Love Comes Softly," GoodReads, October 8, 2008, https://www.goodreads.com/review/show/34866918.

75. Janette Oke, "Interview," Christianbooks.com, n.d. Currently available at https://janetteoke.weebly.com/interview-with-janette -oke.html.

76. Neal, *Romancing God*, 30–31.

Chapter 2

1. Frank Peretti, *This Present Darkness* (1986; reprint, Wheaton, IL: Tyndale House, 2001), 88.

2. "Bestsellers from B. Dalton Bookseller," *Christianity Today*, April 6, 1984, 56.

3. Lovecraft, *Supernatural Horror in Literature* (Mineola, NY: Dover, 1973), 14.

4. Stephen King, "Not Guilty," *New York Times*, October 24, 1976, http://www.nytimes.com/1976/10/24/archives/not-guilty.html.

5. Doreen Carvajal, "Who Can Afford Him? Stephen King Goes in Search of a New Publisher," *New York Times*, October 27, 1997, http://www.nytimes.com/1997/10/27/business/who-can-afford-him-steph en-king-goes-in-search-of-a-new-publisher.html.

6. Good News Publishers, *Where There Is a Vision: The Inspiring Story of God's Faithfulness through Fifty Years of Publishing the Good News* (Westchester, IL: Good News Publishers, 1988), 30.

7. Jan Dennis and Lane Dennis, preface to *Whatever Happened to the Human Race?*, by Francis A. Schaeffer and C. Everett Koop (Wheaton, IL: Crossway Books, 1979), x.

8. "Singer's Plug Puts 'This Present Darkness' in Spotlight," *Los Angeles Times*, September 23, 1989, http://articles.latimes.com/1989 -09-23/local/me-550_1_present-darkness.

9. Daniel K. Williams, *God's Own Party: The Making of the Christian Right* (New York: Oxford University Press, 2010); Matthew Avery Sutton, *American Apocalypse: A History of Modern Evangelicalism* (Cambridge, MA: Harvard University Press, 2014).

10. Barry Hankins, *Jesus and Gin: Evangelicalism, the Roaring Twenties, and Today's Culture Wars* (New York: Palgrave Macmillan, 2010).

11. See William J. Bray, "Recollection of the 1948 Campaign," Truman Library, August 1964, https://www.trumanlibrary.gov/library /oral-histories/brayw; Truman Reelection Campaign, "Foot-Notes on the Opportunities of the White House in the Political Battles of 1948," Truman Library, n.d., https://www.trumanlibrary.gov/library /research-files/footnotes-political-battles-1948; Williams, *God's Own Party*, 19, 39, 36–39.

12. Barry Hankins, *Francis Schaeffer and the Shaping of Evangelical America* (Grand Rapids: Eerdmans, 2008), Kindle location 105.

13. Philip Yancy, "Schaeffer on Schaeffer, Part I: An Interview," *Christianity Today*, March 23, 1979, 21.

14. Francis Schaeffer, *The God Who Is There*, in *The Complete Works of Francis Schaeffer: A Christian Worldview*, vol. 1, *A Christian View of Philosophy and Culture* (Wheaton, IL: Crossway Books, 1982), 8. For a historical account of Christian fundamentalism, see Timothy E. W. Gloege, *Guaranteed Pure: Moody Bible Institute, Business, and the Making of Modern Evangelicalism* (Chapel Hill: University of North Carolina Press, 2015).

15. Schaeffer, *The God Who Is There*, 9.

16. Francis Schaeffer, *He Is There and He Is Not Silent*, in *The Complete Works of Francis Schaeffer*, vol. 1, *A Christian View of Philosophy and Culture*, 275–384, here 338.

17. Schaeffer, *The God Who Is There*, 10.

18. Schaeffer, *The God Who Is There*, 138.

19. Schaeffer, *The God Who Is There*, 143.

20. Schaeffer, *He Is There and He Is Not Silent*, 291.

21. Hankins, *Francis Schaeffer*, 43.

22. Francis Schaeffer, *Whatever Happened to the Human Race*, in *The Complete Works of Francis Schaeffer: A Christian Worldview*, vol. 5, *A Christian View of the West* (Wheaton, IL: Crossway Books, 1982), 281–410, here 354–55.

23. Schaeffer, *The God Who Is There*, 55.

24. Philip Yancey, "Francis Schaeffer: A Prophet for Our Time?" *Christianity Today*, March 23, 1979, 18.

25. H. H. Gerth and C. Wright Mills, *From Max Weber: Essays in Sociology* (New York: Oxford University Press, 1946), 323–59. See also Rogers Brubaker, *The Limits of Rationality: An Essay on the Social and Moral Thought of Max Weber* (London: Allen & Unwin, 1984).

26. Walter Lippmann, *The Public Philosophy* (Boston: Little, Brown,

1955), 109, 110. See also George Marsden, *The Twilight of the American Enlightenment: The 1950s and the Crisis of Liberal Belief* (New York: Basic Books, 2014), 47.

27. Lippmann, *The Public Philosophy*, 112.

28. Schaeffer, *The God Who Is There*, 138.

29. Hankins, *Francis Schaeffer*, 75.

30. Hankins, *Francis Schaeffer*, 76.

31. Marsden, *Twilight of the American Enlightenment*, 141.

32. Hankins, *Francis Schaeffer*, xv.

33. Good News Publishers, *Where There Is a Vision*, 72.

34. Good News Publishers, *Where There Is a Vision*, 78–79.

35. Good News Publishers, *Where There Is a Vision*, 79.

36. Frank Peretti, *The Wounded Spirit* (Nashville: Word, 2000), 191.

37. Focus on the Family, "What We Believe (feat. Mr. Frank Peretti)," *Focus on the Family Daily Radio Broadcast*, August 28, 2014.

38. Frank Peretti, "The Chair" (address at Liberty University Convocation, October 21, 2005), YouTube video, https://youtu.be /M-YQXFkN8aY.

39. Peretti, "The Chair."

40. Quoted in Hankins, *Francis Schaeffer*, 112, and in Francis Schaeffer, *Death in the City*, in *The Complete Works of Francis Schaeffer: A Christian Worldview*, vol. 4, *A Christian View of the Church* (Wheaton, IL: Crossway Books, 1982), 217.

41. Peretti, *This Present Darkness*, 88.

42. Peretti, *This Present Darkness*, 88.

43. Good News Publishers, *Where There Is a Vision*, 83.

44. Good News Publishers, *Where There Is a Vision*, 83, 101–2.

45. Sandra Blakeslee, "Christian Publishing Industry Does Hard Sell on Religion," *New York Times*, July 19, 1987.

46. Peretti, *This Present Darkness*, 466. Hereafter, page references to this work will be given in parentheses in the text.

47. Daniel Radosh, *Rapture Ready: Adventures in the Parallel Universe of Christian Pop Culture* (New York: Scribner, 2008), 111.

48. Edward E. Plowman, "Is Morality All Right? The New Religious Lobbies Say 'Yes'—with Impact," *Christianity Today*, November 2, 1979, 78.

49. Jason C. Bivens, *Religion of Fear: The Politics of Horror in Conservative Evangelicalism* (Oxford: Oxford University Press, 2008), 178.

50. Mikhail M. Bakhtin, *The Dialogic Imagination*, ed. Michael Holquist, trans. Caryl Emerson and Matthew Holquist (Austin: University of Texas Press, 1989); see also Simon Dentith, *Bakhtinian Thought* (London: Routledge, 1995).

51. See Carol Clover, *Men, Women, and Chainsaws: Gender in the Modern Horror Film* (Princeton: Princeton University Press, 1992), 21–64.

52. "Susan Wingate and Joshua Graham Interview Frank Peretti," Dialogue: Between the Lines, BlogTalk Radio, April 5, 2012, http://www.blogtalkradio.com/dialogue/2012/04/05/dialogue-between-the-lines.

53. Amy Grant and Vince Gill, interviewed by Larry King, *CNN Larry King Live*, December 6, 2003, http://transcripts.cnn.com/TRANSCRIPTS/0312/06/lkl.00.html.

54. Bob Millard, *Amy Grant: The Life of a Pop Star* (New York: Doubleday, 1986/1996), 176.

55. Richard Harrington, "Joyful Noise," *Washington Post*, June 9, 1985, https://www.washingtonpost.com/archive/lifestyle/style/1985/06/09/joyful-noise/a2ebd8d4-c35d-49f2-92db-077e9c436bf7/?utm_term=.c0eaed36750b.

56. Chris Willman, "Amy Grant: Hint of Shadow for a Christian Singer; Gospel/Pop Star Isn't All Spiritual Happy Talk, and Neither Is Her Latest Album," *Los Angeles Times*, November 6, 1988, http://articles.latimes.com/1988-11-06/entertainment/ca-111_1_amy-grant/2.

57. Michael Goldberg, "Grant Brings Gospel into the '80s," *South Florida Sun Sentinel*, June 7, 1985, http://articles.sun-sentinel.com/1985-06-07/features/8501230021_1_amy-grant-gospel-music-christian-music/2.

58. Jack Keiley, "The Gospel of Grant," *Iowa City Press Citizen*, November 9, 1985.

59. Millard, *Amy Grant*, 183–89.

60. Pat Curry, "'Real' Life Suits Amy Grant," *Deerfield Beach (FL) Sun Sentinel*, December 9, 1988.

61. Curry, "'Real' Life Suits Amy Grant."

62. Peter Gardella, "Spiritual Warfare in the Fiction of Frank Peretti," in *Religion in the United States in Practice*, vol. 2, ed. Colleen McDannell (Princeton: Princeton University Press, 2001), 328–45, here 329; Andrew Abrams, "Moved by the Spirit of the Lord, Frank Peretti Writes Theological Thrillers That Sell to High Heaven," *People*, June 18, 1990.

63. Wingate and Graham interview.

64. Gene Edward Veith, "This Present (and Future) Peretti," *World Magazine*, October 25, 1997, https://world.wng.org/1997/10/this_present_and_future_peretti.

65. Wingate and Graham interview; Edwin McDowell, "Book Notes," *New York Times*, June 28, 1989, http://www.nytimes.com/1989/06/28/books/book-notes-484889.html.

66. "Singer's Plug Puts 'This Present Darkness' in Spotlight."

67. Bruce Bickle and Stan Jantz, *His Time, His Way: The CBA Story; 1950–1999* (Colorado Springs: CBA, 1999), 94.

68. Carol Johnson, "Saving Stories," *Charisma*, August 1, 2011, https://www.charismamag.com/site-archives/1465-0911-magazine-articles/features/14421--saving-stories.

69. "The Top 50 Books That Have Shaped Evangelicals." *Christianity Today*, October 6, 2006, https://www.christianitytoday.com/ct/2006/october/23.51.html.

70. Justin Taylor, email to the author, March 8, 2018.

71. Focus on the Family, "Foundational Values," https://www.focusonthefamily.com/about/foundational-values.

72. Focus on the Family, "What We Believe (feat. Mr. Frank Peretti),"

Focus on the Family Broadcast, April 29, 1998, https://www.focusonthe family.com/episodes/broadcast/what-we-believe-part-1-of-2/.

73. Veith, "This Present (and Future) Peretti."

74. See George Marsden, *Reforming Fundamentalism: Fuller Seminary and the New Evangelicalism* (Grand Rapids: Eerdmans, 1987), 292–95; David Walker McConeghy, "Geographies of Prayer: Place and Religion in Modern America" (PhD diss., University of California Santa Barbara, 2013).

75. See James M. Collins, *Exorcism and Deliverance Ministry in the Twentieth Century* (Eugene, OR: Wipf & Stock, 2009), 41–55.

76. Veith, "This Present (and Future) Peretti."

77. "Jeanette's Reviews: This Present Darkness," GoodReads, July 24, 2009, https://www.goodreads.com/review/show/63595115 ?book_show_action=false&page=1.

78. "Sherae's Reviews: This Present Darkness," GoodReads, April 26, 2012, https://www.goodreads.com/review/show/319636591 ?book_show_action=false&page=1.

79. "Annette's Reviews: This Present Darkness," GoodReads, December 8, 2008, https://www.goodreads.com/review/show/39596324 ?book_show_action=true.

80. "Angie's Reviews: This Present Darkness," GoodReads, May 9, 2011, https://www.goodreads.com/review/show/166757196 ?book_show_action=false.

81. "Marsha Anne's Reviews: This Present Darkness," GoodReads, January 17, 2011, https://www.goodreads.com/review/show /141528762?book_show_action=false&page=1.

82. "Danyell's Reviews: This Present Darkness," GoodReads, February 23, 2008, https://www.goodreads.com/review/show/16192810 ?book_show_action=false&page=1.

83. Mark Noll, *The Scandal of the Evangelical Mind* (Grand Rapids: Eerdmans, 1994), 140–41.

Chapter 3

1. Paul C. Gutjahr, "No Longer Left Behind," *Book History* 4 (2002): 209–36.

2. Judith Lynn, "Peretti's Back with a More Ghoulish Tale," *Panama City (FL) News Herald*, September 16, 1995, https://newspaperarchive.com/panama-city-news-herald-sep-16-1995-p-18/.

3. Daniel Silliman, "Publishers and Profit Motives: The Economic History of *Left Behind*," in *Religion and the Marketplace in the United States*, ed. Jan Stievermann et al. (New York: Oxford University Press, 2015), 165–88.

4. Jeff Gerke, "Please Welcome . . . Jerry B. Jenkins," Where the Map Ends, accessed December 2, 2020, http://www.wherethemap ends.com/Interviews/jerry_jenkins.htm.

5. "Jerry Jenkins on Writing the Left Behind Series," LeftBehind.com, November 20, 2003.

6. Joanna Penn, "Writing Christian Fiction and Success over a Long Career with Jerry B. Jenkins," The Creative Pen, August 14, 2017, https://www.thecreativepenn.com/2017/08/14/writing-christian-fiction-long-career-jerry-b-jenkins/.

7. Crawford Gribben, *Writing the Rapture Prophecy Fiction in Evangelical America* (New York: Oxford University Press, 2009), 33.

8. Penn, "Writing Christian Fiction and Success over a Long Career with Jerry B. Jenkins."

9. Jerry B. Jenkins, *Writing for the Soul: Instruction and Advice from an Extraordinary Writing Life* (Cincinnati: Writer's Digest Books, 2006), 3.

10. Jenkins, *Writing for the Soul*, 163.

11. Silliman, "Publishers and Profit Motives," 171.

12. Tim LaHaye, *No Fear of the Storm: Why Christians Will Escape All the Tribulation* (Sisters, OR: Multnomah, 1992), 19, 18.

13. LaHaye, *No Fear of the Storm*, 16.

14. John G. Turner, *Bill Bright and Campus Crusade for Christ: The*

Renewal of Evangelicalism in Postwar America (Chapel Hill: University of North Carolina Press, 2008), 30–31.

15. LaHaye, *No Fear of the Storm*, 16.

16. LaHaye, *No Fear of the Storm*, 235. LaHaye took his early church history from Dallas Theological Seminary's John Walvoord. For scholarly studies of the eschatologies of the early church, see Charles Hill, *Regnum Caelorum: Patterns of Millennial Thought in Early Christianity* (Grand Rapids: Eerdmans, 2001), and Brian Daley, *The Hope of the Early Church: A Handbook of Patristic Eschatology* (Grand Rapids: Baker Books, 2002).

17. LaHaye, *No Fear of the Storm*, 66.

18. Paul S. Boyer, *When Time Shall Be No More: Prophecy Belief in Modern American Culture* (Cambridge, MA: Belknap Press of Harvard University Press, 1992), 148, 298.

19. Hal Lindsey, *The Late Great Planet Earth* (New York: Bantam Books, 1973), frontispiece.

20. LaHaye, *No Fear of the Storm*, 147.

21. LaHaye, "Remarks," Council for National Policy, Policy Council, October 2, 2010.

22. LaHaye, *No Fear of the Storm*, 146.

23. LaHaye, *No Fear of the Storm*, 136.

24. Heather Hendershot, *What's Fair on the Air? Cold War Right-Wing Broadcasting and the Public Interest* (Chicago: University of Chicago Press, 2011), 1–4.

25. Robert Welch, *The Blue Book of the John Birch Society* (Appleton, WI: John Birch Society, 1961), 60.

26. LaHaye, *No Fear of the Storm*, 147.

27. Matthew Avery Sutton, *American Apocalypse: A History of Modern Evangelicalism* (Cambridge, MA: Belknap Press of Harvard University Press, 2017), xiii–xiv.

28. LaHaye, *No Fear of the Storm*, 241.

29. LaHaye, *No Fear of the Storm*, 242.

30. Tim LaHaye and Jerry B. Jenkins, *Left Behind: A Novel of the Earth's Last Days* (Carol Stream, IL: Tyndale House, 1995), 389.

31. LaHaye and Jenkins, *Left Behind*, 397–98.

32. Penn, "Writing Christian Fiction and Success over a Long Career with Jerry B. Jenkins."

33. Jenkins, *Writing for the Soul*, 128.

34. See Wolfgang Iser on the self-disclosure of fictionality, *The Fictive and the Imaginary: Charting Literary Anthropology* (Baltimore: Johns Hopkins University Press, 1993), 11–13.

35. Peter L. Berger, *The Heretical Imperative: Contemporary Possibilities of Religious Affirmation* (Garden City, NY: Anchor, 1979), 15.

36. Berger, *The Heretical Imperative*, 28.

37. Charles Taylor, *A Secular Age* (Cambridge, MA: Belknap Press of Harvard University Press, 2007), 11.

38. Lee Strobel, *The Case for Christ: A Journalist's Personal Investigation of the Evidence for Jesus* (Grand Rapids: Zondervan, 1998), 18.

39. William Lane Craig, *Reasonable Faith: Christian Truth and Apologetics*, 3rd ed. (Wheaton, IL: Crossway Books, 2008), 18.

40. Nathan Schneider, *God in Proof: The Story of a Search from the Ancients to the Internet* (Berkeley: University of California Press, 2013), 207.

41. Josh McDowell, *Evidence That Demands a Verdict: Historical Evidences for the Christian Faith* (Arrowhead Springs, CA: Campus Crusade for Christ, 1972), iii.

42. Bill Bright, foreword to *Evidence That Demands a Verdict*, by Josh McDowell, i–ii, here i.

43. John G. Stackhouse Jr., "By Their Books Ye Shall Know Them," *Christianity Today*, September 16, 1996, http://www.christianitytoday.com/ct/1996/september16/6ta058.html?share=2pzkqeEtoNgR2zTX5iExOecmO6s%2bXPoo.

44. "The Top 50 Books That Have Shaped Evangelicals," *Christianity Today*, October 6, 2006, https://www.christianitytoday.com/ct/2006/october/23.51.html.

45. For a history of *Mere Christianity*, see George M. Marsden, *C. S. Lewis's "Mere Christianity": A Biography* (Princeton: Princeton University Press, 2016).

46. Alister McGrath, *C. S. Lewis: A Life* (Carol Stream, IL: Tyndale House, 2013), 205, 206.

47. Bob Smietana, "C. S. Lewis Superstar," *Christianity Today*, November 23, 2005, https://www.christianitytoday.com/ct/2005/december/9.28.html.

48. McGrath, *C. S. Lewis*, 257.

49. McGrath, *C. S. Lewis*, 255.

50. McGrath, *C. S. Lewis*, 253.

51. McGrath, *C. S. Lewis*, 259.

52. J. I. Packer, "Still Surprised by Lewis," *Christianity Today*, September 7, 1998, http://www.christianitytoday.com/ct/1998/september7/8ta054.html?share=2pzkqeEtoNg1CEF3F7ghfObHtcy2Bg52.

53. Mark A. Noll, *The Scandal of the Evangelical Mind* (Grand Rapids: Eerdmans, 1995), 218.

54. David W. Stowe, *No Sympathy for the Devil: Christian Pop Music and the Transformation of American Evangelicalism* (Chapel Hill: University of North Carolina Press, 2011), 226.

55. Chuck Colson, *Born Again* (Grand Rapids: Baker Books, 1976), 124.

56. C. S. Lewis, *Mere Christianity* (1952; reprint, New York: HarperCollins, 2001), 52.

57. Colson, *Born Again*, 136.

58. Colson, *Born Again*, 140.

59. Josh McDowell and Cristóbal Krusen, *Undaunted: One Man's Real-Life Journey from Unspeakable Memories to Unbelievable Grace* (Carol Stream, IL: Tyndale House, 2012), 92.

60. McDowell and Krusen, *Undaunted*, 87.

61. McDowell and Krusen, *Undaunted*, 127.

62. Josh McDowell, *More Than a Carpenter* (Carol Stream, IL: Tyndale House, 1977), 124.

63. McDowell, *Evidence That Demands a Verdict*, 108.

64. McDowell, *Evidence That Demands a Verdict*, 109.

65. McDowell, *More Than a Carpenter*, 33.

66. Hugh B. Urban, "America, Left Behind: Bush, the Neocon-servatives, and Evangelical Christian Fiction," *Journal of Religion & Society* 8 (2006): 3, 4.

67. Urban, "America, Left Behind," 10.

68. Joan Didion, "Mr. Bush & the Divine," *New York Review of Books* 50, no. 17 (2003): 81–86, here 82.

69. Stephen Bates, "The Jesus Market," *Weekly Standard*, December 16, 2002, http://www.weeklystandard.com/the-jesus-market/article/3260.

70. Carl E. Olson, "The 12th Coming of Less-Than-Glorious Fiction," *National Review*, April 2, 2004, http://www.nationalreview.com/article/210135/12th-coming-less-glorious-fiction-carl-e-olson; Carl E. Olson, "Not with a Biblical Bang . . . ," *National Review*, December 29, 2003, http://www.nationalreview.com/article/208982/not-biblical-bang-carl-e-olson?target=author&tid=901377.

71. Didion, "Mr. Bush & the Divine," 86.

72. Amy Hungerford, *Postmodern Belief: American Literature and Religion since 1960* (Princeton: Princeton University Press, 2010), 120.

73. LaHaye and Jenkins, *Left Behind*, 3. Hereafter, page references to this work will be given in parentheses in the text.

74. Jenkins, *Writing for the Soul*, 130–31.

75. The novel uses the New King James Version of the text.

76. Jenkins, *Writing for the Soul*, 137.

77. Jenkins, *Writing for the Soul*, 6.

78. Cindy Crosby, "Left Behind Fuels Growth at Tyndale House," *Publishers Weekly*, May 10, 2001, https://www.publishersweekly.com/pw/print/20010507/38487-left-behind-fuels-growth-at-tyndale-house.html.

79. Amy Johnson Frykholm, *Rapture Culture: "Left Behind" in Evangelical America* (New York: Oxford University Press, 2004), 46.

80. Silliman, "Publishers and Profit Motives," 53.

81. See Bethany Moreton, *To Serve God and Wal-Mart: The Making of Christian Free Enterprise* (Cambridge, MA: Harvard University Press, 2010).

82. Silliman, "Publishers and Profit Motives," 171–83.

83. Silliman, "Publishers and Profit Motives," 178–80.

84. Penn, "Writing Christian Fiction and Success over a Long Career with Jerry B. Jenkins."

85. Ann Byle, "LaHaye, Co-author of Left Behind Series, Leaves a Lasting Impact," *Publishers Weekly*, July 27, 2016, https://www.publish ersweekly.com/pw/by-topic/industry-news/religion/article/71026 -lahaye-co-author-of-left-behind-series-leaves-a-lasting-impact.html.

86. "Q&A with Norm Rohrer," Evangelical Press Association, March 7, 1997, https://www.evangelicalpress.com/rohrer/.

87. Tim LaHaye and Jerry B. Jenkins, with Norman B. Rohrer, *These Will Not Be Left Behind: True Stories of Changed Lives* (Carol Stream, IL: Tyndale House, 2003), 5.

88. LaHaye and Jenkins, with Rohrer, *These Will Not Be Left Behind*, 6.

89. LaHaye and Jenkins, with Rohrer, *These Will Not Be Left Behind*, 4.

90. LaHaye and Jenkins, with Rohrer, *These Will Not Be Left Behind*, 5.

91. Frykholm, *Rapture Culture*, 133.

92. Frykholm, *Rapture Culture*, 87.

93. "Melissa's Reviews: Left Behind," GoodReads, April 1, 2008, https://www.goodreads.com/review/show/19231295?book_show_ac tion=false&from_review_page=1.

94. "Lesmana's Reviews: Left Behind," GoodReads, April 20, 2007, https://www.goodreads.com/review/show/817806?book_show _action=false&from_review_page=1.

95. "Nick Black's Reviews: Left Behind," Good Reads, April 18, 2009, https://www.goodreads.com/review/show/53194000?book _show_action=true&from_review_page=1.

96. James Bielo, *Emerging Evangelicals: Faith, Modernity, and the*

Desire for Authenticity (New York: New York University Press, 2011), 143.

97. Fred Clark, "Left Behind Index (the Whole Thing)," *Slacktivist*, November 5, 2015, http://www.patheos.com/blogs/slacktivist/2015/11/05/left-behind-index-the-whole-thing/.

98. Fred Clark, "Left Behind: Pretrib Porno," *Slacktivist*, October 18, 2003, http://www.patheos.com/blogs/slacktivist/2003/10/18/left-behind-pretrib-porno/.

99. Fred Clark, "L. B.: Freeze Frame, Roll Credits," *Slacktivist*, September 19, 2008, http://www.patheos.com/blogs/slacktivist/2008/09/19/lb-freeze-frame/.

100. Clark, "L. B.: Freeze Frame, Roll Credits."

101. "Lexi's Reviews: Left Behind," GoodReads, November 29, 2014, https://www.goodreads.com/review/show/1118841993?book_show_action=false&from_review_page=1.

Chapter 4

1. Ane Mulligan, "Author Interview: Beverly Lewis," *Novel Rocket*, July 26, 2007, https://novelrocket.com/2007/07/author-interview-beverly-lewis.html/.

2. Beverly Lewis, *Holly's Heart*, vols. 1–3 (Minneapolis: Bethany House, 2008).

3. Mulligan, "Author Interview."

4. C. J. Darlington, "Beverly Lewis Interview," Title Trakk.

5. "Amish Gone Wild?" Beliefnet.

6. "Getting to Know Beverly Lewis," *Amish Country News*, February 2010, http://www.amishnews.com/coverstory_pg4-5.pdf.

7. Jennifer McClure, "Conversation: Beverly Lewis," *Pentecostal Evangel*, May 13, 2007, http://pentecostalevangel.ag.org/Conversations2007/4853_Lewis.cfm.

8. See Valerie Weaver-Zercher, *Thrill of the Chaste: The Allure of Amish Romance Novels* (Baltimore: Johns Hopkins University Press, 2013), 261n44.

9. Eric Gorski, "From Amish to Vampires, Christian Fiction Expands," *Mansfield (OH) News-Journal*, July 18, 2009.

10. Nancy M. Tischler, *Encyclopedia of Contemporary Christian Fiction: From C. S. Lewis to "Left Behind"* (Santa Barbara, CA: ABC-CLIO, 2009), 196.

11. McClure, "Conversation."

12. Gloria Gaither, "Beverly Lewis: The Plain Truth," *Homecoming Magazine*, December 1, 2012, http://www.homecomingmagazine.com /article/beverly-lewis-the-plain-truth/.

13. Mulligan, "Author Interview."

14. Beverly Lewis, *The Shunning* (Bloomington, MN: Bethany House, 1997), 17. Hereafter, page references to this work will be given in parentheses in the text.

15. Sarah Wendell and Candy Tan, *Beyond Heaving Bosoms: The Smart Bitches' Guide to Romance Novels* (New York: Simon & Schuster, 2009), 54.

16. McClure, "Conversation."

17. Charles Taylor, *A Secular Age* (Cambridge, MA: Belknap Press of Harvard University Press, 2007), 474–75.

18. Lizabeth Cohen, *A Consumers' Republic: The Politics of Mass Consumption in Postwar America* (New York: Random House, 2003), 299.

19. Gustav Niebuhr, "The Gospels of Management: The Minister as Marketer; Learning from Business," *New York Times*, April 18, 1995, https://www.nytimes.com/1995/04/18/us/megachurches-second-ar ticle-series-gospels-management-minister-marketer-learning.html; Michael Lewis, "God Is in the Packaging," *New York Times Magazine*, July 21, 1996, https://www.nytimes.com/1996/07/21/magazine/the -capitalist-god-is-in-the-packaging.html.

20. Lynne Hybels and Bill Hybels, *Rediscovering Church: The Story and Vision of Willow Creek Community Church* (Grand Rapids: Zondervan, 1995), 59.

21. Hybels and Hybels, *Rediscovering Church*, 33.

22. Hybels and Hybels, *Rediscovering Church*, 57–58.

23. Hybels and Hybels, *Rediscovering Church*, 63.

24. Hybels and Hybels, *Rediscovering Church*, 67.

25. Gustav Niebuhr, "Where Religion Gets a Big Dose of Shopping-Mall Culture," *New York Times*, April 16, 1995, https://www.nytimes.com/1995/04/16/us/where-religion-gets-a-big-dose-of-shopping-mall-culture.html.

26. Hybels and Hybels, *Rediscovering Church*, 68–70; G. A. Pritchard, *Willow Creek Seeker Services: Evaluating a New Way of Doing Church* (Grand Rapids: Baker Books, 1996), 49–55.

27. Russell Chandler, "'Customer' Poll Shapes Church," *Los Angeles Times*, December 11, 1989, https://www.newspapers.com/image/405760345/.

28. Mary Beth Sammons, "Packing 'em in at Willow Creek," *Chicago Tribune*, April 3, 1994, https://www.newspapers.com/image/167335547.

29. Niebuhr, "The Minister as Marketer."

30. Michael Lewis, "God Is in the Packaging."

31. Michael Lewis, "God Is in the Packaging."

32. Sammons, "Packing 'em in at Willow Creek."

33. Hybels and Hybels, *Rediscovering Church*, 51.

34. Pritchard, *Willow Creek Seeker Services*, 220.

35. Debra Hale, "Mass Appeal," *Eau Claire (WI) Leader-Telegram*, January 20, 1996, https://www.newspapers.com/image/361457692.

36. Joe Engelkemier, "Willow Creek," *Ministry*, May 1991, https://www.ministrymagazine.org/archive/1991/05/willow-creek.

37. Andy Nash, "Revisiting Willow Creek," *Ministry*, December 1998, https://www.ministrymagazine.org/archive/1998/12/revisiting-willow-creek.

38. Hybels and Hybels, *Rediscovering Church*, 169, 188.

39. Pritchard, *Willow Creek Seeker Services*, 39.

40. Hybels and Hybels, *Rediscovering Church*, 81.

41. Hybels and Hybels, *Rediscovering Church*, 77.

42. Pritchard, *Willow Creek Seeker Services*, 40.

43. Pritchard, *Willow Creek Seeker Services*, 41.

44. Bob Smietana, "Hybels Heir Quits Willow as New Accusations Arise before Global Leadership Summit," *Christianity Today*, August 5, 2018, https://www.christianitytoday.com/news/2018/august/bill-hybels-steve-carter-resigns-willow-creek-gls-summit.html. See also Manya Brachear Pashman and Jeff Coen, "After Years of Inquiries, Willow Creek Pastor Denies Misconduct Allegations," *Chicago Tribune*, March 23, 2018, http://www.chicagotribune.com/news/local/breaking/ct-met-willow-creek-pastor-20171220-story.html; Manya Brachear Pashman and Jeff Coen, "Hybels Steps Down from Willow Creek Following Allegations of Misconduct," *Chicago Tribune*, April 11, 2018, http://www.chicagotribune.com/news/local/breaking/ct-met-hybels-willow-creek-resigns-20180410-story.html.

45. Hybels and Hybels, *Rediscovering Church*, 106.

46. Hybels and Hybels, *Rediscovering Church*, 112.

47. Hybels and Hybels, *Rediscovering Church*, 114.

48. Pritchard, *Willow Creek Seeker Services*, 217.

49. Pritchard, *Willow Creek Seeker Services*, 118–19.

50. Hybels and Hybels, *Rediscovering Church*, 122.

51. Barbara Bradley, "Marketing That New-Time Religion," *Los Angeles Times Magazine*, December 10, 1995, https://www.newspapers.com/image/155388626.

52. Rick Warren, *Purpose-Driven Church: Growth without Compromising Your Message and Vision* (Grand Rapids: Zondervan, 1995), 169–72.

53. Shayne Lee and Phillip Sinitiere, *Holy Mavericks: Evangelical Innovators and the Spiritual Marketplace* (New York: New York University Press, 2009), 133.

54. Jeffrey L. Sheler, *The Prophet of Purpose: The Life of Rick Warren* (New York: Doubleday, 2009), 114–15.

55. Warren, *Purpose-Driven Church*, 230.

56. Sheler, *The Prophet of Purpose*, 128.

57. Bradley, "Marketing That New-Time Religion."

58. Stephen Buttry and Gene Erb, "Sales Tactics Fill Pews," *Des Moines Register*, December 27, 1998, https://www.newspapers.com/image/130855819.

59. Rob Walker, "Consumed: 'The Purpose-Driven Life,'" *New York Times Magazine*, April 11, 2004, https://www.nytimes.com/2004/04/11/magazine/the-way-we-live-now-4-11-04-consumed-the-purpose-driven-life.html.

60. Malcolm Gladwell, "Tipping-Point Growth," *Leadership Excellence* 23, no. 9 (September 2006): 6–7.

61. Bradley, "Marketing That New-Time Religion."

62. Warren, *Purpose-Driven Church*, 40.

63. Sheler, *The Prophet of Purpose*, 118–21, 135–36, 144, 149–54, 173–77.

64. Warren, *Purpose-Driven Church*, 27.

65. Warren, *The Purpose-Driven Life: What on Earth Am I Here For?* (Grand Rapids: Zondervan, 2002), 18.

66. David Weaver-Zercher, *The Amish in the American Imagination* (Baltimore: Johns Hopkins University Press, 2001), 20.

67. David Weaver-Zercher, *The Amish in the American Imagination*, 31.

68. David Weaver-Zercher, *The Amish in the American Imagination*, 36.

69. See Beverly Seaton, "Helen Reimensnyder Martin's 'Caricatures' of Pennsylvania Germans," *Pennsylvania Magazine of German History and Biography* 104 (1980): 86–95.

70. Helen Reimensnyder Martin, *Sabina: A Story of the Amish* (New York: Century Company, 1905), 231.

71. Valerie Weaver-Zercher, *Thrill of the Chaste*, 25–32.

72. David Weaver-Zercher, *The Amish in the American Imagination*, 68, 70.

73. Katherine Milhous, "Visit Pennsylvania Where Prerevolutionary Costumes Still Survive," Work Projects Administration Poster Collection (Library of Congress), circa 1936.

74. See Jan Stievermann, "Defining the Limits of American Liberty: Pennsylvania's German Peace Churches during the Revolution," in *A Peculiar Mixture: German-Language Cultures and Identities in Eighteenth Century America*, ed. Jan Stievermann and Oliver Scheidung (Philadelphia: Pennsylvania State University Press, 2013), 207–45.

75. Katherine Milhous, "Colonial Pennsylvania Exists To-day in Many Churches, Costumes, Crafts of the German Sectarians," Work Projects Administration Poster Collection (Library of Congress), circa 1936.

76. David Weaver-Zercher, *The Amish in the American Imagination*, 83.

77. See Albert Jay Nock, "Utopia in Pennsylvania: The Amish," in *Snoring as a Fine Art and Twelve Other Essays* (Auburn, AL: Ludwig von Mises Institute, 2007), 29–42.

78. Russell Kirk, "The Best Form of Government," *Catholic World* 192 (December 1960): 156–63.

79. Brian James Daugherity, "From Desegregation to Integration: The History of the United States Supreme Court's Historic *Green v. New Kent County School Board, Virginia*, Decision (1968)" (College of William & Mary, September 2003), http://www.memphis.edu/ben hooks/creative-works/pdfs/daugherity.pdf.

80. Russell Kirk and James McClellan, *The Political Principles of Robert A. Taft* (1967; reprint, New Brunswick: NJ: Transaction, 2010), 74–75.

81. Russell Kirk, "Ten Conservative Principles," *The Imaginative Conservative*, accessed December 7, 2020, http://www.theimagina tiveconservative.org/ten-conservative-principles.

82. Russell Kirk, "Amish Faith Threatened by School Bureaucrats," *Indianapolis Star*, October 19, 1965, https://www.newspapers.com /image/105503123/.

83. Russell Kirk, "No Appeal for the Amish," *Allentown (PA) Morning Call*, November 27, 1967, https://www.newspapers.com/image /281613987/.

84. Russell Kirk, "More Justice for the Amish," *Danville (VA) Register*, September 24, 1967, https://www.newspapers.com/image /24346398/.

85. Shawn Francis Peters, *The Yoder Case: Religious Freedom, Education, and Parental Rights* (Lawrence: University of Kansas Press, 2003), 111.

86. William C. Lindholm, "The National Committe for Amish Religious Freedom," in *The Amish and the State*, ed. Donald B. Kraybill, 2nd ed. (Baltimore: Johns Hopkins University Press, 2003), 109–24; Peters, *The Yoder Case*, 50–59.

87. Peters, *The Yoder Case*, 172, 175.

88. See "Racial Exclusion by Religious Schools: Brown v. Dade Christian Schools, Inc.," *Harvard Law Review* 91, no. 4 (February 1978): 879–86.

89. David Weaver-Zercher, *The Amish in the American Imagination*, 188.

90. McClure, "Conversation."

91. "Getting to Know Beverly Lewis," in Beverly Lewis, *The Shunning*.

92. Mulligan, "Author Interview."

93. Beverly Lewis, *The Shunning*, 258.

94. Beverly Lewis, *The Shunning*, 57–58.

95. "Amish Gone Wild?"

96. Mulligan, "Author Interview."

97. Beverly Lewis, *The Shunning*, 70.

98. Beverly Lewis, *The Shunning*, 243.

99. Mulligan, "Author Interview."

100. Valerie Weaver-Zercher, *Thrill of the Chaste*, 46.

101. David Ivanovich, "Christian Booksellers: Balancing Ministry and the Market," *McAllen (TX) Monitor*, July 21, 1995, https://www .newspapers.com/image/330837495/.

102. Leslie Brown, "Ministry, Not Money, Motivates Christian Bookstores," *Montgomery (AL) Advertiser*, June 10, 1995, https://www .newspapers.com/image/260601534; "Baptist Book Store Opens,"

Montgomery (AL) Advertiser, December 4, 1994, https://www.news papers.com/image/259981709/.

103. Angie Kiesling, "Religion Publishing: These Little Stores Went to Market—Together," *Publishers Weekly*, January 15, 2001, https://www.publishersweekly.com/pw/print/20010115/25098-re ligion-publishing-these-little-stores-went-to-market-together.html.

104. "Christian Stores Market Their Wares," *Waterloo (IA) Courier*, September 20, 1995.

105. Todd Leopold, "The Death and Life of a Great American Bookstore," CNN, September 12, 2011.

106. Laura J. Miller, *Reluctant Capitalists: Bookselling and the Culture of Consumption* (Chicago: University of Chicago Press, 2007), 50.

107. Mulligan, "Author Interview."

108. Beverly Lewis, *The Confession*, 282.

109. Beverly Lewis, *The Reckoning* (Bloomington, MN: Bethany House, 1998), 132.

110. Beverly Lewis, *The Reckoning*, 172.

111. Beverly Lewis, *The Reckoning*, 172.

112. "Gold / Platinum / Diamond Book Awards," Christian Book Expo, n.d., http://christianbookexpo.com/salesawards/gpd-past -winners.php.

113. Valerie Weaver-Zercher, *Thrill of the Chaste*, 4.

114. Valerie Weaver-Zercher, *Thrill of the Chaste*, 5.

115. Valerie Weaver-Zercher, *Thrill of the Chaste*, 6.

116. "Mary O'Brien's Reviews: The Shunning," GoodReads, October 25, 2011, https://www.goodreads.com/review/show/227363594 ?book_show_action=false&from_review_page=2.

117. "Meg's Reviews: The Shunning," GoodReads, May 21, 2012, https://www.goodreads.com/review/show/334184312?book_show_ac tion=false&from_review_page=1.

118. "Adrienne's Reviews: The Shunning," GoodReads, March 20, 2010, https://www.goodreads.com/review/show/94981773 ?book_show_action=false&from_review_page=1.

119. "Katie's Reviews: The Shunning," GoodReads, March 21,

2015, https://www.goodreads.com/review/show/1233278633?book _show_action=false&from_review_page=2.

120. "Becky's Reviews: The Shunning," GoodReads, March 16, 2015, https://www.goodreads.com/review/show/1229637127?book _show_action=false&from_review_page=1.

121. Valerie Weaver-Zercher, *Thrill of the Chaste*, 206.

122. Valerie Weaver-Zercher, *Thrill of the Chaste*, 54.

123. "Nancy's Reviews: The Shunning," GoodReads, August 9, 2009, https://www.goodreads.com/review/show/66809878?book _show_action=false&from_review_page=1.

124. "Amy's Reviews: The Shunning," GoodReads, May 15, 2012, https://www.goodreads.com/review/show/330388637?book_show _action=false&from_review_page=1.

125. Valerie Weaver-Zercher, *Thrill of the Chaste*, 107.

126. See Timothy Aubry, *Reading as Therapy: What Contemporary Fiction Does for Middle-Class Americans* (Iowa City: University of Iowa Press, 2011); Mathew S. Hedstrom, *The Rise of Liberal Religion: Book Culture and American Spirituality in the Twentieth Century* (New York: Oxford University Press, 2013); and Erin A. Smith, *What Would Jesus Read? Popular Religious Books and Everyday Life in Twentieth-Century America* (Chapel Hill: University of North Carolina Press, 2015).

127. Smith, *What Would Jesus Read?*, 7.

128. Beverly Lewis, *The Shunning*, 282.

129. "Andrea's Reviews: The Shunning," GoodReads, October 24, 2008, https://www.goodreads.com/review/show/36103190?book _show_action=false&from_review_page=1.

130. "Kw's Reviews: The Shunning," GoodReads, December 8, 2016, https://www.goodreads.com/review/show/1833978280?book _show_action=false&from_review_page=1.

131. "Brendygirl's Reviews: The Shunning," GoodReads, January 14, 2013, https://www.goodreads.com/review/show/227749496?book _show_action=false&from_review_page=1.

132. "Pamela's Reviews: The Reckoning," GoodReads, November 23, 2013, https://www.goodreads.com/review/show/772029063? book_show_action=false&from_review_page=3.

133. McClure, "Conversation."

134. Gaither, "Beverly Lewis."

135. Traci L. Miller, "Author Visits Alexandria for Book Signing," *Anderson (IN) Herald Bulletin*, April 10, 2018, http://www.heraldbulle tin.com/news/local_news/author-visits-alexandria-for-book-signing /article_91140de4-9f23-52e5-838b-523cc2bf8917.html.

Chapter 5

1. "Paul Young—Pt. 1—Sexually Abused Missionary Kid," Pure Passion Media, April 8, 2011, https://www.youtube.com/watch?v =lCL36ErvBBE.

2. "Paul Young—Pt. 2—Pastor Commits Adultery," Pure Passion Media, April 8, 2011, https://www.youtube.com/watch?v=QNFPh YEvgSc.

3. See The Alliance, "A Movement for God: An Introduction to the History and Thought of the Christian and Missionary Alliance" (Colorado Springs: National Church Ministries, 2006), and Melvin E. Dieter, *The Holiness Movement of the Nineteenth Century* (Metuchen, NJ: Scarecrow, 1980).

4. Jennifer Bensley, "The Dani Church of Irian Jaya and the Challenge It Is Facing Today" (MA thesis, Monash Asia Institute, Monash Univeristy, Melbourne, Australia, 1994), 21, http://papuaweb.org/dlib /s123/bensley/.

5. See Michael Alan Park, "Peaceful Warriors and Cannibal Farmers," in *Introducing Anthropology: An Integrated Approach*, 6th ed. (New York: McGraw Hill, 2014), 343–52, and Russell T. Hitt, *Cannibal Valley* (New York: Harper & Row, 1962).

6. Bensley, "The Dani Church of Irian Jaya," 25.

7. "Paul Young Shares His Story," Mariner's Church, Irvine, CA, July 1, 2008, https://youtu.be/G-BB2ylI8EU.

8. "Paul Young—Pt. 1."

9. "Paul Young—Pt. 1."

10. "Paul Young Shares His Story."

11. Sarah Eekhoff Zylstra, "When Sexual Abuse Comes to Light," *Christianity Today*, February 20, 2014, https://www.christianitytoday.com/ct/2014/march/sexual-abuse-comes-to-light.html.

12. Geoffrey B. Stearns et al., "Mamou—Final Report of the Independent Commission of Inquiry," Missionary Kids Safety Net, November 15, 1997, http://mksafetynet.org/content/mamou-final-report-independent-commission-inquiry.

13. Wess Stafford, "A Candle in the Darkness," *Christianity Today*, May 7, 2010, https://www.christianitytoday.com/ct/2010/may/9.23.html.

14. "Paul Young—Pt. 2."

15. Motoko Rich, "Christian Novel Is Surprise Best Seller," *New York Times*, June 24, 2008, https://www.nytimes.com/2008/06/24/books/24shack.html?em&ex=1214452800&en=40f16df7490a912f&ei=5070.

16. Paul Young, "The Hope and Healing Behind 'The Shack,'" *Guideposts*, July 8, 2009, https://www.guideposts.org/better-living/positive-living/emotional-and-mental-health/the-hope-and-healing-behind-the-shack.

17. "Paul Young—Pt. 1."

18. William Paul Young, *The Shack* (Newbury Park, CA: Windblown Media, 2007), 206. Hereafter, page references to this work will be placed in parentheses in the text. All ellipses are original.

19. James Wood, *The Broken Estate: Essays on Literature and Belief* (New York: Picador, 2010), xxi.

20. David Foster Wallace, *The Pale King* (London: Penguin, 2011), 68.

21. See Roland Barthes, "The Death of the Author," Aspen no. 5+6 (1967), http://www.ubu.com/aspen/aspen5and6/index.html, and Mi-

chel Foucault, "What Is an Author?" in *The Foucault Reader*, ed. Paul Rabinow (New York: Random House, 1984), 101–20.

22. Charles Trueheart, "Welcome to the Next Church," *Atlantic Monthly* 278, no. 2 (1996): 37–58; Douglas B. Sosnik, Matthew J. Dowd, and Ron Fournier, *Applebee's America: How Successful Political, Business, and Religious Leaders Connect with the New American Community* (New York: Simon & Schuster, 2006), 118–19; Stephen P. Miller, *The Age of Evangelicalism: America's Born-Again Years* (Oxford: Oxford University Press, 2014), 104–5.

23. Mark Driscoll, *Confessions of a Reformission Rev.: Hard Lessons from an Emerging Missional Church* (Grand Rapids: Zondervan, 2006), 10. See also Dan Kimball, *Emerging Worship: Creating New Worship Gatherings for Emerging Generations* (El Cajon, CA: emergentYS, 2004), xi.

24. Adam Sweatman, "A Generous Heterodoxy: Emergent Village and the Emerging Milleau" (presentation, Annual Meeting of the American Academy of Religion, Atlanta, November 21–24, 2015). See also Ed Stetzer, "The Emerging/Emergent Church: A Missiological Perspective," *Journal for Baptist Theology and Ministry* 5, no. 2 (2008): 63–97.

25. Tony Jones, *New Christians: Dispatches from the Emergent Frontier* (San Francisco: Jossey-Bass, 2008), 43.

26. Jones, *New Christians*, 43.

27. Brad Cecil, "Minister in the Emerging Postmodern World," PowerPoint presentation, 1999, http://www.slideshare.net/knightopia/ministry-in-the-emerging-postmodern-world/.

28. Driscoll, *Confessions*, 203–5n10. Tony Jones credits Cecil with introducing emergent Christians to John Caputo (Jones, *New Christians*, 41).

29. Driscoll, *Confessions*, 22.

30. Jean-François Lyotard, *The Postmodern Condition: A Report on Knowledge*, trans. Geoff Bennington and Brian Massumi (Manchester: Manchester University Press, 1989), xxiv.

31. Lyotard, *The Postmodern Condition*, xxv.

32. Tim Keel, *Intuitive Leadership: Embracing a Paradigm of Narrative, Metaphor, and Chaos* (Grand Rapids: Baker Books, 2007), 33.

33. Cecil, "Minister in the Emerging Postmodern World."

34. Lynn Neary, "Youth and Religion," *All Things Considered*, National Public Radio, March 1, 1999, https://web.archive.org/web/20010418221244/http://www.marshill.fm/who/articles/nprtranscript.htm.

35. Lori Leibovich, "Generation," *Mother Jones*, July/August 1998, https://www.motherjones.com/politics/1998/07/generation/.

36. Donald Miller, *Blue Like Jazz* (Nashville: Nelson, 2003), 133.

37. Phil Johnson, "Fed Up," *Pyromaniacs* (blog), October 25, 2006, http://teampyro.blogspot.com/2006/10/fed-up.html.

38. Jones, *New Christians*, 48. See also Brad Cecil, "Politics of Love," Axxess.org, November 19, 2008, http://axxess.org/?p=51, and "In Defense of Driscoll," Axxess.org, March 15, 2009, http://axxess.org/?p=80.

39. Jason Bailey, "Men Are from Mars Hill," *Christianity Today*, July 4, 2006, https://www.christianitytoday.com/ct/2006/julyweb-only/127-52.0.html.

40. Molly Worthen, "Who Would Jesus Smack Down?" *New York Times*, January 6, 2009, https://www.nytimes.com/2009/01/11/magazine/11punk-t.html.

41. Tony Jones, "Some Thoughts about Mark Driscoll," *Theoblogy*, September 4, 2014, http://www.patheos.com/blogs/tonyjones/2014/09/04/some-thoughts-about-mark-driscoll/; Jones, *New Christians*, 48.

42. Brad Smith, "What's Next with the Terra Nova Project," Young Leaders.com, April 19, 2001, http://web.archive.org/web/20010419192307/http://www.youngleader.org/WhatsNext.htm.

43. Jones, *New Christians*, 49.

44. Smith, "What's Next with the Terra Nova Project."

45. Brian D. McLaren, *A New Kind of Christian: A Tale of Two Friends on a Spiritual Journey* (San Francisco: Jossey-Bass, 2001), 18.

46. McLaren, *A New Kind of Christian*, 19.

47. McLaren, *A New Kind of Christian*, xiii–xiv.

48. McLaren, *A New Kind of Christian*, xvii.

49. Jones, *New Christians*, 50. See also Phyllis Tickle, *The Great Emergence: How Christianity Is Changing and Why* (Grand Rapids: Baker Books, 2008), 164.

50. James Ruark, *House of Zondervan* (Grand Rapids: Zondervan, 2006), 200.

51. "Emergent Village Resources for Communities of Faith Series," Baker Publishing Group, n.d., http://bakerpublishinggroup .com/series/emersion-emergent-village-resources-for-communiti es-of-faith.

52. Miller, *Blue Like Jazz*, viii.

53. Rob Bell, *Velvet Elvis: Repainting the Christian Faith* (Grand Rapids: Zondervan, 2005), 11.

54. John Leland, "Center Stage for a Pastor Where It's Rock That Usually Rules," *New York Times*, July 8, 2006, https://www.nytimes .com/2006/07/08/us/08minister.html?_r=1&oref=slogin.

55. Tony Jones, *Postmodern Youth Ministry* (El Cajon, CA: Youth Specialties, 2001), 12.

56. Jones, *Postmodern Youth Ministry*, 29.

57. Jones, *Postmodern Youth Ministry*, 231.

58. Leonard Sweet, Brian D. McLaren, and Jerry Haselmayer, *A Is for Abductive: The Language of the Emerging Church* (Grand Rapids: Zondervan, 2003), 16.

59. Sweet, McLaren, and Haselmayer, *A Is for Abductive*, 16, 29.

60. Sweet, McLaren, and Haselmayer, *A Is for Abductive*, 31.

61. Rick Warren, foreword to *The Emerging Church: Vintage Christianity for a New Generation*, by Dan Kimball (Grand Rapids: Zondervan, 2003), 7.

62. Brian McLaren, foreword to *The Emerging Church*, by Dan Kimball, 9.

63. Kimball, *The Emerging Church*, 14.

64. Gerardo Marti and Gladys Ganiel, *The Deconstructed Church:*

Understanding Emergent Christianity (New York: Oxford University Press, 2014), 108, 99.

65. James Bielo, *Emerging Evangelicals: Faith, Modernity, and the Desire for Authenticity* (New York: New York University Press, 2011), 29.

66. Bielo, *Emerging Evangelicals*, 53, 55.

67. Bielo, *Emerging Evangelicals*, 143.

68. Brad Cummings and Wayne Jacobsen, "Meet the Author of *The Shack*," *The God Journey* (podcast), May 18, 2018, https://www.the godjourney.com/2007/05/18/meet-the-author-of-the-shack/.

69. Cummings and Jacobsen, "Meet the Author of *The Shack*."

70. Brad Cummings and Wayne Jacobsen, "The Journey Begins," *The God Journey* (podcast), March 19, 2005.

71. Marco R. della Cava, "Podcasting: It's All Over the Dial," *USA Today*, February 8, 2005, https://www.thegodjourney.com/2005/03 /19/first-webcast-released/.

72. Cummings and Jacobsen, "Meet the Author of *The Shack*."

73. Martin D. Singer and Allison Hart Seivers, "First Amended Complaint, Jacobsen et al. v. Young et al.," C. D. Calif. 2010, case no. CV 10-3246 JFW (JCx), 3.

74. John 3:8.

75. Lauren Streib, "Paul Young's Publishing Miracle," *Forbes*, June 4, 2009, http://www.forbes.com/forbes/2009/0622/celebrity -09-shack-religious-thriller-paul-young-publishing-miracle.html.

76. Jordan E. Rosenfeld, "William P. Young's Cinderella Story," *Writer's Digest*, January 13, 2009, http://www.writersdigest.com/writ ing-articles/by-writing-level/published-author/william-p-young.

77. Motoko Rich, "Christian Novel Is Surprise Best Seller," *New York Times*, June 24, 2008, http://www.nytimes.com/2008/06/24 /books/24shack.html?_r=0.

78. Cathy Lynn Grossman, "*Shack* Opens Doors, But Critics Call Book 'Scripturally Incorrect," *USA Today*, May 28, 2008, http://usa today30.usatoday.com/news/religion/2008-05-28-the-shack_N.htm.

79. Hachette Book Group v. Windblown Media, C. D. Calif. 2010, First Amended Complaint, Document 14, case no. CV10-03534 JFW (JCx), http://ia600302.us.archive.org/0/items/gov.uscourts.cacd .472377/gov.uscourts.cacd.472377.14.0.pdf, 6.

80. Streib, "Paul Young's Publishing Miracle."

81. "Shack Author Signs for New Book with Hachette," *Publishers Weekly*, August 22, 2011; Marcia Z. Nelson, "Howard Books Signs 'Shack' Author to New Deal," *Publishers Weekly*, October 2, 2014.

82. Rich, "Christian Novel Is Surprise Best Seller."

83. *Hachette*, 8.

84. Jay Leno, *The Tonight Show with Jay Leno*, NBC, May 23, 2008.

85. Oprah Winfrey, *The Oprah Winfrey Show*, ABC, October 24, 2008.

86. Andy Butcher, "Where Is Christian Publishing Heading? ECPA Chairman Dwight Baker Discusses the Current Publishing Landscape, Trends, and Future," *CBA Retailers & Resources*, January 2016, 20–24, here 24.

87. Christian Book Expo, "ECPA Christian Bestsellers Archives," November 2015, http://christianbookexpo.com/bestseller/archives .php.

88. Chuck Colson, "Stay Out of the Shack," *BreakPoint*, May 5, 2008, http://www.christianheadlines.com/news/stay-out-of-the -shack-11575218.html.

89. Tim Challies, "A Readers Review of the Shack," Challies.com, May 2008.

90. R. Albert Mohler, "The Shack—the Missing Art of Evangelical Discernment," Al Mohler, January 27, 2010, http://www.albert mohler.com/2010/01/27/the-shack-the-missing-art-of-evangelical -discernment/; see also "A Look at 'The Shack,'" Albert Mohler, April 11, 2008, http://www.albertmohler.com/2008/05/26/a-look-at -the-shack-2/.

91. Mark Driscoll, "Trinity: God Is," Mars Hill, March 30, 2008, http://marshill.se/marshill/media/doctrine/trinity-god-is/the-shack.

92. Paul Young, *Lies We Believe about God* (New York: Simon & Schuster, 2017), 65.

93. "Nancy Mure's Reviews: The Shack," GoodReads, January 3, 2016, https://www.goodreads.com/review/show/1493750475?book _show_action=false.

94. "Pam Whitman's Reviews: The Shack," GoodReads, January 6, 2016, https://www.goodreads.com/review/show/1498134584? book_show_action=false.

95. "Heather's Reviews: The Shack," GoodReads, January 2, 2015, https://www.goodreads.com/review/show/1491009722?book_show _action=false; "Denisa's Reviews: The Shack," GoodReads, January 6, 2016, https://www.goodreads.com/review/show/1498191471 ?book_show_action=false; "Julie's Reviews: The Shack," Good-Reads, January 3, 2016, https://www.goodreads.com/review/show /1493387249?book_show_action=false.

96. "Vue's Reviews: The Shack," GoodReads, January 5, 2016, https://www.goodreads.com/review/show/1497418254?book_show _action=false.

97. Pete Enns, "Interview with William Paul Young: Reimagining the God of the Bible," *The Bible for Normal People* (podcast), season 2, episode 41, July 14, 2020, https://peteenns.com/reimagining-the-go d-of-the-bible-with-william-paul-young/.

98. Zach Dundas, "The Gospel of Paul," *Portland Monthly*, November 2008, https://www.pdxmonthly.com/articles/2009/5/19/1108 -paul-young.

99. John A. McDonald, "Best-Selling Author William Paul Young Breaks the Rules, Heals the Hearts," *Birmingham (AL) News*, updated March 28, 2019, http://blog.al.com/living-news/2009/09/bestselling _author_william_pau.html.

100. Marcia Z. Nelson, "After 'The Shack,' a Crossroads: William

Paul Young," *Publishers Weekly*, September 21, 2012, https://www.pub
lishersweekly.com/pw/by-topic/authors/profiles/article/54046-after
-the-shack-cross-roads-william-paul-young.html.

101. Dundas, "The Gospel of Paul."

Conclusion

1. Douglas Todd, "'I'm Not a Republican, I'm a Canadian,' Says
Shack Author," *Vancouver (BC) Sun*, January 20, 2013, https://van
couversun.com/news/staff-blogs/im-not-republican-im-canadian
-says-shack-author.

2. Frank Peretti, "A Pathway to Peace," Facebook, May 5, 2005,
https://www.facebook.com/20531316728/posts/101540099905
06729/.

3. Jeremy Weber, "Died: Tim LaHaye, Author Who 'Left Behind'
a Long Legacy," *Christianity Today*, July 25, 2016, https://www.chris
tianitytoday.com/news/2016/july/tim-lahaye-dies-left-behind-co
author-stroke.html.

4. Kristin Kobes Du Mez, *Jesus and John Wayne: How White Evangelicals Corrupted a Faith and Fractured a Nation* (New York: Liveright
Publishing, 2020), 1.

5. Cindy Crosby, "How to Save the Christian Bookstore," *Christianity Today*, April 11, 2008, https://www.christianitytoday.com/ct
/2008/april/18.22.html.

6. Chris Freeman, "Christian Bookstore Closing after 35 Years,"
Northwest (IL) Herald, May 23, 2009, https://www.newspapers.com
/image/205314111/.

7. Ann Byle, "Christian Retail Show a Skip for Some, a Must for
Others," *Publishers Weekly*, May 9, 2011, https://www.publisher
sweekly.com/pw/by-topic/industry-news/religion/article/47127
-christian-retail-show-a-skip-for-some-a-must-for-others.html.

8. "Anna Myrl Long," *Inland Valley (CA) Daily Bulletin*, January 5, 2012.

9. Jim Harger, "Nation's Largest Christian Bookstore and Gift Chain Files for Chapter 11 Bankruptcy Protection," *MLive* (Grand Rapids, MI), February 13, 2015, https://www.mlive.com/business/west-michigan/index.ssf/2015/02/nations_largest_christian_book.html.

10. Ann Byle, "Details of Family Christian Stores' New Ownership Plan Emerge," *Publishers Weekly*, July 21, 2015, https://www.publishersweekly.com/pw/by-topic/industry-news/religion/article/67563-details-of-family-christian-stores-new-ownership-plan-emerge.html.

Index